LAW, CRIME AND LAW ENFORCEMENT

FORFEITURE, CONSPIRACY, VENUE: FEDERAL CRIME LAW

LAW, CRIME AND LAW ENFORCEMENT

Additional books in this series can be found on Nova's website under the Series tab.

Additional E-books in this series can be found on Nova's website under the E-books tab.

LAW, CRIME AND LAW ENFORCEMENT

FORFEITURE, CONSPIRACY, VENUE: FEDERAL CRIME LAW

RYAN E. MCGOWAN
AND
COLIN H. GROVSTEN
EDITORS

Nova Science Publishers, Inc.
New York

For permission to use material from this book please contact us:
Telephone 631-231-7269; Fax 631-231-8175
Web Site: http://www.novapublishers.com

LIBRARY OF CONGRESS CATALOGING-IN-PUBLICATION DATA

Forfeiture, conspiracy, venue : federal crime law / editors, Ryan E. McGowan and Colin H. Grovsten.
p. cm.
Includes index.
"CRS report for Congress prepared for members and committees of Congress."
ISBN 978-1-61209-315-4 (hardcover)
1. Criminal law--United States. 2. Conspiracy--United States. 3. Forfeiture--United States. 4. Venue--United States. I. McGowan, Ryan E. II. Grovsten, Colin H. III. Library of Congress. Congressional Research Service.
KF9205.6.F67 2010
345.73--dc22
2010051559

Published by Nova Science Publishers, Inc. + New York

CONTENTS

PREFACE

This new book examines U.S. federal crime law with a focus on the law enforcement tool of forfeiture; federal conspiracy law and venue. Forfeiture redirects property worth hundreds of millions of dollars from criminal to lawful uses. Federal conspiracy laws rest on the belief that criminal schemes are equally or more reprehensible than the substantive offenses to which they are devoted. Additionally, federal law promises criminal defendants a proper venue, that is, trial in the district in which the federal crime was committed.

Chapter 1- Forfeiture has long been an effective law enforcement tool. Congress and state legislatures have authorized its use for over two hundred years. Every year, it redirects property worth hundreds of millions of dollars from criminal to lawful uses. Forfeiture law has always been somewhat unique. Legislative bodies, commentators and the courts, however, had begun to examine its eccentricities in greater detail because under some circumstances it could be not only harsh but unfair. The Civil Asset Forfeiture Reform Act, P.L. 106-185, 114 Stat. 202 (2000) is a product of that reexamination.

Chapter 2- Zacarias Moussaoui, members of the Colombian drug cartels, members of organized crime, and some of the former Enron executives have at least one thing in common: they all have federal conspiracy convictions. The essence of conspiracy is an agreement of two or more persons to engage in some form of prohibited misconduct. The crime is complete upon agreement, although some statutes require prosecutors to show that at least one of the conspirators has taken some concrete step or committed some overt act in furtherance of the scheme. There are dozens of federal conspiracy statutes. One, 18 U.S.C. 371, outlaws conspiracy to commit some other federal crime. The others outlaw conspiracy to engage in various specific forms of proscribed conduct. General Section 371 conspiracies are punishable by imprisonment for not more than five years; drug trafficking, terrorist, and racketeering conspiracies all carry the same penalties as their underlying substantive offenses, and thus are punished more severely than are Section 371 conspiracies. All are subject to fines of not more than $250,000 (not more than $500,000 for organizations), most may serve as the basis for a restitution order, and some for a forfeiture order.

Chapter 3- Federal law promises criminal defendants a proper venue, that is, trial in the district in which the federal crime was committed. A crime is committed in any district in which any of its "conduct" elements are committed. Some offenses are committed entirely within a single district; there they must be tried. Others begin in one district and are completed in another. They may be tried where they occur unless Congress has limited the choice of venue for the particular offense. Still others, while fully committed in one district, continue on through one or more other districts. They too may be tried where they occur unless Congress elected to limit where they may be tried. Conspiracy is one of the continuing offenses, and so it may be tried in any district in which an overt act in its furtherance is committed.

In: Forfeiture, Conspiracy, Venue: Federal Crime Law ISBN: 978-1-61209-315-4
Editors: Ryan E. McGowan and Colin H. Grovsten

Chapter 1

CRIME AND FORFEITURE

Charles Doyle

SUMMARY

Forfeiture has long been an effective law enforcement tool. Congress and state legislatures have authorized its use for over two hundred years. Every year, it redirects property worth hundreds of millions of dollars from criminal to lawful uses. Forfeiture law has always been somewhat unique. Legislative bodies, commentators and the courts, however, had begun to examine its eccentricities in greater detail because under some circumstances it could be not only harsh but unfair. The Civil Asset Forfeiture Reform Act, P.L. 106-185, 114 Stat. 202 (2000) is a product of that reexamination.

Modern forfeiture follows one of two procedural routes. Although crime triggers all forfeitures, they are classified as civil forfeitures or criminal forfeitures according to the nature of the procedure which ends in confiscation. Civil forfeiture is an in rem proceeding. The property is the defendant in the case. Unless the statute provides otherwise, the innocence of the owner is irrelevant—it is enough that the property was involved in a violation to which forfeiture attaches. As a matter of expedience and judicial economy, Congress often allows administrative forfeiture in uncontested civil confiscation cases. Criminal forfeiture is an in personam proceeding, and confiscation is only possible upon the conviction of the owner of the property.

The Supreme Court has held that authorities may seize moveable property without prior notice or an opportunity for a hearing but that real property owners are entitled as a matter of due process to preseizure notice and the chance for a hearing. As a matter of due process, innocence may be irrelevant in the case of an individual who entrusts his or her property to someone who uses the property for criminal purposes. Although some civil forfeitures may be considered punitive for purposes of the Eighth Amendment's excessive fines clause, civil forfeitures do not implicate the Fifth Amendment's double jeopardy clause unless they are so utterly punitive as to belie remedial classification.

The statutes governing the disposal of forfeited property may authorize destruction of property, or transfer for governmental purposes, or deposit of the property or the proceeds from its sale in a special fund. Intergovernmental transfers and the use of special funds are hallmarks of federal forfeiture. Every year federal agencies transfer hundreds of millions of dollars worth of property to state, local, and foreign law enforcement officials in compensation for their contribution to joint enforcement efforts.

This report is available in an abridged form, without citations, footnotes, or appendices, as CRS Report RS22005, *Crime and Forfeiture: In Short*, by Charles Doyle.

INTRODUCTION

This is an overview of federal forfeiture law.[1] It sketches the origins and general attributes of forfeiture, describes the distribution of the hundreds of millions of dollars it generates, and identifies some of the constitutional issues it raises.

BACKGROUND

Congress and state legislatures have authorized the use of forfeiture for over two hundred years. Forfeiture law has always been somewhat unique. Its increased use has highlighted its eccentricities and attendant policy concerns.

Present forfeiture law has its roots in early English law. It is reminiscent of three early English procedures: deodands, forfeiture of estate or common law forfeiture, and statutory or commercial forfeiture.[2]

At early common law, the object that caused the death of a human being—the ox that gored, the knife that stabbed, or the cart that crushed—was confiscated as a deodand.[3] Coroners' inquests and grand juries, bound with the duty to determine the cause of death, were obligated to identify the offending object and determine its value.[4] The Crown distributed the proceeds realized from the confiscation of the animal or deadly object for religious and charitable purposes in the name of the deceased.[5]

Although deodands were not unknown in the American colonies,[6] they appear to have fallen into disuse or been abolished by the time of the American Revolution or shortly thereafter.[7] In spite of their limited use in this country, deodands and the practice of treating the offending animal or object as the defendant have frequently been cited to illustrate the characteristics of modern civil forfeiture.[8]

Forfeiture of estate or common law forfeiture, unlike deodands, focused solely on a human offender. At common law, anyone convicted and attained for treason or a felony forfeited all his lands and personal property.[9] Attainder, the judicial declaration of civil death, occurred as a consequence of the pronouncement of final sentence for treason or felony.[10] In colonial America, common law forfeitures were rare.[11] After the Revolution, the Constitution restricted the use of common law forfeiture in cases of treason, and Congress restricted its use, by statute, in the case of other crimes.[12]

The third antecedent of modern forfeiture, statutory or commercial forfeiture, figured prominently in cases in admiralty and on the revenue side of the Exchequer in pre-colonial England.[13] It was used fairly extensively against smuggling and other revenue evasion schemes in the American colonies and has been used ever since.[14] In most instances, the statutes called for *in rem* confiscation proceedings in which, as with deodands, the offending object is the defendant; occasionally, they established *in personam* procedures where confiscation occurs as the result of the conviction of the owner of the property.[15]

Although contemporary American forfeiture law owes much to the law of deodands and the law of forfeiture of estate, it is clearly a descendant of English statutory or commercial forfeiture.[16]

MODERN FORFEITURE LAW

Property and Trigger Crimes

Modern forfeiture is a creature of statute. While there are some common themes and general patterns concerning the crimes that trigger forfeiture, the property subject to confiscation, and the procedures associated with forfeiture, the federal forfeiture statutes are matters of legislative choice and can vary greatly.[17]

Virtually every kind of property, real or personal, tangible or intangible, may be subject to confiscation under the appropriate circumstances.[18] The laws that call for the confiscation of contraband per se, property whose very possession has been outlawed, were at one time the most prevalent and can still be found.[19] Property—particularly vehicles—used to facilitate the commission of a crime and without which violation would be less likely, has long been the target of confiscatory statutes as well.[20]

In some instances, Congress has focused upon the profits of crime and authorized the confiscation of the direct and indirect proceeds of illegal activities.[21] And under some circumstances, it has authorized the forfeiture of substitute assets, when the tainted property subject to confiscation under a particular statute has become unavailable.[22]

Traditionally, the crimes that triggered forfeiture were those that threatened the government's revenue interest, *e.g.*, smuggling, tax evasion, hunting or fishing without a license, or those crimes which because of their perceived threat to public health or morals might have been considered public nuisances subject to abatement, *e.g*., gambling, or dealing in obscene material, or illicit drug use.

Beginning with the racketeering statutes, a number of jurisdictions have created another category of forfeiture warranting offenses—crimes that involve substantial economic gain for the defendant even if not at the expense of government revenues, but which may greatly enhance government revenues, *e.g*., racketeering and money laundering.[23] A prime example of this approach is the Civil Asset Forfeiture Reform Act (CAFRA),[24] which makes forfeitable the proceeds from any of the crimes upon which a money laundering or RICO prosecution might be based.[25]

Following the terrorist attacks on September 11, 2001, Congress authorized the confiscation of another type of crime-related property—property owned by certain terrorists regardless of whether the property is traceable, used to facilitate, or connected in any other way to any practical crime.[26]

Federal confiscation ordinarily begins with a federal crime. Federal law, however, permits the confiscation of property located in the United States, derived from or used to facilitate various crimes committed in violation of foreign law overseas.[27] The qualifying felonies include public corruption, crimes of violence, drug trafficking, gun running, bank fraud, and child prostitution.[28]

Civil Procedure

Forfeiture follows one of three procedural routes. Although crime triggers all forfeitures, they are classified as civil forfeitures or criminal forfeitures according to the nature of the judicial procedure which ends in confiscation or administrative forfeitures if confiscation occurs without judicial proceedings.

Civil forfeiture is ordinarily the product of a civil, in rem proceeding in which the property is treated as the offender.[29] Within the confines of due process and the language of the applicable statutes, the guilt or innocence of the property owner is irrelevant; it is enough that the property was involved in a violation to which forfeiture attaches in the manner in which statute demands.[30] Criminal forfeiture proceedings, on the other hand, are in personam proceedings, and confiscation is only possible upon the conviction of the owner of the property[31] and only to the extent of defendant's interest in the property.[32]

Historically, most forfeiture statutes called for civil forfeiture. The procedure for forfeiture varies according to the statute which authorizes confiscation. Although each usually contains a few procedural features, the drug, money laundering, and several other civil forfeiture statutes fill in their procedural gaps by cross-reference to the regime established under the customs laws.[33] CAFRA contains generally applicable procedures and thus reduces the extent to which civil forfeiture procedural matters are resolved by reference solely to the customs laws.[34]

As a general rule, since the proceedings are in rem, actual or constructive possession of the property by the court is a necessary first step in any confiscation proceeding.[35] The arrest of the property may be accomplished either by warrant under the Federal Rules of Criminal Procedure or; if judicial proceedings have been filed, by a warrant under the Supplemental Rules of Certain Admiralty and Maritime Claims; or without warrant, if there is probable cause and other grounds under which the Fourth Amendment permits a warrantless arrest; or pursuant to equivalent authority under state law.[36] Because realty cannot ordinarily be seized until after the property owner has been given an opportunity for a hearing,[37] the procedure differs slightly in the case of real property.[38]

Where the seizure of the property causes an undue hardship, CAFRA affords an owner the opportunity to petition the court for release of the property pending the completion of forfeiture proceedings.[39] Conversely, the government may be entitled to a restraining or protective order to preserve the property pending the completion of forfeiture proceedings.[40]

In the interests of expediency and judicial economy, Congress has sometimes authorized the use of administrative forfeiture as the first step after seizure in uncontested cases.[41] The procedure requires that those with an interest in the property be notified and given an opportunity to request judicial forfeiture proceedings;[42] notice of the seizure but not of the government's intent to seek confiscation is not in itself sufficient.[43] If there are no properly filed claims, the property is summarily declared forfeited.[44] If the government has failed to provide adequate notice or failed to honor some other due process obligation, the declaration of administrative forfeiture may be set aside.[45] When an administrative forfeiture is set aside for want of notice, section 983(e) gives the government 60 days to initiate judicial forfeiture proceedings notwithstanding the expiration of an otherwise applicable statute of limitations.[46]

CAFRA establishes a timetable for administrative forfeitures under which the government must notify those with a property interest of its intent to confiscate within 60 days of seizure.[47]

Thereafter, the property owner has at least 35 days within which to file a claim and request a judicial hearing.[48] The government has 90 days within which to initiate judicial proceedings after the receipt of a claim.[49] In customs or tax cases or cases that predate the passage of CAFRA, due process dictates the speed with which the government must act to initiate forfeiture proceedings following seizure of the property.[50]

When administrative forfeiture is unavailable, or when a claimant has successfully sought judicial proceedings, or when the government has elected not to proceed administratively, the government may begin civil judicial proceedings by filing either a complaint or a libel against the property.[51] Property owners have 30 days after the government's filing to submit a claim,[52] and 20 days thereafter to tender their answer.[53]

The period within which a claimant must register his or her intent to contest may be a fairly narrow window, and the courts may consider time of the essence, as long as the government has made reasonable efforts to notify interested parties.[54] Even if the government sustains no appreciable damage, a claim not promptly filed may be a claim lost.[55]

In money laundering and other civil forfeitures governed by CAFRA, the government must establish that the property is subject to confiscation by a preponderance of the evidence.[56] In cases such as those arising under the customs laws and cases filed before the effective date of CAFRA amendments, the government must establish probable cause to believe that the property is subject to forfeiture.[57] If the government overcomes this initial obstacle, the burden shifts to the claimant, who must establish standing[58] and, by a preponderance of the evidence, that his or her interest in the property is not subject to a declaration of forfeiture.[59]

A claimant may successfully challenge confiscation on several grounds. He or she may be able to show that the predicate criminal offense did not occur or that his or her property lacks the statutorily required nexus to the crime.[60] For example, when the government claims that property is forfeitable because it was used to commit or to facilitate the commission of a crime, it must "establish that there was a substantial connection between the property and the offense."[61] A claimant's innocence or even acquittal only bars civil forfeiture to the extent that a statute permits or due process requires.[62] For most civil forfeitures, other than those arising under the tax or customs laws,[63] CAFRA establishes two "innocent owner" defenses—one for claimants with an interest in the property at the time the forfeiture-triggering offense occurred and the other for claimants with an interest acquired after the forfeiture-triggering offense occurred.[64] The first is available to claimants either who were unaware that their property was being criminally used or who did all that could be reasonably expected of them to prevent criminal use of their property.[65] The second is for good faith purchasers who did not know of the taint on the property at the time they acquired their interest.[66]

When the court determines that the property is not subject to forfeiture, it must be released to its owner, assuming the property can be lawfully possessed by its owner.[67] Regardless of the statutory procedure initially invoked, prevailing claimants may be entitled to compensation for damages to the property incurred while in federal custody,[68] attorneys' fees,[69] post-judgment interest, and in some instances pre-judgment interest.[70] Where the property is declared forfeited, its disposal is a matter of statute.[71]

The Attorney General and the Secretary of the Treasury enjoy wide latitude to transfer confiscated property to state, local, and foreign law enforcement agencies to the extent of their participation of in the case,[72] although both must be assured that the transfers will encourage law enforcement cooperation.[73]

At one time, this "equitable sharing" transfer authority could not be used unless the Attorney General was convinced that confiscated property "[was] not so transferred to circumvent any requirement of State law that prohibits forfeiture or limits use or disposition of property forfeited to State or local agencies," 21 U.S.C. 881(e)(3)(B)(1988 ed.). The restriction addressed sometimes controversial adoptive forfeitures.[74]

Adoptive forfeiture occurs when property is forfeitable under federal law and the Department of Justice "adopts," for processing under federal law, a forfeiture case brought to it by state or local law enforcement officials and in which the United States is not otherwise involved. Federal adoption is sometimes attractive because of the speed afforded by federal administrative forfeiture. It may also be attractive because forfeiture would be impossible or more difficult under state law or because law enforcement agencies would not share as extensively in the bounty of a successful forfeiture under state law.

The circumvention restriction is no longer in effect, but the Treasury and Justice Departments insist that state and local law enforcement agencies indicate the law enforcement purposes to which the transferred property is to be devoted and that the transfer will increase and not supplant law enforcement resources.[75]

Criminal Procedure

Once less frequently invoked than civil forfeiture, criminal forfeiture appears to have become the procedure of choice when judicial proceedings are required.[76] CAFRA added to the federal crimes punishable by criminal forfeiture, various offenses involving unlawful money transmission,[77] counterfeiting,[78] identify fraud,[79] credit card fraud,[80] computer fraud,[81] theft related to motor vehicles,[82] health care fraud,[83] telemarketing fraud,[84] bank fraud,[85] and immigration-related offenses.[86] Perhaps more significantly, a bridge statute, 28 U.S.C. 2461(c), exists which permits confiscation using criminal forfeiture procedures whenever civil forfeiture is authorized elsewhere.[87]

Like civil forfeiture, criminal forfeiture is a creature of statute. Unlike civil forfeiture, criminal forfeiture follows as a consequence of conviction.[88] It is punishment, even though it may also serve remedial purposes very effectively.[89] While civil forfeiture treats the property as the defendant, confiscating the interests of the innocent and guilty alike, criminal forfeiture traditionally consumes only the property interests of the convicted defendant,[90] and only with respect to the crime for which he is convicted.[91] When the property subject to confiscation is unavailable following the defendant's conviction, however, the court may order the confiscation of other property belonging to the defendant in its stead (substitute assets).[92]

The indictment or information upon which the conviction is based must list the property which the government asserts is subject to confiscation,[93] and the defendant is entitled to a jury finding of the necessary connection between the crime of conviction and the property to be confiscated.[94] Since the court's jurisdiction does not depend upon initial control of the res, it need not be seized before forfeiture is declared.[95] Although the courts are authorized to issue pretrial restraining orders to prevent depletion or transfer of property which the government contends is subject to confiscation,[96] many are hesitant to issue pre-trial restraining orders covering substitute property.[97] And there may be some lingering uncertainty as to whether such orders can be issued when the government has opted to use the good offices of the bridge statute[98] to accomplish what would otherwise be a civil forfeiture in conjunction with the criminal prosecution of the property owner.

Originally, section 2461(c) permitted criminal forfeiture under statutes that authorized civil forfeiture but that made no provision for criminal forfeiture.[99] In such cases, it declared that "upon conviction, the court shall order the forfeiture of the property in accordance with the procedures set forth in section 413 of the Controlled Substances Act (21 U.S.C. 853), other than subsection (d) of that section," 28 U.S.C. 2461(c) (2000 ed.). Section 853(e), then as now, authorized pretrial restraining orders, so it might seem that they should be available in section 2461 cases.

Not so, said the Second Circuit. In section 2461(c) cases, the Federal Rules of Criminal Procedure, which do not include authority to issue pretrial restraining orders, govern prior to conviction; only after conviction does section 853 dictate the procedural path.[100] The Court found confirmation of its view by contrasting the language of section 2461(c) with that of 18 U.S.C. 982, which the courts have concluded does authorize such pretrial restraining orders.

Section 982 states that "the forfeiture of property under this section, *including any seizure and disposition of property and any related judicial or administrative proceeding shall be governed by section 853*."[101] "In contrast, section 2461(c) state[d] only that '*upon conviction*, the court shall order the forfeiture of the property in accordance with the procedures set forth in section 853.'"[102]

Shortly thereafter, the current version of section 2461(c) appeared, unexplained, in the conference report on the bill subsequently enacted as the USA PATRIOT Improvement and Reauthorization Act.[103] The new language permits criminal forfeiture under the procedures of section 2461(c) whenever a civil forfeiture is authorized, regardless of whether the statute that authorizes the civil forfeiture also authorizes criminal forfeiture under different procedures.[104] It thus permits the government to elect to use section 2461(c)'s criminal forfeiture procedures even where alternative criminal forfeiture procedures were already available, hence perhaps its "uniform procedures" caption in the Act.[105]

Section 2461 cases aside, the defense to criminal forfeiture differs somewhat from the defense to civil forfeiture. For example, since conviction is a prerequisite to confiscation, acquittal will ordinarily preclude forfeiture. Third party interests are less likely to be cut off by virtue of the property's proximity to criminal conduct simply because only the defendant's interest in the property is subject to confiscation and because bona fide purchaser exceptions are more common. Bona fide purchaser exceptions protect a good faith purchaser who acquired the property after commission of the offense—at which time title to the property vested in the United States—but before the declaration of forfeiture.[106]

After conviction of the defendant, the government may elect to seek either confiscation of forfeitable property or a money judgment in the amount of its value.[107] If the government seeks confiscation, the court must determine whether the statutory nexus between the property and the crime of conviction exists,[108] a determination presented to the jury at the defendant's request.[109] If the government instead seeks a money judgment, the court must determine the amount the defendant must pay.[110] At that point, the court issues a preliminary forfeiture order or order for a money judgment against the defendant in favor of the government.[111] Upon the issuance of a preliminary forfeiture order, the government must proclaim its intent to dispose of the property and notify any third parties known to have an interest in the property.[112] Third parties with claims to the forfeited property, other than the defendant, are then entitled to a judicial hearing,[113] provide they file timely petition asserting their claims.[114]

Third party claims may be grounded either in an assertion that they possessed a superior interest in the property at the time confiscation-trigger misconduct occurred or that they are good faith purchases.[115] The courts will not recognize the unsecured claims of general creditors to the property,[116] but will look to state law to determine whether a third party has the requisite superior interest in the property.[117] Regardless of whether third parties assert a superior interest or the status of a good faith purchaser, they bear the burden of establishing their claim by a preponderance of the evidence.[118]

When the government is awarded a money judgment, it is not limited to the forfeitable assets the defendant has on hand at the time but may enforce the judgment against future and perhaps alternative assets as well.[119] In such cases, the courts are divided over the question of whether the government may enforce the judgment like any other judgment creditor or instead is limited to substitute assets and then only if the tainted assets are unavailable.[120]

Disposition of Forfeited Assets

Generally

Disposal of forfeited property is ordinarily a matter of statute as well. The pertinent statute may require that the proceeds of a confiscation be devoted to a single purpose, such as the support of education or deposit in the general fund. The statute may call for the destruction of property that can not be lawfully possessed;[121] or authorize rewards, the settlement of claims against the property; or remission or mitigation.[122] Intergovernmental transfers and the use of special funds, however, are the hallmarks of the more prominent federal forfeiture statutes. Under their authority, the Attorney General and the Secretary of the Treasury enjoy considerable discretion to transfer confiscated property to state, local, and foreign law enforcement agencies.[123]

They direct lion's share of confiscated cash or the proceeds from the sale of confiscated property to the Department of Justice Asset Forfeiture Fund,[124] and the Department of the Treasury Forfeiture Fund.[125]

Federal Funds

The Comprehensive Crime Control Act of 1984 changed the way in which the federal government deals with revenues realized from the collection of fines and forfeitures.[126] Prior to the Act, virtually all of the money realized from fines and forfeitures, like most federal revenues, was deposited in the general fund of the United States Treasury. Through the enactment of annual appropriation bills, Congress permitted the money in the general fund to be spent to finance the activities it had authorized by statute.[127]

The Crime Control legislation created three new funds to receive revenues collected as part of the federal criminal law enforcement process, and Congress added a fourth a few years later. The Customs Forfeiture Fund, which became the Department of the Treasury Forfeiture Fund, and the Department of Justice Asset Forfeiture Fund collect confiscated cash and the proceeds from other forfeitures which are devoted to federal and state law enforcement purposes. The Treasury and Justice Department Funds, together receive over $1.5 billion per year.[128]

Department of Justice Asset Forfeiture Fund

Congress created the Department of Justice Asset Forfeiture Fund[129] as part of the Comprehensive Crime Control Act of 1984.[130] The Department of Justice administers the Fund, which receives confiscated cash and the proceeds from forfeitures conducted under the laws enforced or administered by the Department of Justice and the Department of Justice's equitable share of forfeitures conducted by other state, federal, or foreign law enforcement agencies.[131]

Before confiscated cash or the proceeds from the sale of other confiscated property is paid into the Fund, the Attorney General may often authorize it to be transferred to or shared with other federal, state, local, or foreign law enforcement agencies who have participated in the investigation or proceedings that resulted in confiscation.[132]

After money has been paid into the Fund, the Attorney General may use it to pay:

- forfeiture related expenses,
- rewards to informants in illicit drug cases,[133]
- rewards to informants in forfeiture cases,[134]
- liens and mortgages against forfeited property,
- remission and mitigation in forfeiture cases,
- to equip cars, boats and planes for law enforcement purposes,[135]
- to purchase evidence of money laundering or of federal drug crimes,
- to pay state and local real estate taxes on forfeited property;
- to pay overtime, travel, training and the like for assisting state and local law enforcement personnel;
- federal correctional construction costs,
- the Special Forfeiture Fund,[136] and
- to pay for joint state, local and federal cooperative law enforcement operations. 28 U.S.C. 524(c).[137]

In the past, Congress has occasionally directed that the Fund be made available during a particular year and for a specific law enforcement purpose in anticipation of a surplus in the Fund after the statutory purposes had been served.[138] More recently, however, it has authorized the Attorney General to tap this "super surplus" for any law enforcement or Justice Department purpose.[139]

Although once money has been appropriated it may be spent in any fiscal year, access to the Fund is subject to annual appropriation for purposes of awarding rewards, purchasing evidence, and refitting of law enforcement vehicles.[140] For other purposes, Congress has enacted a permanent appropriation.[141]

Record-keeping functions are performed under contract paid out of the Fund, but as a general rule the Department of Justice has not used the Fund to pay the salaries and expenses of the United States Marshals Service personnel responsible for management of the seized assets and the Fund. Except in the case of equitable sharing where they are covered by the administrative fee, those costs have generally been handled through the overall salaries and expenses appropriation for the Marshals Service.[142]

Department of the Treasury Forfeiture Fund

The Department of the Treasury Forfeiture Fund began as the Customs Forfeiture Fund and was also created by the Comprehensive Crime Control Act.[143] It is administered by the Secretary of the Treasury and receives deposits of forfeited currency and proceeds from forfeitures under laws enforced or administered by the Department of the Treasury or the Coast Guard, amounts received by the Department of the Treasury or the Coast Guard as an equitable share of a forfeiture conducted by other authorities, or income realized from investments on behalf of the Fund.[144] Earlier plans to merge the Justice and Treasury Department Funds[145] have yet to be acted upon.

Before confiscated cash or the proceeds from the sale of other confiscated property are paid into the Fund, the Secretary of the Treasury may also authorize transfer of the property to other federal, state, local, or foreign law enforcement agencies who assisted in its forfeiture.[146]

After money has been paid into the Fund, the Secretary of the Treasury makes one portion available to the Coast Guard in an amount reflecting its contributions.[147] The moneys available for the Coast Guard may be used to equip cars, boats and planes for law enforcement purposes, to pay overtime and similar expenses for state and local law enforcement officers in a joint operation, and to satisfy environmental requirements before sinking hazards to navigation.[148]

The Fund is otherwise available to the Secretary of the Treasury for a number of purposes, including paying:

- expenses associated with the forfeiture,
- claims against the property,
- liens and mortgages against forfeited property,[149]
- remission and mitigation,
- rewards for information concerning violations of the customs laws,[150]
- rewards for information or assistance resulting in a Department of Treasury forfeiture,
- to equip cars, boats and planes for law enforcement purposes,
- to purchase evidence of various crimes traditionally within the jurisdiction of the Department,[151]
- to reimburse the expenses of private individuals associated with Department law enforcement activities,

- for equitable sharing, if not accomplished prior to deposit in the Fund,[152]
- for "overtime salaries, travel, fuel, training, equipment, and other similar costs of State and local law enforcement officers that are incurred in joint law enforcement operations;" and
- to train foreign law enforcement personnel in Department forfeiture related matters.[153]

Congress has established a permanent appropriation to pay for forfeiture-related expenses, for the settlement of claims, liens, and mortgages, for remission and mitigation, rewards under the customs laws, and equitable sharing.[154]

Special Forfeiture Fund

The Special Forfeiture Fund, initially a depository of forfeiture proceeds, was created to fund the Office of National Drug Control Policy (the "drug czar").[155] The Office is now funded by direct appropriations, and the Fund, through which various drug-related programs are funded by directed appropriation, is no longer a recipient of forfeiture proceeds.[156]

Crime Victims Fund

The Justice Department's Office for Victims of Crime in the Office of Justice Programs administers the Crime Victims Fund created by the Crime Control Act, P.L. 98-473, §1402, 98 Stat. 2170 (1984).[157] The Fund receives revenues collected as fines for violations of federal criminal law, as special assessments against misdemeanor offenders, as a consequence of jumping bail,[158] and from the operation of the espionage provisions,[159] and the "Son of Sam" forfeiture provisions.[160] The Fund is available for grants to the States for crime victim compensation and assistance programs, for HHS child-abuse prevention and treatment grants, and to reimburse the courts for administrative costs.[161]

CONSTITUTIONAL CONSIDERATIONS

Until recently, it could safely be said that the Constitution afforded state and federal governments extraordinary latitude to enact and enforce forfeiture statutes; forfeiture often seemed unusual, sometimes severe, and occasionally unfair, yet with rare exceptions it was not unconstitutional. In 1993, the Court handed down a series of decisions that seemed to signal its uneasiness with the trends in forfeiture law.[162] Thereafter, it announced another series of opinions that seem to deny any inclination to totally repudiate the government's broad forfeiture authority,[163] yet in terms that incrementally began to define the constitutional borders of that authority.[164]

Eighth Amendment

The Eighth Amendment states in its entirety that "[e]xcessive bail shall not be required, nor excessive fines imposed, nor cruel and unusual punishments inflicted." The lower courts had on several occasions held that criminal forfeitures are subject to Eighth Amendment analysis,[165] but Eighth Amendment concerns were generally considered irrelevant in civil forfeiture cases because the Amendment was thought to be limited to criminal punishments while civil forfeitures were remedial and thus neither criminal nor punishments.[166]

This changed in 1993 when the Supreme Court announced that the Eighth Amendment's excessive fines clause applies not only to criminal forfeitures but to some civil forfeitures as well.[167] The full impact of those decisions remained uncertain initially, because the Court declined to articulate a test by which to measure particular forfeitures against the clause's proscriptions.[168] It subsequently selected in *Bajakajian* the standard used as the measure under the parallel cruel and unusual punishment clause of the Eighth Amendment: "a punitive forfeiture violates the Excessive Fines Clause if it is grossly disproportionate to the gravity of a defendant's offense."[169] Subsequent federal appellate courts tend to measure the facts before them against those in *Bajakajian*. Several circuits begin with a standard distilled from the factors there;[170] others simply point to a stark factual differences between *Bajakajian* and the cases before them.[171] In either case, a punitive forfeiture ordinarily will not be considered an excessive fine, if it is distinguishable on one or more of the grounds *Bajakajian* mentioned as indicative of gross disproportionality, *e.g.,* a single crime, unrelated to any other criminality, causing relatively little harm, but resulting in a forfeiture greatly disproportionate to the authorized fine.[172]

Double Jeopardy

Historically, the procedure used to accomplish forfeiture made a difference for purposes of the Fifth Amendment's double jeopardy clause.[173] Where confiscation was accomplished through civil, in rem proceedings against the property, a prior trial of the property owner resulting in either acquittal or conviction was no bar to subsequent forfeiture proceedings.[174] Where conviction was a prerequisite to forfeiture, if double jeopardy precluded further trial and conviction, it likewise precluded forfeiture.

The Supreme Court's conclusion in *Austin* that certain civil forfeitures may be considered punitive for purposes of the Eighth Amendment's excessive fines clause seemed to have obvious double jeopardy implications. In fact, the Court went so far as to note that its past decisions declining to apply the double jeopardy clause to civil forfeitures arose "only in cases where the forfeiture could properly be characterized as remedial."[175] Yet the Court in *United States v. Ursery*, 518 U.S. 267 (1996) reaffirmed its faith in the traditional tests. Forfeitures that Congress has designated as remedial civil sanctions do not implicate double jeopardy concerns unless "the statutory scheme [is] so punitive either in purpose or effect as to negate Congress' intention to establish a civil remedial mechanism," 518 U.S. at 278.[176]

Sixth Amendment

The Sixth Amendment assures the accused in criminal proceedings the right to a jury trial, to the assistance of counsel, and to confrontation accusers. The Supreme Court long ago held that the right to confrontation does not apply in civil forfeiture cases and has not revisited the issue.[177] The right to the assistance of counsel in criminal cases does not prevent the government from confiscating fees paid to counsel;[178] or, upon a probable cause showing, from obtaining a restraining order to freeze assets preventing the payment of attorneys' fees;[179] or entitle an otherwise indigent property owner to the appointment of counsel for substitute asset forfeiture proceedings.[180] The Amendment is by its terms only applicable "in all criminal prosecutions," and consequently there is no constitutionally required right to assistance of counsel in civil forfeiture cases.[181]

The Court's opinion in *Libretti,* to the effect that there is no right to a jury trial on disputed factual issues in criminal forfeiture, rests on a somewhat battered foundation. At the time, it was thought that "there [was] no Sixth Amendment right to jury sentencing, even where the sentence turns on specific finding of fact." 516 U.S. at 49, quoting *McMillan v. Pennsylvania*, 477 U.S. 79, 93 (1986). Thereafter, the Court explained that *McMillan* impermissibly slighted the right to have certain sentencing factors decided by the jury. "Any fact that increases the penalty for a crime beyond the prescribed statutory maximum," the Court declared in *Apprendi v. New Jersey*, 530 U.S. 466, 490 (2000), "must be submitted to a jury, and proved beyond a reasonable doubt." The erosion of *McMillan* notwithstanding, the fact that criminal forfeiture is a penalty *within* "the prescribed statutory maximum" and that Rule 32.2 of the Federal Rules of Criminal Procedure affords an expanded jury determination right would seem to shield federal criminal forfeiture procedures from *Apprendi*-based attacks. Although *Apprendi*'s implications for the preponderance standard might appear slightly more ominous, the federal appellate courts have either explicitly or implicitly declined to apply *Apprendi* to criminal forfeitures.[182]

Due Process

Due process objections can come in such a multitude of variations that general statements are hazardous. More specifically, due process demands that those with an interest in the property the government seeks to confiscate be given notice and opportunity for a hearing to contest.[183] Actual notice is not required but the government's efforts must be "reasonably calculated, under all the circumstances, to apprise" of the opportunity to contest.[184] In some instances, due process permits the initiation of forfeiture proceedings by seizing the personal property in question without first giving the property owner either notice or the prior opportunity of a hearing to contest the seizure and confiscation.[185] But absent exigent circumstances, the owner is entitled to the opportunity for a preseizure hearing in the case of real property where there is no real danger that the property will be spirited away in order to frustrate efforts to secure in rem jurisdiction over it.[186] Due process also requires a pretrial hearing on the forfeitability of property made subject to a postseizure, pretrial restraining order designed to prevent dissipation.[187]

While due process clearly limits at some point the circumstances under which the property of an innocent owner may be confiscated,[188] the Court has declined the opportunity to broadly assert that due process uniformly precludes confiscation of the property of an innocent owner, *Bennis v. Michigan*, 516 U.S. 442 (1996).[189] *Bennis*, however, is a 5-4 decision in which Justice Ginsburg joined the majority but filed a concurring opinion in which she emphasized the importance of the case's somewhat individualistic facts.[190]

Any delay between seizure and hearing offends due process only when it fails to meet the test applied in speedy trial cases: is the delay unreasonable given the length of delay, the reasons for the delay, the claimant's assertion of his or her rights, and prejudice to the claimant?[191]

In other challenges, the lower federal courts have found that due process permits: the procedure of shifting the burden of proof to a forfeiture claimant after the government has shown probable cause and allows use of a probable cause standard in civil forfeitures;[192] postponement of the determination of third-party interests in criminal forfeiture cases until after trial in the main;[193] and fugitive disentitlement under 28 U.S.C. 2466.[194]

Whether in cases occasioned by delay, failure of notice, or want of predeprivational hearing for real property, the lower courts became somewhat ensnarled in the consequences that flow from a finding that the government has violated due process demands in a forfeiture context. Some concluded that the lack of due process voided the purported administrative or judicial forfeiture even if an intervening statute of limitations barred relitigation of confiscation proceedings;[195] others determined that the forfeiture need not be vacated[196] although they sometimes held that the property owner might be entitled to disgorgement or interest.[197] CAFRA resolved the conflict by establishing a timetable within which the government must restart forfeiture proceedings following a claimant's successful motion setting aside an earlier confiscation declaration.[198]

Finally, counsel in *Monsanto* and *Caplin & Drysdale*, challenged on both Sixth Amendment right counsel and Fifth Amendment due process grounds the confiscation of property paid for, and destined to pay for, the services of defense counsel. The Supreme Court rejected both assertions.[199] The Court left open, however, the question of whether due process requires notice and the opportunity for a hearing before a restraining order may be issued.[200] At least two circuits have concluded that absent extraordinary circumstances due process requires notice and an opportunity to be heard prior to the issuance of a restraining order.[201] In the presence of extraordinary circumstances, notice and hearing may be postponed until soon after issuance of the order as long as the opportunity is afforded before trial.[202]

Article III

Section 3 of Article III of the United States Constitution does not appear to threaten most contemporary forfeiture statutes. It provides in part that "no attainder of treason shall work corruption of blood, or forfeiture except during the life of the person attainted." The section on its face seems to restrict forfeiture only in treason cases, but at least one court has suggested a broader scope.[203]

Even if Article III when read in conjunction with the due process clause reaches not only treason but all crimes, its prohibitions run only to forfeiture of estate. They do not address statutory forfeitures of the type currently found in state and federal law. The critical distinction between forfeiture of estate and statutory forfeiture is that in the first all of the defendant's property, related or unrelated to the offense and acquired before, during, or after the crime, is confiscated. In the second, confiscation is only possible if the property is related to the criminal conduct in the manner defined by the statute. Some have suggested that Congress intended to revive forfeiture of estate when it crafted the RICO criminal forfeiture provisions.[204] The courts have nevertheless upheld the RICO provisions in the face of Article III challenges.[205]

Fourth Amendment

Fourth Amendment questions may appear somewhat unsettled. Many statutes reflected the traditional view of contraband that forfeitable property may be seized without observing the normal demands of the Amendment's warrant requirements.[206] The position of the Supreme Court is uncertain[207] and the lower courts are split as to whether purely domestic forfeiture seizures must comply with the warrant requirements in the absence of some other applicable and recognized exception, *e.g.*, seizure of evidence incident to lawful arrest or vehicle seizures.[208] The recent promulgation of Rule G (forfeiture actions in rem) of the Supplemental Admiralty and Maritime Claims to the Federal Rules of Civil Procedure left the issue unresolved.[209]

The point may be academic. Unlawfully seized evidence may not be used in the forfeiture proceedings,[210] but unlawful seizure of the res does not doom the proceedings as long as there is sufficient untainted evidence to support the confiscation.[211]

Ex Post Facto

Neither the states nor the federal government may enact ex post facto laws.[212] The prohibition applies both to laws which make criminal conduct which was innocent when committed and laws which increase the penalties for a crime over those which attached when a crime was committed.[213] The ex post facto bar, however, poses no impediment to the application of a new sanction such as forfeiture to a continuing crime which straddles the date of enactment.[214]

First Amendment

When confiscation involves material entitled to First Amendment protection, more demanding standards must be met. In *Fort Wayne Books, Inc. v. Indiana*, 489 U.S. 46 (1989), the Court held while a single book or film might be seized upon an ex parte probable cause showing, books or films could not be taken completely out of circulation until after an adversary hearing on their obscenity. On the other hand, the First Amendment stands as no bar to the use of criminal forfeiture to punish those convicted of engaging in the commercial exploitation of obscenity,[215] nor to civil forfeiture of the equipment used by an unlicensed radio station.[216]

ATTACHMENTS

18 U.S.C. 981. Civil Forfeiture (Text)

(a)

(1) The following property is subject to forfeiture to the United States:

(A) Any property, real or personal, involved in a transaction or attempted transaction in violation of section 1956, 1957 or 1960 of this title, or any property traceable to such property.

(B) Any property, real or personal, within the jurisdiction of the United States, constituting, derived from, or traceable to, any proceeds obtained directly or indirectly from an offense against a foreign nation, or any property used to facilitate such an offense, if the offense—

(i) involves trafficking in nuclear, chemical, biological, or radiological weapons technology or material, or the manufacture, importation, sale, or distribution of a controlled substance (as that term is defined for purposes of the Controlled Substances Act), or any other conduct described in section 1956(c)(7)(B);

(ii) would be punishable within the jurisdiction of the foreign nation by death or imprisonment for a term exceeding 1 year; and

(iii) would be punishable under the laws of the United States by imprisonment for a term exceeding 1 year, if the act or activity constituting the offense had occurred within the jurisdiction of the United States.

(C) Any property, real or personal, which constitutes or is derived from proceeds traceable to a violation of section 215, 471, 472, 473, 474, 476, 477, 478, 479, 480, 481, 485, 486, 487, 488, 501, 502, 510, 542, 545, 656, 657, 842, 844, 1005, 1006, 1007, 1014, 1028, 1029, 1030, 1032, or 1344 of this title or any offense constituting "specified unlawful activity" (as defined in section 1956(c)(7) of this title), or a conspiracy to commit such offense.

(D) Any property, real or personal, which represents or is traceable to the gross receipts obtained, directly or indirectly, from a violation of—

(i) section 666(a)(1) (relating to Federal program fraud);

(ii) section 1001 (relating to fraud and false statements);

(iii) section 1031 (relating to major fraud against the United States);

(iv) section 1032 (relating to concealment of assets from conservator or receiver of insured financial institution);

(v) section 1341 (relating to mail fraud); or

(vi) section 1343 (relating to wire fraud),

if such violation relates to the sale of assets acquired or held by the Resolution Trust Corporation, the Federal Deposit Insurance Corporation, as conservator or receiver for a financial institution, or any other conservator for a financial institution appointed by the Office of the Comptroller of the Currency or the Office of Thrift Supervision or the National Credit Union Administration, as conservator or liquidating agent for a financial institution.

(E) With respect to an offense listed in subsection (a)(1)(D) committed for the purpose of executing or attempting to execute any scheme or artifice to defraud, or for obtaining money or property by means of false or fraudulent statements, pretenses, representations or promises, the gross receipts of such an offense shall include all property, real or personal, tangible or intangible, which thereby is obtained, directly or indirectly.

(F) Any property, real or personal, which represents or is traceable to the gross proceeds obtained, directly or indirectly, from a violation of—

(i) section 511 (altering or removing motor vehicle identification numbers);

(ii) section 553 (importing or exporting stolen motor vehicles);

(iii) section 2119 (armed robbery of automobiles);

(iv) section 2312 (transporting stolen motor vehicles in interstate commerce); or

(v) section 2313 (possessing or selling a stolen motor vehicle that has moved in interstate commerce).

(G) All assets, foreign or domestic –

(i) of any individual, entity, or organization engaged in planning or perpetrating any Federal crime of terrorism (as defined in section 2332b(g)(5)) against the United States, citizens or residents of the United States, or their property, and all assets, foreign or domestic, affording any person a source of influence over any such entity or organization;

(ii) acquired or maintained by any person with the intent and for the purpose of supporting, planning, conducting, or concealing Federal crime of terrorism (as defined in section 2332b(g)(5)) against the United States, citizens or residents of the United States, or their property; or

(iii) derived from, involved in, or used or intended to be used to commit any Federal crime of terrorism (as defined in section 2332b(g)(5)) against the United States, citizens or residents of the United States, or their property.

(iv) of any individual, entity, or organization engaged in planning or perpetrating any act of international terrorism (as defined in section 2331) against an international organization (as defined in section 209 of the State Department Basic Authorities Act of 1956 (22 U.S.C. 4309(b)) or against any foreign Government. Where the property sought for forfeiture is located beyond the territorial boundaries of the United States, an act in furtherance of such planning or perpetration must have occurred within the jurisdiction of the United States.

(H) Any property, real or personal, involved in a violation or attempted violation, or which constitutes or is derived from proceeds traceable to a violation, of section 2339C of this title.

(2) For purposes of paragraph (1), the term "proceeds" is defined as follows:

(A) In cases involving illegal goods, illegal services, unlawful activities, and telemarketing and health care fraud schemes, the term "proceeds" means property of any kind obtained directly or indirectly, as the result of the commission of the offense giving rise to forfeiture, and any property traceable thereto, and is not limited to the net gain or profit realized from the offense.

(B) In cases involving lawful goods or lawful services that are sold or provided in an illegal manner, the term "proceeds" means the amount of money acquired through the illegal transactions resulting in the forfeiture, less the direct costs incurred in providing the goods or services. The claimant shall have the burden of proof with respect to the issue of direct costs. The direct costs shall not include any part of the overhead expenses of the entity providing the goods or services, or any part of the income taxes paid by the entity.

(C) In cases involving fraud in the process of obtaining a loan or extension of credit, the court shall allow the claimant a deduction from the forfeiture to the extent that the loan was repaid, or the debt was satisfied, without any financial loss to the victim.

(b)

(1) Except as provided in section 985, any property subject to forfeiture to the United States under subsection (a) may be seized by the Attorney General and, in the case of property involved in a violation investigated by the Secretary of the Treasury or the United States Postal Service, the property may also be seized by the Secretary of the Treasury or the Postal Service, respectively.

(2) Seizures pursuant to this section shall be made pursuant to a warrant obtained in the same manner as provided for a search warrant under the Federal Rules of Criminal Procedure, except that a seizure may be made without a warrant if—

(A) a complaint for forfeiture has been filed in the United States district court and the court issued an arrest warrant in rem pursuant to the Supplemental Rules for Certain Admiralty and Maritime Claims;

(B) there is probable cause to believe that the property is subject to forfeiture and—

(i) the seizure is made pursuant to a lawful arrest or search; or

(ii) another exception to the Fourth Amendment warrant requirement would apply; or

(C) the property was lawfully seized by a State or local law enforcement agency and transferred to a Federal agency.

(3) Notwithstanding the provisions of rule 41(a) of the Federal Rules of Criminal Procedure, a seizure warrant may be issued pursuant to this subsection by a judicial officer in any district in which a forfeiture action against the property may be filed under section 1355(b) of title 28, and may be executed in any district in which the property is found, or transmitted to the central authority of any foreign state for service in accordance with any treaty or other international agreement. Any motion for the return of property seized under this section shall be filed in the district court in which the seizure warrant was issued or in the district court for the district in which the property was seized.

(4)

(A) If any person is arrested or charged in a foreign country in connection with an offense that would give rise to the forfeiture of property in the United States under this section or under the Controlled Substances Act, the Attorney General may apply to any Federal judge or magistrate judge in the district in which the property is located for an ex parte order restraining the property subject to forfeiture for not more than 30 days, except that the time may be extended for good cause shown at a hearing conducted in the manner provided in rule 43(e) of the Federal Rules of Civil Procedure.

(B) The application for the restraining order shall set forth the nature and circumstances of the foreign charges and the basis for belief that the person arrested or charged has property in the United States that would be subject to forfeiture, and shall contain a statement that the restraining order is needed to preserve the availability of property for such time as is necessary to receive evidence from the foreign country or elsewhere in support of probable cause for the seizure of the property under this subsection.

(c) Property taken or detained under this section shall not be repleviable, but shall be deemed to be in the custody of the Attorney General, the Secretary of the Treasury, or the Postal Service, as the case may be, subject only to the orders and decrees of the court or the official having jurisdiction thereof. Whenever property is seized under this subsection, the Attorney General, the Secretary of the Treasury, or the Postal Service, as the case may be, may—

(1) place the property under seal;

(2) remove the property to a place designated by him; or

(3) require that the General Services Administration take custody of the property and remove it, if practicable, to an appropriate location for disposition in accordance with law.

(d) For purposes of this section, the provisions of the customs laws relating to the seizure, summary and judicial forfeiture, condemnation of property for violation of the customs laws, the disposition of such property or the proceeds from the sale of such property under this section, the remission or mitigation of such forfeitures, and the compromise of claims (19 U.S.C. 1602 et seq.), insofar as they are applicable and not inconsistent with the provisions of this section, shall apply to seizures and forfeitures incurred, or alleged to have been incurred, under this section, except that such duties as are imposed upon the customs officer or any other person with respect to the seizure and forfeiture of property under the customs laws shall be performed with respect to seizures and forfeitures of property under this section by such officers, agents, or other persons as may be authorized or designated for that purpose by the Attorney General, the Secretary of the Treasury, or the Postal Service, as the case may be. The Attorney General shall have sole responsibility for disposing of petitions for remission or mitigation with respect to property involved in a judicial forfeiture proceeding.

(e) Notwithstanding any other provision of the law, except section 3 of the Anti Drug Abuse Act of 1986, the Attorney General, the Secretary of the Treasury, or the Postal Service, as the case may be, is authorized to retain property forfeited pursuant to this section, or to transfer such property on such terms and conditions as he may determine—

(1) to any other Federal agency;
(2) to any State or local law enforcement agency which participated directly in any of the acts which led to the seizure or forfeiture of the property;
(3) in the case of property referred to in subsection (a)(1)(C), to any Federal financial institution regulatory agency—
    (A) to reimburse the agency for payments to claimants or creditors of the institution; and
    (B) to reimburse the insurance fund of the agency for losses suffered by the fund as a result of the receivership or liquidation;
(4) in the case of property referred to in subsection (a)(1)(C), upon the order of the appropriate Federal financial institution regulatory agency, to the financial institution as restitution, with the value of the property so transferred to be set off against any amount later recovered by the financial institution as compensatory damages in any State or Federal proceeding;
(5) in the case of property referred to in subsection (a)(1)(C), to any Federal financial institution regulatory agency, to the extent of the agency's contribution of resources to, or expenses involved in, the seizure and forfeiture, and the investigation leading directly to the seizure and forfeiture, of such property;
(6) as restoration to any victim of the offense giving rise to the forfeiture, including, in the case of a money laundering offense, any offense constituting the underlying specified unlawful activity; or
(7) In the case of property referred to in subsection (a)(1)(D), to the Resolution Trust Corporation, the Federal Deposit Insurance Corporation, or any other Federal financial institution regulatory agency (as defined in section 8(e)(7)(D) of the Federal Deposit Insurance Act).

The Attorney General, the Secretary of the Treasury, or the Postal Service, as the case may be, shall ensure the equitable transfer pursuant to paragraph (2) of any forfeited property to the appropriate State or local law enforcement agency so as to reflect generally the contribution of any such agency participating directly in any of the acts which led to the seizure or forfeiture of such property. A decision by the Attorney General, the Secretary of the Treasury, or the Postal Service pursuant to paragraph (2) shall not be subject to review. The United States shall not be liable in any action arising out of the use of any property the custody of which was transferred pursuant to this section to any non-Federal agency. The Attorney General, the Secretary of the Treasury, or the Postal Service may order the discontinuance of any forfeiture proceedings under this section in favor of the institution of forfeiture proceedings by State or local authorities under an appropriate State or local statute. After the filing of a complaint for forfeiture under this section, the Attorney General may seek dismissal of the complaint in favor of forfeiture proceedings under State or local law. Whenever forfeiture proceedings are discontinued by the United States in favor of State or local proceedings, the United States may transfer custody and possession of the seized property to the appropriate State or local official immediately upon the initiation of the proper actions by such officials. Whenever forfeiture proceedings are discontinued by the United States in favor of State or local proceedings, notice shall be sent to all known interested parties advising them of the discontinuance or dismissal. The United States shall not be liable in any action arising out of the seizure, detention, and transfer of seized property to State or local officials. The United States shall not be liable in any action arising out of a transfer under paragraph (3), (4), or (5) of this subsection.

(f) All right, title, and interest in property described in subsection (a) of this section shall vest in the United States upon commission of the act giving rise to forfeiture under this section.

(g)

(1) Upon the motion of the United States, the court shall stay the civil forfeiture proceeding if the court determines that civil discovery will adversely affect the ability of the Government to conduct a related criminal investigation or the prosecution of a related criminal case.

(2) Upon the motion of a claimant, the court shall stay the civil forfeiture proceeding with respect to that claimant if the court determines that—

(A) the claimant is the subject of a related criminal investigation or case;

(B) the claimant has standing to assert a claim in the civil forfeiture proceeding; and

(C) continuation of the forfeiture proceeding will burden the right of the claimant against self-incrimination in the related investigation or case.

(3) With respect to the impact of civil discovery described in paragraphs (1) and (2), the court may determine that a stay is unnecessary if a protective order limiting discovery would protect the interest of one party without unfairly limiting the ability of the opposing party to pursue the civil case. In no case, however, shall the court impose a protective order as an alternative to a stay if the effect of such protective order would be to allow one party to pursue discovery while the other party is substantially unable to do so.

(4) In this subsection, the terms "related criminal case" and "related criminal investigation" mean an actual prosecution or investigation in progress at the time at which the request for the stay, or any subsequent motion to lift the stay is made. In determining whether a criminal case or investigation is "related" to a civil forfeiture proceeding, the court shall consider the degree of similarity between the parties, witnesses, facts, and circumstances involved in the two proceedings, without requiring an identity with respect to any one or more factors.

(5) In requesting a stay under paragraph (1), the Government may, in appropriate cases, submit evidence ex parte in order to avoid disclosing any matter that may adversely affect an ongoing criminal investigation or pending criminal trial.

(6) Whenever a civil forfeiture proceeding is stayed pursuant to this subsection, the court shall enter any order necessary to preserve the value of the property or to protect the rights of lienholders or other persons with an interest in the property while the stay is in effect.

(7) A determination by the court that the claimant has standing to request a stay pursuant to paragraph (2) shall apply only to this subsection and shall not preclude the Government from objecting to the standing of the claimant by dispositive motion or at the time of trial.

(h) In addition to the venue provided for in section 1395 of title 28 or any other provision of law, in the case of property of a defendant charged with a violation that is the basis for forfeiture of the property under this section, a proceeding for forfeiture under this section may be brought in the judicial district in which the defendant owning such property is found or in the judicial district in which the criminal prosecution is brought.

(i)

(1) Whenever property is civilly or criminally forfeited under this chapter, the Attorney General or the Secretary of the Treasury, as the case may be, may transfer the forfeited personal property or the proceeds of the sale of any forfeited personal or real property to any foreign country which participated directly or indirectly in the seizure or forfeiture of the property, if such a transfer—

(A) has been agreed to by the Secretary of State;

(B) is authorized in an international agreement between the United States and the foreign country; and

(C) is made to a country which, if applicable, has been certified under section 481(h) of the Foreign Assistance Act of 1961.

A decision by the Attorney General or the Secretary of the Treasury pursuant to this paragraph shall not be subject to review. The foreign country shall, in the event of a transfer of property or proceeds of sale of property under this subsection, bear all expenses incurred by the United States in the seizure, maintenance, inventory, storage, forfeiture, and disposition of the property, and all transfer costs. The payment of all such expenses, and the transfer of assets pursuant to this paragraph, shall be upon such terms and conditions as the Attorney General or the Secretary of the Treasury may, in his discretion, set.

(2) The provisions of this section shall not be construed as limiting or superseding any other authority of the United States to provide assistance to a foreign country in obtaining property related to a crime committed in the foreign country, including property which is sought as evidence of a crime committed in the foreign country.

(3) A certified order or judgment of forfeiture by a court of competent jurisdiction of a foreign country concerning property which is the subject of forfeiture under this section and was determined by such court to be the type of property described in subsection (a)(1)(B) of this section, and any certified recordings or transcripts of testimony taken in a foreign judicial proceeding concerning such order or judgment of forfeiture, shall be admissible in evidence in a proceeding brought pursuant to this section. Such certified order or judgment of forfeiture, when admitted into evidence, shall constitute probable cause that the property forfeited by such order or judgment of forfeiture is subject to forfeiture under this section and creates a rebuttable presumption of the forfeitability of such property under this section.

(4) A certified order or judgment of conviction by a court of competent jurisdiction of a foreign country concerning an unlawful drug activity which gives rise to forfeiture under this section and any certified recordings or transcripts of testimony taken in a foreign judicial proceeding concerning such order or

judgment of conviction shall be admissible in evidence in a proceeding brought pursuant to this section. Such certified order or judgment of conviction, when admitted into evidence, creates a rebuttable presumption that the unlawful drug activity giving rise to forfeiture under this section has occurred.

(5) The provisions of paragraphs (3) and (4) of this subsection shall not be construed as limiting the admissibility of any evidence otherwise admissible, nor shall they limit the ability of the United States to establish probable cause that property is subject to forfeiture by any evidence otherwise admissible.

(j) For purposes of this section—

(1) the term "Attorney General" means the Attorney General or his delegate; and

(2) the term "Secretary of the Treasury" means the Secretary of the Treasury or his delegate.

(k) Interbank accounts.—

(1) In general.—

(A) In general.—For the purpose of a forfeiture under this section or under the Controlled Substances Act (21 U.S.C. 801 et seq.), if funds are deposited into an account at a foreign bank, and that foreign bank has an interbank account in the United States with a covered financial institution (as defined in section 5318(j)(1) of title 31), the funds shall be deemed to have been deposited into the interbank account in the United States, and any restraining order, seizure warrant, or arrest warrant in rem regarding the funds may be served on the covered financial institution, and funds in the interbank account, up to the value of the funds deposited into the account at the foreign bank, may be restrained, seized, or arrested.

(B) Authority to suspend.—The Attorney General, in consultation with the Secretary of the Treasury, may suspend or terminate a forfeiture under this section if the Attorney General determines that a conflict of law exists between the laws of the jurisdiction in which the foreign bank is located and the laws of the United States with respect to liabilities arising from the restraint, seizure, or arrest of such funds, and that such suspension or termination would be in the interest of justice and would not harm the national interests of the United States.

(2) No requirement for Government to trace funds.—If a forfeiture action is brought against funds that are restrained, seized, or arrested under paragraph (1), it shall not be necessary for the Government to establish that the funds are directly traceable to the funds that were deposited into the foreign bank, nor shall it be necessary for the Government to rely on the application of section 984.

(3) Claims brought by owner of the funds.—If a forfeiture action is instituted against funds restrained, seized, or arrested under paragraph (1), the owner of the funds deposited into the account at the foreign bank may contest the forfeiture by filing a claim under section 983.

(4) Definitions.—For purposes of this subsection, the following definitions shall apply:

(A) Interbank account.—The term "interbank account" has the same meaning as in section 984(c)(2)(B).

(B) Owner.—

(i) In general.—Except as provided in clause (ii), the term "owner"—

(I) means the person who was the owner, as that term is defined in section 983(d)(6), of the funds that were deposited into the foreign bank at the time such funds were deposited; and

(II) does not include either the foreign bank or any financial institution acting as an intermediary in the transfer of the funds into the interbank account.

(ii) Exception.—The foreign bank may be considered the "owner" of the funds (and no other person shall qualify as the owner of such funds) only if—

(I) the basis for the forfeiture action is wrongdoing committed by the foreign bank; or

(II) the foreign bank establishes, by a preponderance of the evidence, that prior to the restraint, seizure, or arrest of the funds, the foreign bank had discharged all or part of its obligation to the prior owner of the funds, in which case the foreign bank shall be deemed the owner of the funds to the extent of such discharged obligation.

18 U.S.C. 982. Criminal Forfeiture (Text)

(a)

(1) The court, in imposing sentence on a person convicted of an offense in violation of section 1956, 1957, or 1960 of this title, shall order that the person forfeit to the United States any property, real or personal, involved in such offense, or any property traceable to such property.

(2) The court, in imposing sentence on a person convicted of a violation of, or a conspiracy to violate –

(A) section 215, 656, 657, 1005, 1006, 1007, 1014, 1341, 1343, or 1344 of this title, affecting a financial institution, or

(B) section 471, 472, 473, 474, 476, 477, 478, 479, 480, 481, 485, 486, 487, 488, 501, 502, 510, 542, 545, 842, 844, 1028, 1029, or 1030 of this title, shall order that the person forfeit to the United States any property constituting, or derived from, proceeds the person obtained directly or indirectly, as the result of such violation.

(3) The court, in imposing a sentence on a person convicted of an offense under –

(A) section 666(a)(1) (relating to Federal program fraud);

(B) section 1001 (relating to fraud and false statements);

(C) section 1031 (relating to major fraud against the United States);

(D) section 1032 (relating to concealment of assets from conservator, receiver, or liquidating agent of insured financial institution);

(E) section 1341 (relating to mail fraud); or

(F) section 1343 (relating to wire fraud), involving the sale of assets acquired or held by the Resolution Trust Corporation, the Federal Deposit Insurance

Corporation, as conservator or receiver for a financial institution or any other conservator for a financial institution appointed by the Office of the Comptroller of the Currency or the Office of Thrift Supervision, or the National Credit Union Administration, as conservator or liquidating agent for a financial institution, shall order that the person forfeit to the United States any property, real or personal, which represents or is traceable to the gross receipts obtained, directly or indirectly, as a result of such violation.

(4) With respect to an offense listed in subsection (a)(3) committed for the purpose of executing or attempting to execute any scheme or artifice to defraud, or for obtaining money or property by means of false or fraudulent statements, pretenses, representations, or promises, the gross receipts of such an offense shall include any property, real or personal, tangible or intangible, which is obtained, directly or indirectly, as a result of such offense.

(5) The court, in imposing sentence on a person convicted of a violation or conspiracy to violate –

(A) section 511 (altering or removing motor vehicle identification numbers);

(B) section 553 (importing or exporting stolen motor vehicles);

(C) section 2119 (armed robbery of automobiles);

(D) section 2312 (transporting stolen motor vehicles in interstate commerce); or

(E) section 2313 (possessing or selling a stolen motor vehicle that has moved in interstate commerce); shall order that the person forfeit to the United States any property, real or personal, which represents or is traceable to the gross proceeds obtained, directly or indirectly, as a result of such violation.

(6)

(A) The court, in imposing sentence on a person convicted of a violation of, or conspiracy to violate, section 274(a), 274A(a)(1), or 274A(a)(2) of the Immigration and Nationality Act or section 554, 1425, 1426, 1427, 1541, 1542, 1543, 1544, or 1546 of this title, or a violation of, or conspiracy to violate, section 1028 of this title if committed in connection with passport or visa issuance or use, shall order that the person forfeit to the United States, regardless of any provision of State law –

(i) any conveyance, including any vessel, vehicle, or aircraft used in the commission of the offense of which the person is convicted; and

(ii) any property real or personal –

(I) that constitutes, or is derived from or is traceable to the proceeds obtained directly or indirectly from the commission of the offense of which the person is convicted; or

(II) that is used to facilitate, or is intended to be used to facilitate, the commission of the offense of which the person is convicted.

(B) The court, in imposing sentence on a person described in subparagraph (A), shall order that the person forfeit to the United States all property described in that subparagraph.

(7) The court, in imposing sentence on a person convicted of a Federal health care offense, shall order the person to forfeit property, real or personal, that constitutes or is derived, directly or indirectly, from gross proceeds traceable to the commission of the offense.

(8) The court, in sentencing a defendant convicted of an offense under section 1028, 1029, 1341, 1342, 1343, or 1344, or of a conspiracy to commit such an offense, if the offense involves telemarketing (as that term is defined in section 2325), shall order that the defendant forfeit to the United States any real or personal property –

(A) used or intended to be used to commit, to facilitate, or to promote the commission of such offense; and

(B) constituting, derived from, or traceable to the gross proceeds that the defendant obtained directly or indirectly as a result of the offense.

(b)

(1) The forfeiture of property under this section, including any seizure and disposition of the property and any related judicial or administrative proceeding, shall be governed by the provisions of section 413 (other than subsection (d) of that section) of the Comprehensive Drug Abuse Prevention and Control Act of 1970 (21 U.S.C. 853).

(2) The substitution of assets provisions of subsection 413(p) shall not be used to order a defendant to forfeit assets in place of the actual property laundered where such defendant acted merely as an intermediary who handled but did not retain the property in the course of the money laundering offense unless the defendant, in committing the offense or offenses giving rise to the forfeiture, conducted three or more separate transactions involving a total of $100,000 or more in any twelve month period.

18 U.S.C. 983. General Rules for Civil Forfeiture Proceedings (Text)

(a) *Notice; claim; complaint.*—

(1)

(A)

(i) Except as provided in clauses (ii) through (v), in any nonjudicial civil forfeiture proceeding under a civil forfeiture statute, with respect to which the Government is required to send written notice to interested parties, such notice shall be sent in a manner to achieve proper notice as soon as practicable, and in no case more than 60 days after the date of the seizure.

(ii) No notice is required if, before the 60-day period expires, the Government files a civil judicial forfeiture action against the property and provides notice of that action as required by law.

(iii) If, before the 60-day period expires, the Government does not file a civil judicial forfeiture action, but does obtain a criminal indictment containing an allegation that the property is subject to forfeiture, the Government shall either –

(I) send notice within the 60 days and continue the nonjudicial civil forfeiture proceeding under this section; or

(II) terminate the nonjudicial civil forfeiture proceeding, and take the steps necessary to preserve its right to maintain custody of the property as provided in the applicable criminal forfeiture statute.

(iv) In a case in which the property is seized by a State or local law enforcement agency and turned over to a Federal law enforcement agency for the purpose of forfeiture under Federal law, notice shall be sent not more than 90 days after the date of seizure by the State or local law enforcement agency.

(v) If the identity or interest of a party is not determined until after the seizure or turnover but is determined before a declaration of forfeiture is entered, notice shall be sent to such interested party not later than 60 days after the determination by the Government of the identity of the party or the party's interest.

(B) A supervisory official in the headquarters office of the seizing agency may extend the period for sending notice under subparagraph (A) for a period not to exceed 30 days (which period may not be further extended except by a court), if the official determines that the conditions in subparagraph (D) are present.

(C) Upon motion by the Government, a court may extend the period for sending notice under subparagraph (A) for a period not to exceed 60 days, which period may be further extended by the court for 60-day periods, as necessary, if the court determines, based on a written certification of a supervisory official in the headquarters office of the seizing agency, that the conditions in subparagraph (D) are present.

(D) The period for sending notice under this paragraph may be extended only if there is reason to believe that notice may have an adverse result, including –

(i) endangering the life or physical safety of an individual;

(ii) flight from prosecution;

(iii) destruction of or tampering with evidence;

(iv) intimidation of potential witnesses; or

(v) otherwise seriously jeopardizing an investigation or unduly delaying a trial.

(E) Each of the Federal seizing agencies conducting nonjudicial forfeitures under this section shall report periodically to the Committees on the Judiciary of the House of Representatives and the Senate the number of occasions when an extension of time is granted under subparagraph (B).

(F) If the Government does not send notice of a seizure of property in accordance with subparagraph (A) to the person from whom the property was seized, and no extension of time is granted, the Government shall return the property to that person without prejudice to the right of the Government to commence a forfeiture proceeding at a later time. The Government shall not be required to return contraband or other property that the person from whom the property was seized may not legally possess.

(2)

(A) Any person claiming property seized in a nonjudicial civil forfeiture proceeding under a civil forfeiture statute may file a claim with the appropriate official after the seizure.

(B) A claim under subparagraph (A) may be filed not later than the deadline set forth in a personal notice letter (which deadline may be not earlier than 35 days after the date the letter is mailed), except that if that letter is not received, then a claim may be filed not later than 30 days after the date of final publication of notice of seizure.

(C) A claim shall –

(i) identify the specific property being claimed;

(ii) state the claimant's interest in such property; and

(iii) be made under oath, subject to penalty of perjury.

(D) A claim need not be made in any particular form. Each Federal agency conducting nonjudicial forfeitures under this section shall make claim forms generally available on request, which forms shall be written in easily understandable language.

(E) Any person may make a claim under subparagraph (A) without posting bond with respect to the property which is the subject of the claim.

(3)

(A) Not later than 90 days after a claim has been filed, the Government shall file a complaint for forfeiture in the manner set forth in the Supplemental Rules for Certain Admiralty and Maritime Claims or return the property pending the filing of a complaint, except that a court in the district in which the complaint will be filed may extend the period for filing a complaint for good cause shown or upon agreement of the parties.

(B) If the Government does not –

(i) file a complaint for forfeiture or return the property, in accordance with subparagraph (A); or

(ii) before the time for filing a complaint has expired—

(I) obtain a criminal indictment containing an allegation that the property is subject to forfeiture; and

(II) take the steps necessary to preserve its right to maintain custody of the property as provided in the applicable criminal forfeiture statute,

the Government shall promptly release the property pursuant to regulations promulgated by the Attorney General, and may not take any further action to effect the civil forfeiture of such property in connection with the underlying offense.

(C) In lieu of, or in addition to, filing a civil forfeiture complaint, the Government may include a forfeiture allegation in a criminal indictment. If criminal forfeiture is the only forfeiture proceeding commenced by the Government, the Government's right to continued possession of the property shall be governed by the applicable criminal forfeiture statute.

(D) No complaint may be dismissed on the ground that the Government did not have adequate evidence at the time the complaint was filed to establish the forfeitability of the property.

(4)

(A) In any case in which the Government files in the appropriate United States district court a complaint for forfeiture of property, any person claiming an interest in the seized property may file a claim asserting such person's interest in the property in the manner set forth in the Supplemental Rules for Certain Admiralty and Maritime Claims, except that such claim may be filed not later than 30 days after the date of service of the Government's complaint or, as applicable, not later than 30 days after the date of final publication of notice of the filing of the complaint.

(B) A person asserting an interest in seized property, in accordance with subparagraph (A), shall file an answer to the Government's complaint for forfeiture not later than 20 days after the date of the filing of the claim.

(b) *Representation.* –

(1)

(A) If a person with standing to contest the forfeiture of property in a judicial civil forfeiture proceeding under a civil forfeiture statute is financially unable to obtain representation by counsel, and the person is represented by counsel appointed under section 3006A of this title in connection with a related criminal case, the court may authorize counsel to represent that person with respect to the claim.

(B) In determining whether to authorize counsel to represent a person under subparagraph (A), the court shall take into account such factors as –

(i) the person's standing to contest the forfeiture; and

(ii) whether the claim appears to be made in good faith.

(2)

(A) If a person with standing to contest the forfeiture of property in a judicial civil forfeiture proceeding under a civil forfeiture statute is financially unable to obtain representation by counsel, and the property subject to forfeiture is real property that is being used by the person as a primary residence, the court, at the request of the person, shall insure that the person is represented by an attorney for the Legal Services Corporation with respect to the claim.

(B)

(i) At appropriate times during a representation under subparagraph (A), the Legal Services Corporation shall submit a statement of reasonable attorney fees and costs to the court.

(ii) The court shall enter a judgment in favor of the Legal Services Corporation for reasonable attorney fees and costs submitted pursuant to clause (i) and treat such judgment as payable under section 2465 of title 28, United States Code, regardless of the outcome of the case.

(3) The court shall set the compensation for representation under this subsection, which shall be equivalent to that provided for court-appointed representation under section 3006A of this title.

(c) *Burden of proof.*—In a suit or action brought under any civil forfeiture statute for the civil forfeiture of any property –

(1) the burden of proof is on the Government to establish, by a preponderance of the evidence, that the property is subject to forfeiture;

(2) the Government may use evidence gathered after the filing of a complaint for forfeiture to establish, by a preponderance of the evidence, that property is subject to forfeiture; and

(3) if the Government's theory of forfeiture is that the property was used to commit or facilitate the commission of a criminal offense, or was involved in the commission of a criminal offense, the Government shall establish that there was a substantial connection between the property and the offense.

(d) *Innocent owner defense.* –

(1) An innocent owner's interest in property shall not be forfeited under any civil forfeiture statute. The claimant shall have the burden of proving that the claimant is an innocent owner by a preponderance of the evidence.

(2)

(A) With respect to a property interest in existence at the time the illegal conduct giving rise to forfeiture took place, the term "innocent owner" means an owner who –

(i) did not know of the conduct giving rise to forfeiture; or

(ii) upon learning of the conduct giving rise to the forfeiture, did all that reasonably could be expected under the circumstances to terminate such use of the property.

(B)

(i) For the purposes of this paragraph, ways in which a person may show that such person did all that reasonably could be expected may include demonstrating that such person, to the extent permitted by law –

(I) gave timely notice to an appropriate law enforcement agency of information that led the person to know the conduct giving rise to a forfeiture would occur or has occurred; and

(II) in a timely fashion revoked or made a good faith attempt to revoke permission for those engaging in such conduct to use the property or took reasonable actions in consultation with a law enforcement agency to discourage or prevent the illegal use of the property.

(ii) A person is not required by this subparagraph to take steps that the person reasonably believes would be likely to subject any person (other than the person whose conduct gave rise to the forfeiture) to physical danger.

(3)

(A) With respect to a property interest acquired after the conduct giving rise to the forfeiture has taken place, the term "innocent owner" means a person who, at the time that person acquired the interest in the property –

(i) was a bona fide purchaser or seller for value (including a purchaser or seller of goods or services for value); and

(ii) did not know and was reasonably without cause to believe that the property was subject to forfeiture.

(B) An otherwise valid claim under subparagraph (A) shall not be denied on the ground that the claimant gave nothing of value in exchange for the property if –

(i) the property is the primary residence of the claimant;

(ii) depriving the claimant of the property would deprive the claimant of the means to maintain reasonable shelter in the community for the claimant and all dependents residing with the claimant;

(iii) the property is not, and is not traceable to, the proceeds of any criminal offense; and

(iv) the claimant acquired his or her interest in the property through marriage, divorce, or legal separation, or the claimant was the spouse or legal dependent of a person whose death resulted in the transfer of the property to the claimant through inheritance or probate,

except that the court shall limit the value of any real property interest for which innocent ownership is recognized under this subparagraph to the value necessary to maintain reasonable shelter in the community for such claimant and all dependents residing with the claimant.

(4) Notwithstanding any provision of this subsection, no person may assert an ownership interest under this subsection in contraband or other property that it is illegal to possess.

(5) If the court determines, in accordance with this section, that an innocent owner has a partial interest in property otherwise subject to forfeiture, or a joint tenancy or tenancy by the entirety in such property, the court may enter an appropriate order –

(A) severing the property;

(B) transferring the property to the Government with a provision that the Government compensate the innocent owner to the extent of his or her ownership interest once a final order of forfeiture has been entered and the property has been reduced to liquid assets; or

(C) permitting the innocent owner to retain the property subject to a lien in favor of the Government to the extent of the forfeitable interest in the property.

(6) In this subsection, the term "owner"—

(A) means a person with an ownership interest in the specific property sought to be forfeited, including a leasehold, lien, mortgage, recorded security interest, or valid assignment of an ownership interest; and

(B) does not include –

(i) a person with only a general unsecured interest in, or claim against, the property or estate of another;

(ii) a bailee unless the bailor is identified and the bailee shows a colorable legitimate interest in the property seized; or

(iii) a nominee who exercises no dominion or control over the property.

(e) *Motion to set aside forfeiture.* –

(1) Any person entitled to written notice in any nonjudicial civil forfeiture proceeding under a civil forfeiture statute who does not receive such notice may file a motion to set aside a declaration of forfeiture with respect to that person's interest in the property, which motion shall be granted if –

(A) the Government knew, or reasonably should have known, of the moving party's interest and failed to take reasonable steps to provide such party with notice; and

(B) the moving party did not know or have reason to know of the seizure within sufficient time to file a timely claim.

(2)

(A) Notwithstanding the expiration of any applicable statute of limitations, if the court grants a motion under paragraph (1), the court shall set aside the declaration of forfeiture as to the interest of the moving party without prejudice to the right of the Government to commence a subsequent forfeiture proceeding as to the interest of the moving party.

(B) Any proceeding described in subparagraph (A) shall be commenced –

(i) if nonjudicial, within 60 days of the entry of the order granting the motion; or

(ii) if judicial, within 6 months of the entry of the order granting the motion.

(3) A motion under paragraph (1) may be filed not later than 5 years after the date of final publication of notice of seizure of the property.

(4) If, at the time a motion made under paragraph (1) is granted, the forfeited property has been disposed of by the Government in accordance with law, the Government may institute proceedings against a substitute sum of money equal to the value of the moving party's interest in the property at the time the property was disposed of.

(5) A motion filed under this subsection shall be the exclusive remedy for seeking to set aside a declaration of forfeiture under a civil forfeiture statute.

(f) *Release of seized property.* –

(1) A claimant under subsection (a) is entitled to immediate release of seized property if –

(A) the claimant has a possessory interest in the property;

(B) the claimant has sufficient ties to the community to provide assurance that the property will be available at the time of the trial;

(C) the continued possession by the Government pending the final disposition of forfeiture proceedings will cause substantial hardship to the claimant, such as preventing the functioning of a business, preventing an individual from working, or leaving an individual homeless;

(D) the claimant's likely hardship from the continued possession by the Government of the seized property outweighs the risk that the property will be destroyed, damaged, lost, concealed, or transferred if it is returned to the claimant during the pendency of the proceeding; and

(E) none of the conditions set forth in paragraph (8) applies.

(2) A claimant seeking release of property under this subsection must request possession of the property from the appropriate official, and the request must set forth the basis on which the requirements of paragraph (1) are met.

(3)

(A) If not later than 15 days after the date of a request under paragraph (2) the property has not been released, the claimant may file a petition in the district court in which the complaint has been filed or, if no complaint has been filed, in the district court in which the seizure warrant was issued or in the district court for the district in which the property was seized.

(B) The petition described in subparagraph (A) shall set forth –

(i) the basis on which the requirements of paragraph (1) are met; and

(ii) the steps the claimant has taken to secure release of the property from the appropriate official.

(4) If the Government establishes that the claimant's claim is frivolous, the court shall deny the petition. In responding to a petition under this subsection on other grounds, the Government may in appropriate cases submit evidence ex parte in order to avoid disclosing any matter that may adversely affect an ongoing criminal investigation or pending criminal trial.

(5) The court shall render a decision on a petition filed under paragraph (3) not later than 30 days after the date of the filing, unless such 30-day limitation is extended by consent of the parties or by the court for good cause shown.

(6) If –

(A) a petition is filed under paragraph (3); and

(B) the claimant demonstrates that the requirements of paragraph (1) have been met, the district court shall order that the property be returned to the claimant, pending completion of proceedings by the Government to obtain forfeiture of the property.

(7) If the court grants a petition under paragraph (3) –

(A) the court may enter any order necessary to ensure that the value of the property is maintained while the forfeiture action is pending, including

(i) permitting the inspection, photographing, and inventory of the property;

(ii) fixing a bond in accordance with rule E(5) of the Supplemental Rules for Certain Admiralty and Maritime Claims; and

(iii) requiring the claimant to obtain or maintain insurance on the subject property; and

(B) the Government may place a lien against the property or file a lis pendens to ensure that the property is not transferred to another person.

(8) This subsection shall not apply if the seized property –

(A) is contraband, currency, or other monetary instrument, or electronic funds unless such currency or other monetary instrument or electronic funds constitutes the assets of a legitimate business which has been seized;

(B) is to be used as evidence of a violation of the law;

(C) by reason of design or other characteristic, is particularly suited for use in illegal activities; or

(D) is likely to be used to commit additional criminal acts if returned to the claimant.

(g) *Proportionality.* –

(1) The claimant under subsection (a)(4) may petition the court to determine whether the forfeiture was constitutionally excessive.

(2) In making this determination, the court shall compare the forfeiture to the gravity of the offense giving rise to the forfeiture.

(3) The claimant shall have the burden of establishing that the forfeiture is grossly disproportional by a preponderance of the evidence at a hearing conducted by the court without a jury.

(4) If the court finds that the forfeiture is grossly disproportional to the offense it shall reduce or eliminate the forfeiture as necessary to avoid a violation of the Excessive Fines Clause of the Eighth Amendment of the Constitution.

(h) *Civil fine.* –

(1) In any civil forfeiture proceeding under a civil forfeiture statute in which the Government prevails, if the court finds that the claimant's assertion of an interest in the property was frivolous, the court may impose a civil fine on the claimant of an amount equal to 10 percent of the value of the forfeited property, but in no event shall the fine be less than $250 or greater than $5,000.

(2) Any civil fine imposed under this subsection shall not preclude the court from imposing sanctions under rule 11 of the Federal Rules of Civil Procedure.

(3) In addition to the limitations of section 1915 of title 28, United States Code, in no event shall a prisoner file a claim under a civil forfeiture statute or appeal a judgment in a civil action or proceeding based on a civil forfeiture statute if the prisoner has, on three or more prior occasions, while incarcerated or detained in any facility, brought an action or appeal in a court of the United States that was dismissed on the grounds that it is frivolous or malicious, unless the prisoner shows extraordinary and exceptional circumstances.

(i) *Civil forfeiture statute defined.*—In this section, the term "civil forfeiture statute" –

(1) means any provision of Federal law providing for the forfeiture of property other than as a sentence imposed upon conviction of a criminal offense; and

(2) does not include –

(A) the Tariff Act of 1930 or any other provision of law codified in title 19;

(B) the Internal Revenue Code of 1986;

(C) the Federal Food, Drug, and Cosmetic Act (21 U.S.C. 301 et seq.);

(D) the Trading with the Enemy Act (50 U.S.C. App. 1 et seq.) or the International Emergency Economic Powers Act (IEEPA) (50 U.S.C. 1701 et seq.); or

(E) section 1 of title VI of the Act of June 15, 1917 (40 Stat. 233; 22 U.S.C. 401).

(j) *Restraining orders; protective orders.* –

(1) Upon application of the United States, the court may enter a restraining order or injunction, require the execution of satisfactory performance bonds, create receiverships, appoint conservators, custodians, appraisers, accountants, or trustees, or take any other action to seize, secure, maintain, or preserve the availability of property subject to civil forfeiture –

(A) upon the filing of a civil forfeiture complaint alleging that the property with respect to which the order is sought is subject to civil forfeiture; or

(B) prior to the filing of such a complaint, if, after notice to persons appearing to have an interest in the property and opportunity for a hearing, the court determines that –

(i) there is a substantial probability that the United States will prevail on the issue of forfeiture and that failure to enter the order will result in the property being destroyed, removed from the jurisdiction of the court, or otherwise made unavailable for forfeiture; and

(ii) the need to preserve the availability of the property through the entry of the requested order outweighs the hardship on any party against whom the order is to be entered.

(2) An order entered pursuant to paragraph (1)(B) shall be effective for not more than 90 days, unless extended by the court for good cause shown, or unless a complaint described in paragraph (1)(A) has been filed.

(3) A temporary restraining order under this subsection may be entered upon application of the United States without notice or opportunity for a hearing when a complaint has not yet been filed with respect to the property, if the United States demonstrates that there is probable cause to believe that the property with respect to which the order is sought is subject to civil forfeiture and that provision of notice will jeopardize the availability of the property for forfeiture. Such a temporary order shall expire not more than 10 days after the date on which it is entered, unless extended for good cause shown or unless the party against whom it is entered consents to an extension for a longer period. A hearing requested concerning an order entered under this paragraph shall be held at the earliest possible time and prior to the expiration of the temporary order.

(4) The court may receive and consider, at a hearing held pursuant to this subsection, evidence and information that would be inadmissible under the Federal Rules of Evidence.

18 U.S.C. 984. Civil Forfeiture of Fungible Property(Text)

(a)

(1) In any forfeiture action in rem in which the subject property is cash, monetary instruments in bearer form, funds deposited in an account in a financial institution (as defined in section 20 of this title), or precious metals –

(A) it shall not be necessary for the Government to identify the specific property involved in the offense that is the basis for the forfeiture; and

(B) it shall not be a defense that the property involved in such an offense has been removed and replaced by identical property.

(2) Except as provided in subsection (b), any identical property found in the same place or account as the property involved in the offense that is the basis for the forfeiture shall be subject to forfeiture under this section.

(b) No action pursuant to this section to forfeit property not traceable directly to the offense that is the basis for the forfeiture may be commenced more than 1 year from the date of the offense.

(c)

(1) Subsection (a) does not apply to an action against funds held by a financial institution in an interbank account unless the account holder knowingly engaged in the offense that is the basis for the forfeiture.

(2) In this subsection –
(A) the term "financial institution" includes a foreign bank (as defined in section 1(b)(7) of the International Banking Act of 1978 (12 U.S.C. 3101(b)(7))); and
(B) the term "interbank account" means an account held by one financial institution at another financial institution primarily for the purpose of facilitating customer transactions.

(d) Nothing in this section may be construed to limit the ability of the Government to forfeit property under any provision of law if the property involved in the offense giving rise to the forfeiture or property traceable thereto is available for forfeiture.

18 U.S.C. 985. Civil Forfeiture of Real Property (Text)

(a) Notwithstanding any other provision of law, all civil forfeitures of real property and interests in real property shall proceed as judicial forfeitures.

(b)
(1) Except as provided in this section –
(A) real property that is the subject of a civil forfeiture action shall not be seized before entry of an order of forfeiture; and
(B) the owners or occupants of the real property shall not be evicted from, or otherwise deprived of the use and enjoyment of, real property that is the subject of a pending forfeiture action.
(2) The filing of a lis pendens and the execution of a writ of entry for the purpose of conducting an inspection and inventory of the property shall not be considered a seizure under this subsection.

(c)
(1) The Government shall initiate a civil forfeiture action against real property by –
(A) filing a complaint for forfeiture;
(B) posting a notice of the complaint on the property; and
(C) serving notice on the property owner, along with a copy of the complaint.
(2) If the property owner cannot be served with the notice under paragraph (1) because the owner –
(A) is a fugitive;
(B) resides outside the United States and efforts at service pursuant to rule 4 of the Federal Rules of Civil Procedure are unavailing; or
(C) cannot be located despite the exercise of due diligence, constructive service may be made in accordance with the laws of the State in which the property is located.
(3) If real property has been posted in accordance with this subsection, it shall not be necessary for the court to issue an arrest warrant in rem, or to take any other action to establish in rem jurisdiction over the property.

(d)
(1) Real property may be seized prior to the entry of an order of forfeiture if –

(A) the Government notifies the court that it intends to seize the property before trial; and

(B) the court –

(i) issues a notice of application for warrant, causes the notice to be served on the property owner and posted on the property, and conducts a hearing in which the property owner has a meaningful opportunity to be heard; or

(ii) makes an ex parte determination that there is probable cause for the forfeiture and that there are exigent circumstances that permit the Government to seize the property without prior notice and an opportunity for the property owner to be heard.

(2) For purposes of paragraph (1)(B)(ii), to establish exigent circumstances, the Government shall show that less restrictive measures such as a lis pendens, restraining order, or bond would not suffice to protect the Government's interests in preventing the sale, destruction, or continued unlawful use of the real property.

(e) If the court authorizes a seizure of real property under subsection (d)(1)(B)(ii), it shall conduct a prompt post-seizure hearing during which the property owner shall have an opportunity to contest the basis for the seizure.

(f) This section –

(1) applies only to civil forfeitures of real property and interests in real property;

(2) does not apply to forfeitures of the proceeds of the sale of such property or interests, or of money or other assets intended to be used to acquire such property or interests; and

(3) shall not affect the authority of the court to enter a restraining order relating to real property.

18 U.S.C. 987. Anti-terrorist Forfeiture Protection (Text)

(a) Right to contest.– An owner of property that is confiscated under any provision of law relating to the confiscation of assets of suspected international terrorists, may contest that confiscation by filing a claim in the manner set forth in the Federal Rules of Civil Procedure (Supplemental Rules for Certain Admiralty and Maritime Claims), and asserting as an affirmative defense that –

(1) the property is not subject to confiscation under such provision of law; or

(2) the innocent owner provisions of section 983(d) of title 18, United States Code, apply to the case.

(b) Evidence.– In considering a claim filed under this section, a court may admit evidence that is otherwise inadmissible under the Federal Rules of Evidence, if the court determines that the evidence is reliable, and that compliance with the Federal Rules of Evidence may jeopardize the national security interests of the United States.

(c) Clarifications.–

(1) Protection of rights.– The exclusion of certain provisions of Federal law from the definition of the term "civil forfeiture statute" in section 983(i) of title 18, United

States Code, shall not be construed to deny an owner of property the right to contest the confiscation of assets of suspected international terrorists under–

(A) subsection (a) of this section;

(B) the Constitution; or

(C) subchapter II of chapter 5 of title 5, United States Code (commonly known as the "Administrative Procedure Act").

(2) Savings clause.– Nothing in this section shall limit or otherwise affect any other remedies that may be available to an owner of property under section 983 of title 18, United States Code, or any other provision of law.

21 U.S.C. 881. Civil Forfeitures (Controlled Substances)(Text)

(a) *Subject property*

The following shall be subject to forfeiture to the United States and no property right shall exist in them:

(1) All controlled substances which have been manufactured, distributed, dispensed, or acquired in violation of this subchapter.

(2) All raw materials, products, and equipment of any kind which are used, or intended for use, in manufacturing, compounding, processing, delivering, importing, or exporting any controlled substance or listed chemical in violation of this subchapter.

(3) All property which is used, or intended for use, as a container for property described in paragraph (1), (2), or (9).

(4) All conveyances, including aircraft, vehicles, or vessels, which are used, or are intended for use, to transport, or in any manner to facilitate the transportation, sale, receipt, possession, or concealment of property described in paragraph (1), (2), or (9).

(5) All books, records, and research, including formulas, microfilm, tapes, and data which are used, or intended for use, in violation of this subchapter.

(6) All moneys, negotiable instruments, securities, or other things of value furnished or intended to be furnished by any person in exchange for a controlled substance or listed chemical in violation of this subchapter, all proceeds traceable to such an exchange, and all moneys, negotiable instruments, and securities used or intended to be used to facilitate any violation of this subchapter.

(7) All real property, including any right, title, and interest (including any leasehold interest) in the whole of any lot or tract of land and any appurtenances or improvements, which is used, or intended to be used, in any manner or part, to commit, or to facilitate the commission of, a violation of this subchapter punishable by more than one year's imprisonment.

(8) All controlled substances which have been possessed in violation of this subchapter.

(9) All listed chemicals, all drug manufacturing equipment, all tableting machines, all encapsulating machines, and all gelatin capsules, which have been imported,

exported, manufactured, possessed, distributed, dispensed, acquired, or intended to be distributed, dispensed, acquired, imported, or exported, in violation of this subchapter or subchapter II of this chapter.

(10) Any drug paraphernalia (as defined in section 863 of this title).

(11) Any firearm (as defined in section 921 of Title 18) used or intended to be used to facilitate the transportation, sale, receipt, possession, or concealment of property described in paragraph (1) or (2) and any proceeds traceable to such property.

(b) *Seizure procedures*

Any property subject to forfeiture to the United States under this section may be seized by the Attorney General in the manner set forth in section 981(b) of Title 18.

(c) *Custody of Attorney General*

Property taken or detained under this section shall not be repleviable, but shall be deemed to be in the custody of the Attorney General, subject only to the orders and decrees of the court or the official having jurisdiction thereof. Whenever property is seized under any of the provisions of this subchapter, the Attorney General may –

(1) place the property under seal;

(2) remove the property to a place designated by him; or

(3) require that the General Services Administration take custody of the property and remove it, if practicable, to an appropriate location for disposition in accordance with law.

(d) *Other laws and proceedings applicable*

The provisions of law relating to the seizure, summary and judicial forfeiture, and condemnation of property for violation of the customs laws; the disposition of such property or the proceeds from the sale thereof; the remission or mitigation of such forfeitures; and the compromise of claims shall apply to seizures and forfeitures incurred, or alleged to have been incurred, under any of the provisions of this subchapter, insofar as applicable and not inconsistent with the provisions hereof; except that such duties as are imposed upon the customs officer or any other person with respect to the seizure and forfeiture of property under the customs laws shall be performed with respect to seizures and forfeitures of property under this subchapter by such officers, agents, or other persons as may be authorized or designated for that purpose by the Attorney General, except to the extent that such duties arise from seizures and forfeitures effected by any customs officer.

(e) *Disposition of forfeited property*

(1) Whenever property is civilly or criminally forfeited under this subchapter the Attorney General may –

(A) retain the property for official use or, in the manner provided with respect to transfers under section 1616a of Title 19, transfer the property to any Federal agency or to any State or local law enforcement agency which participated directly in the seizure or forfeiture of the property;

(B) except as provided in paragraph (4), sell, by public sale or any other commercially feasible means, any forfeited property which is not required to be destroyed by law and which is not harmful to the public;

(C) require that the General Services Administration take custody of the property and dispose of it in accordance with law;

(D) forward it to the Drug Enforcement Administration for disposition (including delivery for medical or scientific use to any Federal or State agency under regulations of the Attorney General); or

(E) transfer the forfeited personal property or the proceeds of the sale of any forfeited personal or real property to any foreign country which participated directly or indirectly in the seizure or forfeiture of the property, if such a transfer –

(i) has been agreed to by the Secretary of State;

(ii) is authorized in an international agreement between the United States and the foreign country; and

(iii) is made to a country which, if applicable, has been certified under section 2291j(b) of Title 22.

(2)

(A) The proceeds from any sale under subparagraph (B) of paragraph (1) and any moneys forfeited under this title shall be used to pay –

(i) all property expenses of the proceedings for forfeiture and sale including expenses of seizure, maintenance of custody, advertising, and court costs; and

(ii) awards of up to $100,000 to any individual who provides original information which leads to the arrest and conviction of a person who kills or kidnaps a Federal drug law enforcement agent.

Any award paid for information concerning the killing or kidnaping of a Federal drug law enforcement agent, as provided in clause (ii), shall be paid at the discretion of the Attorney General.

(B) The Attorney General shall forward to the Treasurer of the United States for deposit in accordance with section 524(c) of Title 28, any amounts of such moneys and proceeds remaining after payment of the expenses provided in subparagraph (A), except that, with respect to forfeitures conducted by the Postal Service, the Postal Service shall deposit in the Postal Service Fund, under section 2003(b)(7) of Title 39, such moneys and proceeds.

(3) The Attorney General shall assure that any property transferred to a State or local law enforcement agency under paragraph (1)(A) –

(A) has a value that bears a reasonable relationship to the degree of direct participation of the State or local agency in the law enforcement effort resulting in the forfeiture, taking into account the total value of all property forfeited and the total law enforcement effort with respect to the violation of law on which the forfeiture is based; and

(B) will serve to encourage further cooperation between the recipient State or local agency and Federal law enforcement agencies.

(4)

(A) With respect to real property described in subparagraph (B), if the chief executive officer of the State involved submits to the Attorney General a request for purposes of such subparagraph, the authority established in such subparagraph is in lieu of the authority established in paragraph (1)(B).

(B) In the case of property described in paragraph (1)(B) that is civilly or criminally forfeited under this subchapter, if the property is real property that is appropriate for use as a public area reserved for recreational or historic purposes or for the preservation of natural conditions, the Attorney General, upon the request of the chief executive officer of the State in which the property is located, may transfer title to the property to the State, either without charge or for a nominal charge, through a legal instrument providing that –

(i) such use will be the principal use of the property; and

(ii) title to the property reverts to the United States in the event that the property is used otherwise.

(f) *Forfeiture and destruction of schedule I and II substances*

(1) All controlled substances in schedule I or II that are possessed, transferred, sold, or offered for sale in violation of the provisions of this subchapter; all dangerous, toxic, or hazardous raw materials or products subject to forfeiture under subsection (a)(2) of this section; and any equipment or container subject to forfeiture under subsection (a)(2) or (3) of this section which cannot be separated safely from such raw materials or products shall be deemed contraband and seized and summarily forfeited to the United States. Similarly, all substances in schedule I or II, which are seized or come into the possession of the United States, the owners of which are unknown, shall be deemed contraband and summarily forfeited to the United States.

(2) The Attorney General may direct the destruction of all controlled substances in schedule I or II seized for violation of this subchapter; all dangerous, toxic, or hazardous raw materials or products subject to forfeiture under subsection (a)(2) of this section; and any equipment or container subject to forfeiture under subsection (a)(2) or (3) of this section which cannot be separated safely from such raw materials or products under such circumstances as the Attorney General may deem necessary.

(g) *Plants*

(1) All species of plants from which controlled substances in schedules I and II may be derived which have been planted or cultivated in violation of this subchapter, or of which the owners or cultivators are unknown, or which are wild growths, may be seized and summarily forfeited to the United States.

(2) The failure, upon demand by the Attorney General or his duly authorized agent, of the person in occupancy or in control of land or premises upon which such species of plants are growing or being stored, to produce an appropriate registration, or proof that he is the holder thereof, shall constitute authority for the seizure and forfeiture.

(3) The Attorney General, or his duly authorized agent, shall have authority to enter upon any lands, or into any dwelling pursuant to a search warrant, to cut, harvest, carry off, or destroy such plants.

(h) *Vesting of title in United States*

All right, title, and interest in property described in subsection (a) of this section shall vest in the United States upon commission of the act giving rise to forfeiture under this section.

(i) *Stay of civil forfeiture proceedings; applicability*
The provisions of section 981(g) of title 18, United States Code, regarding the stay of a civil forfeiture proceeding shall apply to forfeitures under this section.

(j) *Venue*
In addition to the venue provided for in section 1395 of Title 28 or any other provision of law, in the case of property of a defendant charged with a violation that is the basis for forfeiture of the property under this section, a proceeding for forfeiture under this section may be brought in the judicial district in which the defendant owning such property is found or in the judicial district in which the criminal prosecution is brought.

(l) Agreement between Attorney General and Postal Service for performance of functions
The functions of the Attorney General under this section shall be carried out by the Postal Service pursuant to such agreement as may be entered into between the Attorney General and the Postal Service.

21 U.S.C. 853. Criminal Forfeiture (Controlled Substances) (Text)

(a) *Property subject to criminal forfeiture*
Any person convicted of a violation of this subchapter or subchapter II of this chapter punishable by imprisonment for more than one year shall forfeit to the United States, irrespective of any provision of State law –

(1) any property constituting, or derived from, any proceeds the person obtained, directly or indirectly, as the result of such violation;
(2) any of the person's property used, or intended to be used, in any manner or part, to commit, or to facilitate the commission of, such violation; and
(3) in the case of a person convicted of engaging in a continuing criminal enterprise in violation of section 848 of this title, the person shall forfeit, in addition to any property described in paragraph (1) or (2), any of his interest in, claims against, and property or contractual rights affording a source of control over, the continuing criminal enterprise.

The court, in imposing sentence on such person, shall order, in addition to any other sentence imposed pursuant to this subchapter or subchapter II of this chapter, that the person forfeit to the United States all property described in this subsection. In lieu of a fine otherwise authorized by this part, a defendant who derives profits or other proceeds from an offense may be fined not more than twice the gross profits or other proceeds.

(b) *Meaning of term "property"*
Property subject to criminal forfeiture under this section includes –

(1) real property, including things growing on, affixed to, and found in land; and
(2) tangible and intangible personal property, including rights, privileges, interests, claims, and securities.

(c) *Third party transfers*
All right, title, and interest in property described in subsection (a) of this section vests in the United States upon the commission of the act giving rise to forfeiture

under this section. Any such property that is subsequently transferred to a person other than the defendant may be the subject of a special verdict of forfeiture and thereafter shall be ordered forfeited to the United States, unless the transferee establishes in a hearing pursuant to subsection (n) of this section that he is a bona fide purchaser for value of such property who at the time of purchase was reasonably without cause to believe that the property was subject to forfeiture under this section.

(d) *Rebuttable presumption*

There is a rebuttable presumption at trial that any property of a person convicted of a felony under this subchapter or subchapter II of this chapter is subject to forfeiture under this section if the United States establishes by a preponderance of the evidence that –

(1) such property was acquired by such person during the period of the violation of this subchapter or subchapter II of this chapter or within a reasonable time after such period; and

(2) there was no likely source for such property other than the violation of this subchapter or subchapter II of this chapter.

(e) *Protective orders*

(1) Upon application of the United States, the court may enter a restraining order or injunction, require the execution of a satisfactory performance bond, or take any other action to preserve the availability of property described in subsection (a) of this section for forfeiture under this section –

(A) upon the filing of an indictment or information charging a violation of this subchapter or subchapter II of this chapter for which criminal forfeiture may be ordered under this section and alleging that the property with respect to which the order is sought would, in the event of conviction, be subject to forfeiture under this section; or

(B) prior to the filing of such an indictment or information, if, after notice to persons appearing to have an interest in the property and opportunity for a hearing, the court determines that –

(i) there is a substantial probability that the United States will prevail on the issue of forfeiture and that failure to enter the order will result in the property being destroyed, removed from the jurisdiction of the court, or otherwise made unavailable for forfeiture; and

(ii) the need to preserve the availability of the property through the entry of the requested order outweighs the hardship on any party against whom the order is to be entered:

Provided, however, That an order entered pursuant to subparagraph (B) shall be effective for not more than ninety days, unless extended by the court for good cause shown or unless an indictment or information described in subparagraph (A) has been filed.

(2) A temporary restraining order under this subsection may be entered upon application of the United States without notice or opportunity for a hearing when an information or indictment has not yet been filed with respect to the property, if the United States demonstrates that there is probable cause to believe that the property with respect to which the order is sought would, in the event of conviction, be subject to forfeiture under this section and that provision of notice

will jeopardize the availability of the property for forfeiture. Such a temporary order shall expire not more than ten days after the date on which it is entered, unless extended for good cause shown or unless the party against whom it is entered consents to an extension for a longer period. A hearing requested concerning an order entered under this paragraph shall be held at the earliest possible time and prior to the expiration of the temporary order.

(3) The court may receive and consider, at a hearing held pursuant to this subsection, evidence and information that would be inadmissible under the Federal Rules of Evidence.

(f) *Warrant of seizure*

The Government may request the issuance of a warrant authorizing the seizure of property subject to forfeiture under this section in the same manner as provided for a search warrant. If the court determines that there is probable cause to believe that the property to be seized would, in the event of conviction, be subject to forfeiture and that an order under subsection (e) of this section may not be sufficient to assure the availability of the property for forfeiture, the court shall issue a warrant authorizing the seizure of such property.

(g) *Execution*

Upon entry of an order of forfeiture under this section, the court shall authorize the Attorney General to seize all property ordered forfeited upon such terms and conditions as the court shall deem proper. Following entry of an order declaring the property forfeited, the court may, upon application of the United States, enter such appropriate restraining orders or injunctions, require the execution of satisfactory performance bonds, appoint receivers, conservators, appraisers, accountants, or trustees, or take any other action to protect the interest of the United States in the property ordered forfeited. Any income accruing to or derived from property ordered forfeited under this section may be used to offset ordinary and necessary expenses to the property which are required by law, or which are necessary to protect the interests of the United States or third parties.

(h) *Disposition of property*

Following the seizure of property ordered forfeited under this section, the Attorney General shall direct the disposition of the property by sale or any other commercially feasible means, making due provision for the rights of any innocent persons. Any property right or interest not exercisable by, or transferable for value to, the United States shall expire and shall not revert to the defendant, nor shall the defendant or any person acting in concert with him or on his behalf be eligible to purchase forfeited property at any sale held by the United States. Upon application of a person, other than the defendant or a person acting in concert with him or on his behalf, the court may restrain or stay the sale or disposition of the property pending the conclusion of any appeal of the criminal case giving rise to the forfeiture, if the applicant demonstrates that proceeding with the sale or disposition of the property will result in irreparable injury, harm, or loss to him.

(i) *Authority of the Attorney General*

With respect to property ordered forfeited under this section, the Attorney General is authorized to –

(1) grant petitions for mitigation or remission of forfeiture, restore forfeited property to victims of a violation of this subchapter, or take any other action to protect the rights of innocent persons which is in the interest of justice and which is not inconsistent with the provisions of this section;
(2) compromise claims arising under this section;
(3) award compensation to persons providing information resulting in a forfeiture under this section;
(4) direct the disposition by the United States, in accordance with the provisions of section 881(e) of this title, of all property ordered forfeited under this section by public sale or any other commercially feasible means, making due provision for the rights of innocent persons; and
(5) take appropriate measures necessary to safeguard and maintain property ordered forfeited under this section pending its disposition.

(j) *Applicability of civil forfeiture provisions*
Except to the extent that they are inconsistent with the provisions of this section, the provisions of section 881(d) of this title shall apply to a criminal forfeiture under this section.

(k) *Bar on intervention*
Except as provided in subsection (n) of this section, no party claiming an interest in property subject to forfeiture under this section may –
(1) intervene in a trial or appeal of a criminal case involving the forfeiture of such property under this section; or
(2) commence an action at law or equity against the United States concerning the validity of his alleged interest in the property subsequent to the filing of an indictment or information alleging that the property is subject to forfeiture under this section.

(l) *Jurisdiction to enter orders*
The district courts of the United States shall have jurisdiction to enter orders as provided in this section without regard to the location of any property which may be subject to forfeiture under this section or which has been ordered forfeited under this section.

(m) *Depositions*
In order to facilitate the identification and location of property declared forfeited and to facilitate the disposition of petitions for remission or mitigation of forfeiture, after the entry of an order declaring property forfeited to the United States, the court may, upon application of the United States, order that the testimony of any witness relating to the property forfeited be taken by deposition and that any designated book, paper, document, record, recording, or other material not privileged be produced at the same time and place, in the same manner as provided for the taking of depositions under Rule 15 of the Federal Rules of Criminal Procedure.

(n) *Third party interests*
(1) Following the entry of an order of forfeiture under this section, the United States shall publish notice of the order and of its intent to dispose of the property in such manner as the Attorney General may direct. The Government may also, to the extent practicable, provide direct written notice to any person known to have

alleged an interest in the property that is the subject of the order of forfeiture as a substitute for published notice as to those persons so notified.

(2) Any person, other than the defendant, asserting a legal interest in property which has been ordered forfeited to the United States pursuant to this section may, within thirty days of the final publication of notice or his receipt of notice under paragraph (1), whichever is earlier, petition the court for a hearing to adjudicate the validity of his alleged interest in the property. The hearing shall be held before the court alone, without a jury.

(3) The petition shall be signed by the petitioner under penalty of perjury and shall set forth the nature and extent of the petitioner's right, title, or interest in the property, the time and circumstances of the petitioner's acquisition of the right, title, or interest in the property, any additional facts supporting the petitioner's claim, and the relief sought.

(4) The hearing on the petition shall, to the extent practicable and consistent with the interests of justice, be held within thirty days of the filing of the petition. The court may consolidate the hearing on the petition with a hearing on any other petition filed by a person other than the defendant under this subsection.

(5) At the hearing, the petitioner may testify and present evidence and witnesses on his own behalf, and cross-examine witnesses who appear at the hearing. The United States may present evidence and witnesses in rebuttal and in defense of its claim to the property and cross-examine witnesses who appear at the hearing. In addition to testimony and evidence presented at the hearing, the court shall consider the relevant portions of the record of the criminal case which resulted in the order of forfeiture.

(6) If, after the hearing, the court determines that the petitioner has established by a preponderance of the evidence that –

(A) the petitioner has a legal right, title, or interest in the property, and such right, title, or interest renders the order of forfeiture invalid in whole or in part because the right, title, or interest was vested in the petitioner rather than the defendant or was superior to any right, title, or interest of the defendant at the time of the commission of the acts which gave rise to the forfeiture of the property under this section; or

(B) the petitioner is a bona fide purchaser for value of the right, title, or interest in the property and was at the time of purchase reasonably without cause to believe that the property was subject to forfeiture under this section;

the court shall amend the order of forfeiture in accordance with its determination.

(7) Following the court's disposition of all petitions filed under this subsection, or if no such petitions are filed following the expiration of the period provided in paragraph (2) for the filing of such petitions, the United States shall have clear title to property that is the subject of the order of forfeiture and may warrant good title to any subsequent purchaser or transferee.

(o) *Construction*

The provisions of this section shall be liberally construed to effectuate its remedial purposes.

(p) *Forfeiture of substitute property*

(1) In general

Paragraph (2) of this subsection shall apply, if any property described in subsection (a), as a result of any act or omission of the defendant –

(A) cannot be located upon the exercise of due diligence;

(B) has been transferred or sold to, or deposited with, a third party;

(C) has been placed beyond the jurisdiction of the court;

(D) has been substantially diminished in value; or

(E) has been commingled with other property which cannot be divided without difficulty.

(2) Substitute property

In any case described in any of subparagraphs (A) through (E) of paragraph (1), the court shall order the forfeiture of any other property of the defendant, up to the value of any property described in subparagraphs (A) through (E) of paragraph (1), as applicable.

(3) Return of property to jurisdiction

In the case of property described in paragraph (1)(C), the court may, in addition to any other action authorized by this subsection, order the defendant to return the property to the jurisdiction of the court so that the property may be seized and forfeited.

(q) *Restitution for cleanup of clandestine laboratory sites*

The court, when sentencing a defendant convicted of an offense under this subchapter or subchapter II of this chapter involving the manufacture, possession, or the possession with intent to distribute, of amphetamine or methamphetamine, shall –

(1) order restitution as provided in sections 3612 and 3664 of Title 18;

(2) order the defendant to reimburse the United States, the State or local government concerned, or both the United States and the State or local government concerned for the costs incurred by the United States or the State or local government concerned, as the case may be, for the cleanup associated with the manufacture of amphetamine or methamphetamine by the defendant, or on premises or in property that the defendant owns, resides, or does business in; and

(3) order restitution to any person injured as a result of the offense as provided in section 3663A of Title 18.

18 U.S.C. 1963. Criminal Forfeiture (RICO)(Text)

(a) Whoever violates any provision of section 1962 of this chapter shall be fined under this title or imprisoned not more than 20 years (or for life if the violation is based on a racketeering activity for which the maximum penalty includes life imprisonment), or both, and shall forfeit to the United States, irrespective of any provision of State law –

(1) any interest the person has acquired or maintained in violation of section 1962;

(2) any –

(A) interest in;

(B) security of;

(C) claim against; or

(D) property or contractual right of any kind affording a source of influence over; any enterprise which the person has established, operated, controlled, conducted, or participated in the conduct of, in violation of section 1962; and

(3) any property constituting, or derived from, any proceeds which the person obtained, directly or indirectly, from racketeering activity or unlawful debt collection in violation of section 1962.

The court, in imposing sentence on such person shall order, in addition to any other sentence imposed pursuant to this section, that the person forfeit to the United States all property described in this subsection. In lieu of a fine otherwise authorized by this section, a defendant who derives profits or other proceeds from an offense may be fined not more than twice the gross profits or other proceeds.

(b) Property subject to criminal forfeiture under this section includes –
  (1) real property, including things growing on, affixed to, and found in land; and
  (2) tangible and intangible personal property, including rights, privileges, interests, claims, and securities.

(c) All right, title, and interest in property described in subsection (a) vests in the United States upon the commission of the act giving rise to forfeiture under this section. Any such property that is subsequently transferred to a person other than the defendant may be the subject of a special verdict of forfeiture and thereafter shall be ordered forfeited to the United States, unless the transferee establishes in a hearing pursuant to subsection (l) that he is a bona fide purchaser for value of such property who at the time of purchase was reasonably without cause to believe that the property was subject to forfeiture under this section.

(d)
  (1) Upon application of the United States, the court may enter a restraining order or injunction, require the execution of a satisfactory performance bond, or take any other action to preserve the availability of property described in subsection (a) for forfeiture under this section –
    (A) upon the filing of an indictment or information charging a violation of section 1962 of this chapter and alleging that the property with respect to which the order is sought would, in the event of conviction, be subject to forfeiture under this section; or
    (B) prior to the filing of such an indictment or information, if, after notice to persons appearing to have an interest in the property and opportunity for a hearing, the court determines that –
      (i) there is a substantial probability that the United States will prevail on the issue of forfeiture and that failure to enter the order will result in the property being destroyed, removed from the jurisdiction of the court, or otherwise made unavailable for forfeiture; and
      (ii) the need to preserve the availability of the property through the entry of the requested order outweighs the hardship on any party against whom the order is to be entered:

Provided, however, That an order entered pursuant to subparagraph (B) shall be effective for not more than ninety days, unless extended by the court for good cause shown or unless an indictment or information described in subparagraph (A) has been filed.

(2) A temporary restraining order under this subsection may be entered upon application of the United States without notice or opportunity for a hearing when an information or indictment has not yet been filed with respect to the property, if the United States demonstrates that there is probable cause to believe that the property with respect to which the order is sought would, in the event of conviction, be subject to forfeiture under this section and that provision of notice will jeopardize the availability of the property for forfeiture. Such a temporary order shall expire not more than ten days after the date on which it is entered, unless extended for good cause shown or unless the party against whom it is entered consents to an extension for a longer period. A hearing requested concerning an order entered under this paragraph shall be held at the earliest possible time, and prior to the expiration of the temporary order.

(3) The court may receive and consider, at a hearing held pursuant to this subsection, evidence and information that would be inadmissible under the Federal Rules of Evidence.

(e) Upon conviction of a person under this section, the court shall enter a judgment of forfeiture of the property to the United States and shall also authorize the Attorney General to seize all property ordered forfeited upon such terms and conditions as the court shall deem proper. Following the entry of an order declaring the property forfeited, the court may, upon application of the United States, enter such appropriate restraining orders or injunctions, require the execution of satisfactory performance bonds, appoint receivers, conservators, appraisers, accountants, or trustees, or take any other action to protect the interest of the United States in the property ordered forfeited. Any income accruing to, or derived from, an enterprise or an interest in an enterprise which has been ordered forfeited under this section may be used to offset ordinary and necessary expenses to the enterprise which are required by law, or which are necessary to protect the interests of the United States or third parties.

(f) Following the seizure of property ordered forfeited under this section, the Attorney General shall direct the disposition of the property by sale or any other commercially feasible means, making due provision for the rights of any innocent persons. Any property right or interest not exercisable by, or transferable for value to, the United States shall expire and shall not revert to the defendant, nor shall the defendant or any person acting in concert with or on behalf of the defendant be eligible to purchase forfeited property at any sale held by the United States. Upon application of a person, other than the defendant or a person acting in concert with or on behalf of the defendant, the court may restrain or stay the sale or disposition of the property pending the conclusion of any appeal of the criminal case giving rise to the forfeiture, if the applicant demonstrates that proceeding with the sale or disposition of the property will result in irreparable injury, harm or loss to him. Notwithstanding 31 U.S.C. 3302(b), the proceeds of any sale or other disposition of property forfeited under this section and any moneys forfeited shall be used to pay all proper expenses for the forfeiture and the sale, including expenses of seizure, maintenance and custody of the property pending its disposition, advertising and court costs. The

Attorney General shall deposit in the Treasury any amounts of such proceeds or moneys remaining after the payment of such expenses.

(g) With respect to property ordered forfeited under this section, the Attorney General is authorized to –

(1) grant petitions for mitigation or remission of forfeiture, restore forfeited property to victims of a violation of this chapter, or take any other action to protect the rights of innocent persons which is in the interest of justice and which is not inconsistent with the provisions of this chapter;

(2) compromise claims arising under this section;

(3) award compensation to persons providing information resulting in a forfeiture under this section;

(4) direct the disposition by the United States of all property ordered forfeited under this section by public sale or any other commercially feasible means, making due provision for the rights of innocent persons; and

(5) take appropriate measures necessary to safeguard and maintain property ordered forfeited under this section pending its disposition.

(h) The Attorney General may promulgate regulations with respect to –

(1) making reasonable efforts to provide notice to persons who may have an interest in property ordered forfeited under this section;

(2) granting petitions for remission or mitigation of forfeiture;

(3) the restitution of property to victims of an offense petitioning for remission or mitigation of forfeiture under this chapter;

(4) the disposition by the United States of forfeited property by public sale or other commercially feasible means;

(5) the maintenance and safekeeping of any property forfeited under this section pending its disposition; and

(6) the compromise of claims arising under this chapter.

Pending the promulgation of such regulations, all provisions of law relating to the disposition of property, or the proceeds from the sale thereof, or the remission or mitigation of forfeitures for violation of the customs laws, and the compromise of claims and the award of compensation to informers in respect of such forfeitures shall apply to forfeitures incurred, or alleged to have been incurred, under the provisions of this section, insofar as applicable and not inconsistent with the provisions hereof. Such duties as are imposed upon the Customs Service or any person with respect to the disposition of property under the customs law shall be performed under this chapter by the Attorney General.

(i) Except as provided in subsection (l), no party claiming an interest in property subject to forfeiture under this section may –

(1) intervene in a trial or appeal of a criminal case involving the forfeiture of such property under this section; or

(2) commence an action at law or equity against the United States concerning the validity of his alleged interest in the property subsequent to the filing of an indictment or information alleging that the property is subject to forfeiture under this section.

(j) The district courts of the United States shall have jurisdiction to enter orders as provided in this section without regard to the location of any property which may be subject to forfeiture under this section or which has been ordered forfeited under this section.

(k) In order to facilitate the identification or location of property declared forfeited and to facilitate the disposition of petitions for remission or mitigation of forfeiture, after the entry of an order declaring property forfeited to the United States the court may, upon application of the United States, order that the testimony of any witness relating to the property forfeited be taken by deposition and that any designated book, paper, document, record, recording, or other material not privileged be produced at the same time and place, in the same manner as provided for the taking of depositions under Rule 15 of the Federal Rules of Criminal Procedure.

(l)

(1) Following the entry of an order of forfeiture under this section, the United States shall publish notice of the order and of its intent to dispose of the property in such manner as the Attorney General may direct. The Government may also, to the extent practicable, provide direct written notice to any person known to have alleged an interest in the property that is the subject of the order of forfeiture as a substitute for published notice as to those persons so notified.

(2) Any person, other than the defendant, asserting a legal interest in property which has been ordered forfeited to the United States pursuant to this section may, within thirty days of the final publication of notice or his receipt of notice under paragraph (1), whichever is earlier, petition the court for a hearing to adjudicate the validity of his alleged interest in the property. The hearing shall be held before the court alone, without a jury.

(3) The petition shall be signed by the petitioner under penalty of perjury and shall set forth the nature and extent of the petitioner's right, title, or interest in the property, the time and circumstances of the petitioner's acquisition of the right, title, or interest in the property, any additional facts supporting the petitioner's claim, and the relief sought.

(4) The hearing on the petition shall, to the extent practicable and consistent with the interests of justice, be held within thirty days of the filing of the petition. The court may consolidate the hearing on the petition with a hearing on any other petition filed by a person other than the defendant under this subsection.

(5) At the hearing, the petitioner may testify and present evidence and witnesses on his own behalf, and cross-examine witnesses who appear at the hearing. The United States may present evidence and witnesses in rebuttal and in defense of its claim to the property and cross-examine witnesses who appear at the hearing. In addition to testimony and evidence presented at the hearing, the court shall consider the relevant portions of the record of the criminal case which resulted in the order of forfeiture.

(6) If, after the hearing, the court determines that the petitioner has established by a preponderance of the evidence that –

(A) the petitioner has a legal right, title, or interest in the property, and such right, title, or interest renders the order of forfeiture invalid in whole or in part because the right, title, or interest was vested in the petitioner rather than the defendant or was superior to any right, title, or interest of the defendant at the time of the commission of the acts which gave rise to the forfeiture of the property under this section; or

(B) the petitioner is a bona fide purchaser for value of the right, title, or interest in the property and was at the time of purchase reasonably without cause to believe that the property was subject to forfeiture under this section;

the court shall amend the order of forfeiture in accordance with its determination.

(7) Following the court's disposition of all petitions filed under this subsection, or if no such petitions are filed following the expiration of the period provided in paragraph (2) for the filing of such petitions, the United States shall have clear title to property that is the subject of the order of forfeiture and may warrant good title to any subsequent purchaser or transferee.

(m) If any of the property described in subsection (a), as a result of any act or omission of the defendant—

(1) cannot be located upon the exercise of due diligence;
(2) has been transferred or sold to, or deposited with, a third party;
(3) has been placed beyond the jurisdiction of the court;
(4) has been substantially diminished in value; or
(5) has been commingled with other property which cannot be divided without difficulty;

the court shall order the forfeiture of any other property of the defendant up to the value of any property described in paragraphs (1) through (5).

F.R.Crim.P. 32.2. Criminal Forfeiture (Text)

(a) *Notice to the Defendant.* A court must not enter a judgment of forfeiture in a criminal proceeding unless the indictment or information contains notice to the defendant that the government will seek the forfeiture of property as part of any sentence in accordance with the applicable statute.

(b) *Entering a Preliminary Order of Forfeiture.*

(1) In General. As soon as practicable after a verdict or finding of guilty, or after a plea of guilty or nolo contendere is accepted, on any count in an indictment or information regarding which criminal forfeiture is sought, the court must determine what property is subject to forfeiture under the applicable statute. If the government seeks forfeiture of specific property, the court must determine whether the government has established the requisite nexus between the property and the offense. If the government seeks a personal money judgment, the court must determine the amount of money that the defendant will be ordered to pay. The court's determination may be based on evidence already in the record, including any written plea agreement or, if the forfeiture is contested, on evidence or information presented by the parties at a hearing after the verdict or finding of guilt.

(2) *Preliminary Order.* If the court finds that property is subject to forfeiture, it must promptly enter a preliminary order of forfeiture setting forth the amount of any money judgment or directing the forfeiture of specific property without regard to

any third party's interest in all or part of it. Determining whether a third party has such an interest must be deferred until any third party files a claim in an ancillary proceeding under Rule 32.2(c).

(3) *Seizing Property.* The entry of a preliminary order of forfeiture authorizes the Attorney General (or a designee) to seize the specific property subject to forfeiture; to conduct any discovery the court considers proper in identifying, locating, or disposing of the property; and to commence proceedings that comply with any statutes governing third-party rights. At sentencing—or at any time before sentencing if the defendant consents—the order of forfeiture becomes final as to the defendant and must be made a part of the sentence and be included in the judgment. The court may include in the order of forfeiture conditions reasonably necessary to preserve the property's value pending any appeal.

(4) *Jury Determination.* Upon a party's request in a case in which a jury returns a verdict of guilty, the jury must determine whether the government has established the requisite nexus between the property and the offense committed by the defendant.

(c) *Ancillary Proceeding; Entering a Final Order of Forfeiture.*

(1) *In General.* If, as prescribed by statute, a third party files a petition asserting an interest in the property to be forfeited, the court must conduct an ancillary proceeding, but no ancillary proceeding is required to the extent that the forfeiture consists of a money judgment.

(A) In the ancillary proceeding, the court may, on motion, dismiss the petition for lack of standing, for failure to state a claim, or for any other lawful reason. For purposes of the motion, the facts set forth in the petition are assumed to be true.

(B) After disposing of any motion filed under Rule 32.2(c)(1)(A) and before conducting a hearing on the petition, the court may permit the parties to conduct discovery in accordance with the Federal Rules of Civil Procedure if the court determines that discovery is necessary or desirable to resolve factual issues. When discovery ends, a party may move for summary judgment under Federal Rule of Civil Procedure 56.

(2) *Entering a Final Order.* When the ancillary proceeding ends, the court must enter a final order of forfeiture by amending the preliminary order as necessary to account for any third-party rights. If no third party files a timely petition, the preliminary order becomes the final order of forfeiture if the court finds that the defendant (or any combination of defendants convicted in the case) had an interest in the property that is forfeitable under the applicable statute. The defendant may not object to the entry of the final order on the ground that the property belongs, in whole or in part, to a codefendant or third party; nor may a third party object to the final order on the ground that the third party had an interest in the property.

(3) *Multiple Petitions.* If multiple third-party petitions are filed in the same case, an order dismissing or granting one petition is not appealable until rulings are made on all the petitions, unless the court determines that there is no just reason for delay.

(4) *Ancillary Proceeding Not Part of Sentencing.* An ancillary proceeding is not part of sentencing.

(d) *Stay Pending Appeal.* If a defendant appeals from a conviction or an order of forfeiture, the court may stay the order of forfeiture on terms appropriate to ensure that the property remains available pending appellate review. A stay does not delay the ancillary proceeding or the determination of a third party's rights or interests. If the court rules in favor of any third party while an appeal is pending, the court may amend the order of forfeiture but must not transfer any property interest to a third party until the decision on appeal becomes final, unless the defendant consents in writing or on the record.

(e) *Subsequently Located Property; Substitute Property.*

(1) *In General.* On the government's motion, the court may at any time enter an order of forfeiture or amend an existing order of forfeiture to include property that:

(A) is subject to forfeiture under an existing order of forfeiture but was located and identified after that order was entered; or

(B) is substitute property that qualifies for forfeiture under an applicable statute.

(2) *Procedure.* If the government shows that the property is subject to forfeiture under Rule 32.2(e)(1), the court must:

(A) enter an order forfeiting that property, or amend an existing preliminary or final order to include it; and

(B) if a third party files a petition claiming an interest in the property, conduct an ancillary proceeding under Rule 32.2(c).

(3) *Jury Trial Limited.* There is no right to a jury trial under Rule 32.2(e).

28 U.S.C. 524(c). Department of Justice Asset Forfeiture Fund (Text)

(c)

(1) There is established in the United States Treasury a special fund to be known as the Department of Justice Assets Forfeiture Fund (hereafter in this subsection referred to as the "Fund") which shall be available to the Attorney General without fiscal year limitation for the following law enforcement purposes–

(A) the payment, at the discretion of the Attorney General, of any expenses necessary to seize, detain, inventory, safeguard, maintain, advertise, sell, or dispose of property under seizure, detention, or forfeited pursuant to any law enforced or administered by the Department of Justice, or of any other necessary expense incident to the seizure, detention, forfeiture, or disposal of such property including –

(i) payments for –

(I) contract services;

(II) the employment of outside contractors to operate and manage properties or provide other specialized services necessary to dispose of such properties in an effort to maximize the return from such properties; and

(III) reimbursement of any Federal, State, or local agency for any expenditures made to perform the functions described in this clause;

(ii) payments to reimburse any Federal agency participating in the Fund for investigative costs leading to seizures;

(iii) payments for contracting for the services of experts and consultants needed by the Department of Justice to assist in carrying out duties related to asset seizure and forfeiture; and

(iv) payments made pursuant to guidelines promulgated by the Attorney General if such payments are necessary and directly related to seizure and forfeiture program expenses for –

(I) the purchase or lease of automatic data processing systems (not less than a majority of which use will be related to such program);

(II) training;

(III) printing;

(IV) the storage, protection, and destruction of controlled substances; and

(V) contracting for services directly related to the identification of forfeitable assets, and the processing of and accounting for forfeitures;

(B) the payment of awards for information or assistance directly relating to violations of the criminal drug laws of the United States or of sections 1956 and 1957 of title 18, sections 5313 and 5324 of title 31, and section 6050I of the Internal Revenue Code of 1986;

(C) at the discretion of the Attorney General, the payment of awards for information or assistance leading to a civil or criminal forfeiture involving any Federal agency participating in the Fund;

(D) the compromise and payment of valid liens and mortgages against property that has been forfeited pursuant to any law enforced or administered by the Department of Justice, subject to the discretion of the Attorney General to determine the validity of any such lien or mortgage and the amount of payment to be made, and the employment of attorneys and other personnel skilled in State real estate law as necessary;

(E)

(i) for disbursements authorized in connection with remission or mitigation procedures relating to property forfeited under any law enforced or administered by the Department of Justice; and

(ii) for payment for –

(I) costs incurred by or on behalf of the Department of Justice in connection with the removal, for purposes of Federal forfeiture and disposition, of any hazardous substance or pollutant or contaminant associated with the illegal manufacture of amphetamine or methamphetamine; and

(II) costs incurred by or on behalf of a State or local government in connection with such removal in any case in which such State or local government has assisted in a Federal prosecution relating to amphetamine or methamphetamine, to the extent such costs exceed equitable sharing payments made to such State or local government in such case;

(F)

(i) for equipping for law enforcement functions of any Government-owned or leased vessel, vehicle, or aircraft available for official use by any Federal agency participating in the Fund;

(ii) for equipping any vessel, vehicle, or aircraft available for official use by a State or local law enforcement agency to enable the vessel, vehicle, or aircraft to assist law enforcement functions if the vessel, vehicle, or aircraft will be used in a joint law enforcement operation with a Federal agency participating in the Fund; and

(iii) payments for other equipment directly related to seizure or forfeiture, including laboratory equipment, protective equipment, communications equipment, and the operation and maintenance costs of such equipment;

(G) for purchase of evidence of any violation of the Controlled Substances Act, the Controlled Substances Import and Export Act, chapter 96 of title 18, or sections 1956 and 1957 of title 18;

(H) the payment of State and local property taxes on forfeited real property that accrued between the date of the violation giving rise to the forfeiture and the date of the forfeiture order; and

(I) payment of overtime salaries, travel, fuel, training, equipment, and other similar costs of State or local law enforcement officers that are incurred in a joint law enforcement operation with a Federal law enforcement agency participating in the Fund.

Amounts for paying the expenses authorized by subparagraphs (B), (F), and (G) shall be specified in appropriations Acts and may be used under authorities available to the organization receiving the funds. Amounts for other authorized expenditures and payments from the Fund, including equitable sharing payments, are not required to be specified in appropriations acts. The Attorney General may exempt the procurement of contract services under subparagraph (A) under the Fund from section 3709 of the Revised Statutes of the United States (41 U.S.C. 5), title III of the Federal Property and Administrative Services Act of 1949 (41 U.S.C. 251 and following), and other provisions of law as may be necessary to maintain the security and confidentiality of related criminal investigations.

(2) Any award paid from the Fund, as provided in paragraph (1)(B) or (C), shall be paid at the discretion of the Attorney General or his delegate, under existing departmental delegation policies for the payment of awards, except that the authority to pay an award of $250,000 or more shall not be delegated to any person other than the Deputy Attorney General, the Associate Attorney General, the Director of the Federal Bureau of Investigation, or the Administrator of the Drug Enforcement Administration. Any award pursuant to paragraph (1)(B) shall not exceed $500,000. Any award pursuant to paragraph (1)(C) shall not exceed the lesser of $500,000 or one-fourth of the amount realized by the United States from the property forfeited, without both the personal approval of the Attorney General and written notice within 30 days thereof to the Chairmen and ranking

minority members of the Committees on Appropriations and the Judiciary of the Senate and of the House of Representatives.

(3) Any amount under subparagraph (G) of paragraph (1) shall be paid at the discretion of the Attorney General or his delegate, except that the authority to pay $100,000 or more may be delegated only to the respective head of the agency involved.

(4) There shall be deposited in the Fund –

(A) all amounts from the forfeiture of property under any law enforced or administered by the Department of Justice, except all proceeds of forfeitures available for use by the Secretary of the Treasury or the Secretary of the Interior pursuant to section 11(d) of the Endangered Species Act (16 U.S.C. 1540(d)) or section 6(d) of the Lacey Act Amendments of 1981 (16 U.S.C. 3375(d)), or the Postmaster General of the United States pursuant to 39 U.S.C. 2003(b)(7);

(B) all amounts representing the Federal equitable share from the forfeiture of property under any Federal, State, local or foreign law, for any Federal agency participating in the Fund;

(C) all amounts transferred by the Secretary of the Treasury pursuant to section 9703(g)(4)(A)(ii) of title 31; and

(D) all amounts collected –

(i) by the United States pursuant to a reimbursement order under paragraph (2) of section 413(q) of the Controlled Substances Act (21 U.S.C. 853(q)); and

(ii) pursuant to a restitution order under paragraph (1) or (3) of section 413(q) of the Controlled Substances Act [21 U.S.C. 853(q)] for injuries to the United States.

(5) Amounts in the Fund, and in any holding accounts associated with the Fund, that are not currently needed for the purpose of this section shall be kept on deposit or invested in obligations of, or guaranteed by, the United States and all earnings on such investments shall be deposited in the Fund.

(6)

(A) The Attorney General shall transmit to Congress and make available to the public, not later than 4 months after the end of each fiscal year, detailed reports for the prior fiscal year as follows:

(i) A report on total deposits to the Fund by State of deposit.

(ii) A report on total expenses paid from the Fund, by category of expense and recipient agency, including equitable sharing payments.

(iii) A report describing the number, value, and types of properties placed into official use by Federal agencies, by recipient agency.

(iv) A report describing the number, value, and types of properties transferred to State and local law enforcement agencies, by recipient agency.

(v) A report, by type of disposition, describing the number, value, and types of forfeited property disposed of during the year.

(vi) A report on the year-end inventory of property under seizure, but not yet forfeited, that reflects the type of property, its estimated value, and the estimated value of liens and mortgages outstanding on the property.

(vii) A report listing each property in the year-end inventory, not yet forfeited, with an outstanding equity of not less than $1,000,000.

(B) The Attorney General shall transmit to Congress and make available to the public, not later than 2 months after final issuance, the audited financial statements for each fiscal year for the Fund.

(C) Reports under subparagraph (A) shall include information with respect to all forfeitures under any law enforced or administered by the Department of Justice.

(D) The transmittal and publication requirements in subparagraphs (A) and (B) may be satisfied by –

(i) posting the reports on an Internet website maintained by the Department of Justice for a period of not less than 2 years; and

(ii) notifying the Committees on the Judiciary of the House of Representatives and the Senate when the reports are available electronically.

(7) The provisions of this subsection relating to deposits in the Fund shall apply to all property in the custody of the Department of Justice on or after the effective date of the Comprehensive Forfeiture Act of 1983.

(8)

(A) There are authorized to be appropriated such sums as necessary for the purposes described in subparagraphs (B), (F), and (G) of paragraph (1).

(B) Subject to subparagraphs (C) and (D), at the end of each of fiscal years 1994, 1995, and 1996, the Attorney General shall transfer from the Fund not more than $100,000,000 to the Special Forfeiture Fund established by section 6073 of the Anti-Drug Abuse Act of 1988.

(C) Transfers under subparagraph (B) may be made only from the excess unobligated balance and may not exceed one-half of the excess unobligated balance for any year. In addition, transfers under subparagraph (B) may be made only to the extent that the sum of the transfers in a fiscal year and one-half of the unobligated balance at the beginning of that fiscal year for the Special Forfeiture Fund does not exceed $100,000,000.

(D) For the purpose of determining amounts available for distribution at year end for any fiscal year, "excess unobligated balance" means the unobligated balance of the Fund generated by that fiscal year's operations, less any amounts that are required to be retained in the Fund to ensure the availability of amounts in the subsequent fiscal year for purposes authorized under paragraph (1).

(E) Subject to the notification procedures contained in section 605 of P.L. 103-121, and after satisfying the transfer requirement in subparagraph (B) of this paragraph, any excess unobligated balance remaining in the Fund on September 30, 1997 and thereafter shall be available to the Attorney General, without fiscal year limitation, for any Federal law enforcement, litigative/prosecutive, and correctional activities, or any other authorized purpose of the Department of Justice. Any amounts provided pursuant to this subparagraph may be used under authorities available to the organization receiving the funds.

(9)

(A) Following the completion of procedures for the forfeiture of property pursuant to any law enforced or administered by the Department, the Attorney General is authorized, in her discretion, to warrant clear title to any subsequent purchaser or transferee of such property.

(B) For fiscal years 2002 and 2003, the Attorney General is authorized to transfer, under such terms and conditions as the Attorney General shall specify, real or personal property of limited or marginal value, to a State or local government agency, or its designated contractor or transferee, for use to support drug abuse treatment, drug and crime prevention and education, housing, job skills, and other community-based public health and safety programs. Each such transfer shall be subject to satisfaction by the recipient involved of any outstanding lien against the property transferred, but no such transfer shall create or confer any private right of action in any person against the United States.

(10)The Attorney General shall transfer from the Fund to the Secretary of the Treasury for deposit in the Department of the Treasury Forfeiture Fund amounts appropriate to reflect the degree of participation of the Department of the Treasury law enforcement organizations (described in section 9703(p) of title 31) in the law enforcement effort resulting in the forfeiture pursuant to laws enforced or administered by the Department of Justice.

(11)For purposes of this subsection and notwithstanding section 9703 of title 31 or any other law, property is forfeited pursuant to a law enforced or administered by the Department of Justice if it is forfeited pursuant to –

(A) a judicial forfeiture proceeding when the underlying seizure was made by an officer of a Federal law enforcement agency participating in the Department of Justice Assets Forfeiture Fund or the property was maintained by the United States Marshals Service; or

(B) a civil administrative forfeiture proceeding conducted by a Department of Justice law enforcement component or pursuant to the authority of the Secretary of Commerce. [(12) Redesignated (11)]

28 U.S.C. 2461. Mode of Recovery

(a) Whenever a civil fine, penalty or pecuniary forfeiture is prescribed for the violation of an Act of Congress without specifying the mode of recovery or enforcement thereof, it may be recovered in a civil action.

(b) Unless otherwise provided by Act of Congress, whenever a forfeiture of property is prescribed as a penalty for violation of an Act of Congress and the seizure takes place on the high seas or on navigable waters within the admiralty and maritime jurisdiction of the United States, such forfeiture may be enforced by libel in admiralty but in cases of seizures on land the forfeiture may be enforced by a proceeding by libel which shall conform as near as may be to proceedings in admiralty.

(c) If a person is charged in a criminal case with a violation of an Act of Congress for which the civil or criminal forfeiture of property is authorized, the Government may include notice of the forfeiture in the indictment or information pursuant to the Federal Rules of Criminal Procedure. If the defendant is convicted of the offense giving rise to the forfeiture, the court shall order the forfeiture of the property as part of the sentence in the criminal case pursuant to the Federal Rules of Criminal Procedure and section 3554 of title 18, United States Code. The procedures in section 413 of the Controlled Substances Act (21 U.S.C. 853) apply to all stages of a criminal forfeiture proceeding, except that subsection (d) of such section applies only in cases in which the defendant is convicted of a violation of such Act.

28 U.S.C. 2465. Successful Claims; Interest and Attorneys Fees (Text)

(a) Upon the entry of a judgment for the claimant in any proceeding to condemn or forfeit property seized or arrested under any provision of Federal law—
  (1) such property shall be returned forthwith to the claimant or his agent; and
  (2) if it appears that there was reasonable cause for the seizure or arrest, the court shall cause a proper certificate thereof to be entered and, in such case, neither the person who made the seizure or arrest nor the prosecutor shall be liable to suit or judgment on account of such suit or prosecution, nor shall the claimant be entitled to costs, except as provided in subsection (b).

(b)
  (1) Except as provided in paragraph (2), in any civil proceeding to forfeit property under any provision of Federal law in which the claimant substantially prevails, the United States shall be liable for—
    (A) reasonable attorney fees and other litigation costs reasonably incurred by the claimant;
    (B) post-judgment interest, as set forth in section 1961 of this title; and
    (C) in cases involving currency, other negotiable instruments, or the proceeds of an interlocutory sale –
      (i) interest actually paid to the United States from the date of seizure or arrest of the property that resulted from the investment of the property in an interest-bearing account or instrument; and
      (ii) an imputed amount of interest that such currency, instruments, or proceeds would have earned at the rate applicable to the 30-day Treasury Bill, for any period during which no interest was paid (not including any period when the property reasonably was in use as evidence in an official proceeding or in conducting scientific tests for the purpose of collecting evidence), commencing 15 days after the property was seized by a Federal law enforcement agency, or was turned

over to a Federal law enforcement agency by a State or local law enforcement agency.

(2)

(A) The United States shall not be required to disgorge the value of any intangible benefits nor make any other payments to the claimant not specifically authorized by this subsection.

(B) The provisions of paragraph (1) shall not apply if the claimant is convicted of a crime for which the interest of the claimant in the property was subject to forfeiture under a Federal criminal forfeiture law.

(C) If there are multiple claims to the same property, the United States shall not be liable for costs and attorneys fees associated with any such claim if the United States—

(i) promptly recognizes such claim;

(ii) promptly returns the interest of the claimant in the property to the claimant, if the property can be divided without difficulty and there are no competing claims to that portion of the property;

(iii) does not cause the claimant to incur additional, reasonable costs or fees; and

(iv) prevails in obtaining forfeiture with respect to one or more of the other claims.

(D) If the court enters judgment in part for the claimant and in part for the Government, the court shall reduce the award of costs and attorney fees accordingly.

31 U.S.C. 9703 Department of the Treasury Forfeiture Fund (Text)

(a) *In general.*—There is established in the Treasury of the United States a fund to be known as the "Department of the Treasury Forfeiture Fund" (referred to in this section as the "Fund"). The Fund shall be available to the Secretary, without fiscal year limitation, with respect to seizures and forfeitures made pursuant to any law (other than section 7301 or 7302 of the Internal Revenue Code of 1986) enforced or administered by the Department of the Treasury or the United States Coast Guard for the following law enforcement purposes:

(1)

(A) Payment of all proper expenses of seizure (including investigative costs incurred by a Department of the Treasury law enforcement organization leading to seizure) or the proceedings of forfeiture and sale, including the expenses of detention, inventory, security, maintenance, advertisement, or disposal of the property, and if condemned by a court and a bond for such costs was not given, the costs as taxed by the court.

(B) Payment for –

(i) contract services;

(ii) the employment of outside contractors to operate and manage properties or to provide other specialized services necessary to dispose of such properties in an effort to maximize the return from such properties; and
(iii) reimbursing any Federal, State, or local agency for any expenditures made to perform the functions described in this subparagraph.

(C) Awards of compensation to informers under section 619 of the Tariff Act of 1930 (19 U.S.C. 1619).

(D) Satisfaction of –
(i) liens for freight, charges, and contributions in general average, notice of which has been filed with the appropriate Customs officer according to law; and
(ii) subject to the discretion of the Secretary, other valid liens and mortgages against property that has been forfeited pursuant to any law enforced or administered by a Department of the Treasury law enforcement organization. To determine the validity of any such lien or mortgage, the amount of payment to be made, and to carry out the functions described in this subparagraph, the Secretary may employ and compensate attorneys and other personnel skilled in State real estate law.

(E) Payment of amounts authorized by law with respect to remission and mitigation.

(F) Payment of claims of parties in interest to property disposed of under section 612(b) of the Tariff Act of 1930 (19 U.S.C. 1612(b)), in the amounts applicable to such claims at the time of seizure.

(G) Equitable sharing payments made to other Federal agencies, State and local law enforcement agencies, and foreign countries pursuant to section 616(c) of the Tariff Act of 1930 (19 U.S.C. 1616a(c)), section 981 of title 18, or subsection (h) of this section, and all costs related thereto.

(H) Payment for services of experts and consultants needed by a Department of the Treasury law enforcement organization to carry out the organization's duties relating to seizure and forfeiture.

(I) payment of overtime salaries, travel, fuel, training, equipment, and other similar costs of State or local law enforcement officers that are incurred in joint law enforcement operations with a Department of the Treasury law enforcement organization;

(J) payment made pursuant to guidelines promulgated by the Secretary, if such payment is necessary and directly related to seizure and forfeiture program expenses for –
(i) the purchase or lease of automatic data processing systems (not less than a majority of which use will be related to such program);
(ii) training;
(iii) printing; and
(iv) contracting for services directly related to –
(I) the identification of forfeitable assets;
(II) the processing of and accounting for forfeitures; and

(III)the storage, maintenance, protection, and destruction of controlled substances.

(2) At the discretion of the Secretary –

(A) payment of awards for information or assistance leading to a civil or criminal forfeiture involving any Department of the Treasury law enforcement organization participating in the Fund;

(B) purchases of evidence or information by—

(i) a Department of the Treasury law enforcement organization with respect to –

(I) a violation of section 1956 or 1957 of title 18 (relating to money laundering); or

(II) a law, the violation of which may subject property to forfeiture under section 981 or 982 of title 18;

(ii) the United States Customs Service with respect to drug smuggling or a violation of section 542 or 545 of title 18 (relating to fraudulent customs invoices or smuggling);

(iii) the United States Secret Service with respect to a violation of –

(I) section 1028, 1029, or 1030 or title 18;

(II) any law of the United States relating to coins, obligations, or securities of the United States or of a foreign government; or

(III)any law of the United States which the United States Secret Service is authorized to enforce relating to fraud or other criminal or unlawful activity in or against any federally insured financial institution, the Resolution Trust Corporation, or the Federal Deposit Insurance Corporation; and

(iv) the United States Customs Service or the Internal Revenue Service with respect to a violation of chapter 53 of this title (relating to the Bank Secrecy Act).

(C) payment of costs for publicizing awards available under section 619 of the Tariff Act of 1930 (19 U.S.C. 1619);

(D) payment for equipment for any vessel, vehicle, or aircraft available for official use by a Department of the Treasury law enforcement organization to enable the vessel, vehicle, or aircraft to assist in law enforcement functions, and for other equipment directly related to seizure or forfeiture, including laboratory equipment, protective equipment, communications equipment, and the operation and maintenance costs of such equipment;

(E) the payment of claims against employees of the Customs Service settled by the Secretary under section 630 of the Tariff Act of 1930;

(F) payment for equipment for any vessel, vehicle, or aircraft available for official use by a State or local law enforcement agency to enable the vessel, vehicle, or aircraft to assist in law enforcement functions if the vessel, vehicle, or aircraft will be used in joint law enforcement operations with a Department of the Treasury law enforcement organization;

(G) reimbursement of private persons for expenses incurred by such persons in cooperating with a Department of the Treasury law enforcement organization in investigations and undercover law enforcement operations;

(H) payment for training foreign law enforcement personnel with respect to seizure or forfeiture activities of the Department of the Treasury; and

(b) *Limitations*

(1) Any payment made under subparagraph (D) or (E) of subsection (a)(1) with respect to a seizure or a forfeiture of property shall not exceed the value of the property at the time of the seizure.

(2) Any payment made under subsection (a)(1)(G) with respect to a seizure or forfeiture of property shall not exceed the value of the property at the time of disposition.

(3) The Secretary may exempt the procurement of contract services under the Fund from section 3709 of the Revised Statutes of the United States (41 U.S.C. 5), title III of the Federal Property and Administrative Services Act of 1949 (41 U.S.C. 251 et seq.), and other provisions of law as may be necessary to maintain the security and confidentiality of related criminal investigations.

(4) The Secretary shall assure that any equitable sharing payment made to a State or local law enforcement agency pursuant to subsection (a)(1)(G) and any property transferred to a State or local law enforcement agency pursuant to subsection (h) –

(A) has a value that bears a reasonable relationship to the degree of participation of the State or local agency in the law enforcement effort resulting in the forfeiture, taking into account the total value of all property forfeited and the total law enforcement effort with respect to the violation of law on which the forfeiture is based; and

(B) will serve to encourage further cooperation between the recipient State or local agency and Federal law enforcement agencies.

(5) Amounts transferred by the Attorney General pursuant to section 524(c)(1) of title 28, or by the Postmaster General pursuant to section 2003 of title 39, and deposited into the Fund pursuant to subsection (d), shall be available for Federal law enforcement related purposes of the Department of the Treasury law enforcement organizations.

(c) *Funds available to United States Coast Guard*

(1) The Secretary shall make available to the United States Coast Guard, from funds appropriated under subsection (g)(2) in excess of $10,000,000 for a fiscal year, an amount equal to the net proceeds in the Fund derived from seizures by the Coast Guard.

(2) Funds made available under this subsection may be used to –

(A) pay for equipment for any vessel, vehicle, or aircraft available for official use by the United States Coast Guard to enable the vessel, vehicle, or aircraft to assist in law enforcement functions;

(B) pay for equipment for any vessel, vehicle, equipment, or aircraft available for official use by a State or local law enforcement agency to enable the vessel, vehicle, or aircraft to assist in law enforcement functions if the vessel, vehicle, or aircraft will be used in joint law enforcement operations with the United States Coast Guard;

(C) pay for overtime salaries, travel, fuel, training, equipment, and other similar costs of State and local law enforcement officers that are incurred in joint law enforcement operations with the United States Coast Guard;

(D) pay for expenses incurred in bringing vessels into compliance with applicable environmental laws prior to disposal by sinking.

(d) *Deposits and credits*

(1) With respect to fiscal year 1993, there shall be deposited into or credited to the Fund –

(A) all currency forfeited during fiscal year 1993, and all proceeds from forfeitures during fiscal year 1993, under any law enforced or administered by the United States Customs Service or the United States Coast Guard;

(B) all income from investments made under subsection (e); and

(C) all amounts representing the equitable share of the United States Customs Service or the United States Coast Guard from the forfeiture of property under any Federal, State, local, or foreign law.

(2) With respect to fiscal years beginning after fiscal year 1993, there shall be deposited into or credited to the Fund –

(A) all currency forfeited after fiscal year 1993, and all proceeds from forfeitures after fiscal year 1993, under any law (other than sections 7301 and 7302 of the Internal Revenue Code of 1986) enforced or administered by a Department of the Treasury law enforcement organization or the United States Coast Guard;

(B) all income from investments made under subsection (e); and

(C) all amounts representing the equitable share of a Department of the Treasury law enforcement organization or the United States Coast Guard from the forfeiture of property under any Federal, State, local, or foreign law.

(e) *Investments*.—Amounts in the Fund, and in any holding accounts associated with the Fund, which are not currently needed for the purposes of this section may be kept on deposit or invested in obligations of, or guaranteed by, the United States and all earnings on such investments shall be deposited in the Fund.

(f) *Reports to Congress*.—The Secretary shall transmit to the Congress, not later than February 1 of each year –

(1) a report on –

(A) the estimated total value of property forfeited with respect to which funds were not deposited in the Fund during the preceding fiscal year –

(i) under any law enforced or administered by the United States Customs Service or the United States Coast Guard, in the case of fiscal year 1993; and

(ii) under any law enforced or administered by the Department of the Treasury law enforcement organizations or the United States Coast Guard, in the case of fiscal years beginning after 1993; and

(B) the estimated total value of all such property transferred to any State or local law enforcement agency; and

(2) a report on –

(A) the balance of the Fund at the beginning of the preceding fiscal year;

(B) liens and mortgages paid and the amount of money shared with Federal, State, local, and foreign law enforcement agencies during the preceding fiscal year;
(C) the net amount realized from the operations of the Fund during the preceding fiscal year, the amount of seized cash being held as evidence, and the amount of money that has been carried over into the current fiscal year;
(D) any defendant's property, not forfeited at the end of the preceding fiscal year, if the equity in such property is valued at $1,000,000 or more;
(E) the total dollar value of uncontested seizures of monetary instruments having a value of over $100,000 which, or the proceeds of which, have not been deposited into the Fund pursuant to subsection (d) within 120 days after seizure, as of the end of the preceding fiscal year;
(F) the balance of the Fund at the end of the preceding fiscal year;
(G) the net amount, if any, of the excess unobligated amounts remaining in the Fund at the end of the preceding fiscal year and available to the Secretary for Federal law enforcement related purposes;
(H) a complete set of audited financial statements (including a balance sheet, income statement, and cash flow analysis) prepared in a manner consistent with the requirements of the Chief Financial Officers Act of 1990 (P.L. 101-576); and
(I) an analysis of income and expenses showing the revenue received or lost –
(i) by property category (such as general property, vehicles, vessels, aircraft, cash, and real property); and
(ii) by type of disposition (such as sale, remission, cancellation, placement into official use, sharing with State and local agencies, and destruction).

The Fund shall be subject to annual financial audits as authorized in the Chief Financial Officers Act of 1990 (P.L. 101-576).

(g) *Appropriations*
(1) There are hereby appropriated from the Fund such sums as may be necessary to carry out the purposes described in subsection (a)(1).
(2) There are authorized to be appropriated from the Fund to carry out the purposes set forth in subsections (a)(2) and (c) not to exceed –
(A) $25,000,000 for fiscal year 1993; and
(B) $50,000,000 for each fiscal year after fiscal year 1993.
(3)
(A) Subject to subparagraphs (B) and (C), at the end of each of fiscal years 1994, 1995, 1996, and 1997, the Secretary shall transfer from the Fund not more than $100,000,000 to the Special Forfeiture Fund established by section 6073 of the Anti-Drug Abuse Act of 1988.
(B) Transfers pursuant to subparagraph (A) shall be made only from excess unobligated amounts and only to the extent that, as determined by the Secretary, such transfers will not impair the future availability of amounts for the purposes described in subsection (a). Further, transfers under subparagraph (A) may not exceed one-half of the excess unobligated balance for a year. In addition, transfers under subparagraph (A) may be made only to the extent that the sum of the transfers in a fiscal year and one-half of the

unobligated balance at the beginning of that fiscal year for the Special Forfeiture Fund does not exceed $100,000,000.

(C) The Secretary of the Treasury shall reserve an amount not to exceed $30,000,000 from the unobligated balances remaining in the Customs Forfeiture Fund on September 30, 1992, and such amount shall be transferred to the Fund on October 1, 1992, or, if later, the date that is 15 days after the date of the enactment of this section. Such amount shall be available for any expenses or activities authorized under this section. At the end of fiscal year 1993, 1994, 1995, and 1996, the Secretary shall reserve in the Fund an amount not to exceed $50,000,000 of the unobligated balances in the Fund, or, if the Secretary determines that a greater amount is necessary for asset specific expenses, an amount equal to not more than 10 percent of the total obligations from the Fund in the preceding fiscal year. At the end of fiscal year 1997, and at the end of each fiscal year thereafter, the Secretary shall reserve any amounts that are required to be retained in the Fund to ensure the availability of amounts in the subsequent fiscal year for purposes authorized under subsection (a). Unobligated balances remaining pursuant to section 4(B) of 9703(g) shall also be carried forward.

(4)

(A) After reserving any amount authorized by paragraph (3)(C), any unobligated balances remaining in the Fund on September 30, 1993, shall be deposited into the general fund of the Treasury of the United States.

(B) After reserving any amount authorized by paragraph (3)(C) and after transferring any amount authorized by paragraph (3)(A), any unobligated balances remaining in the Fund on September 30, 1994, and on September 30 of each fiscal year thereafter, shall be available to the Secretary, without fiscal year limitation, for transfers pursuant to subparagraph (A)(ii) and for obligation or expenditure in connection with the law enforcement activities of any Federal agency or of a Department of the Treasury law enforcement organization.

(C) Any obligation or expenditure in excess of $500,000 with respect to an unobligated balance described in subparagraph (B) may not be made by the Secretary unless the Appropriations Committees of both Houses of Congress are notified at least 15 days in advance of such obligation or expenditure.

(h) *Retention or transfer of property.* –

(1) The Secretary may, with respect to any property forfeited under any law (other than section 7301 or 7302 of the Internal Revenue Code of 1986) enforced or administered by the Department of the Treasury—

(A) retain any of the property for official use; or

(B) transfer any of the property to –

(i) any other Federal agency; or

(ii) any State or local law enforcement agency that participated directly or indirectly in the seizure or forfeiture of the property.

(2) The Secretary may transfer any forfeited personal property or the proceeds of the sale of any forfeited personal or real property to any foreign country which

participated directly or indirectly in the seizure of forfeiture of the property, if such a transfer –

(A) is one with which the Secretary of State has agreed;

(B) is authorized in an international agreement between the United States and the foreign country; and

(C) is made to a country which, if applicable, has been certified under section 481(h) of the Foreign Assistance Act of 1961 (22 U.S.C. 2291(h)).

(3) Nothing in this section shall affect the authority of the Secretary under section 981 of title 18 or section 616 of the Tariff Act of 1930 (19 U.S.C. 1616a).

(i) *Regulations.*—The Secretary may prescribe such rules and regulations as may be necessary to carry out this section.

(j) *Customs forfeiture fund.*—Notwithstanding any other provision of law –

(1) during any period when forfeited currency and proceeds from forfeitures under any law (other than section 7301 or 7302 of the Internal Revenue Code of 1986) enforced or administered by the Department of the Treasury or the United States Coast Guard, are required to be deposited in the Fund pursuant to this section—

(A) all moneys required to be deposited in the Customs Forfeiture Fund pursuant to section 613A of the Tariff Act of 1930 (19 U.S.C. 1613b) shall instead be deposited in the Fund; and

(B) no deposits or withdrawals may be made to or from the Customs Forfeiture Fund pursuant to section 613A of the Tariff Act of 1930 (19 U.S.C. 1613b); and

(2) any funds in the Customs Forfeiture Fund and any obligations of the Customs Forfeiture Fund on the effective date of the Treasury Forfeiture Act of 1992, shall be transferred to the Fund and all administrative costs of such transfer shall be paid for out of the Fund.

(k) *Limitation of liability.*—The United States shall not be liable in any action relating to property transferred under this section or under section 616 of the Tariff Act of 1930 (19 U.S.C. 1616a) if such action is based on an act or omission occurring after the transfer.

(l) *Authority to warrant title.*—Following the completion of procedures for the forfeiture of property pursuant to any law enforced or administered by the Department of the Treasury, the Secretary is authorized, at the Secretary's discretion, to warrant clear title to any subsequent purchaser or transferee of such forfeited property.

(m) *Forfeited property.*—For purposes of this section and notwithstanding section 524(c)(11) of title 28 or any other law –

(1) during fiscal year 1993, property and currency shall be deemed to be forfeited pursuant to a law enforced or administered by the United States Customs Service if it is forfeited pursuant to—

(A) a judicial forfeiture proceeding when the underlying seizure was made by an officer of the United States Customs Service or the property was maintained by the United States Customs Service; or

(B) a civil administrative forfeiture proceeding conducted by the United States Customs Service; and

(2) after fiscal year 1993, property and currency shall be deemed to be forfeited pursuant to a law enforced or administered by a Department of the Treasury law enforcement organization if it is forfeited pursuant to –

(A) a judicial forfeiture proceeding when the underlying seizure was made by an officer of a Department of the Treasury law enforcement organization or the property was maintained by a Department of the Treasury law enforcement organization; or

(B) a civil administrative forfeiture proceeding conducted by a Department of the Treasury law enforcement organization.

(n) *Transfers to Attorney General and Postmaster General*

(1) The Secretary shall transfer from the Fund to the Attorney General for deposit in the Department of Justice Assets Forfeiture Fund amounts appropriate to reflect the degree of participation of participating Federal agencies in the law enforcement effort resulting in the forfeiture pursuant to laws enforced or administered by a Department of the Treasury law enforcement organization. For purposes of the preceding sentence, a "participating Federal agency" is an agency that participates in the Department of Justice Assets Forfeiture Fund.

(2) The Secretary shall transfer from the Fund to the Postmaster General for deposit in the Postal Service Fund amounts appropriate to reflect the degree of participation of the United States Postal Service in the law enforcement effort resulting in the forfeiture pursuant to laws enforced or administered by a Department of the Treasury law enforcement organization.

(o) *Definitions.*—For purposes of this section –

(1) Department of the Treasury law enforcement organization.—The term "Department of the Treasury law enforcement organization" means the United States Customs Service, the United States Secret Service, the Tax and Trade Bureau, the Internal Revenue Service, the Federal Law Enforcement Training Center, the Financial Crimes Enforcement Network, and any other law enforcement component of the Department of the Treasury so designated by the Secretary.

(2) Secretary.—The term "Secretary" means the Secretary of the Treasury.

42 U.S.C. 10601 Crime Victims Fund (Text)

(a) *Establishment*

There is created in the Treasury a separate account to be known as the Crime Victims Fund (hereinafter in this chapter referred to as the "Fund").

(b) *Fines deposited in Fund; penalties; forfeited appearance bonds*

Except as limited by subsection (c) of this section, there shall be deposited in the Fund –

(1) all fines that are collected from persons convicted of offenses against the United States except –

(A) fines available for use by the Secretary of the Treasury pursuant to –

(i) section 11(d) of the Endangered Species Act (16 U.S.C. 1540(d)); and

(ii) section 6(d) of the Lacey Act Amendments of 1981 (16 U.S.C. 3375(d)); and

(B) fines to be paid into –

(i) the railroad unemployment insurance account pursuant to the Railroad Unemployment Insurance Act (45 U.S.C. 351 et seq.);

(ii) the Postal Service Fund pursuant to sections 2601(a)(2) and 2003 of Title 39 and for the purposes set forth in section 404(a)(7) of Title 39;

(iii) the navigable waters revolving fund pursuant to section 311 of the Federal Water Pollution Control Act (33 U.S.C. 1321); and

(iv) county public school funds pursuant to section 3613 of Title 18;

(2) penalty assessments collected under section 3013 of Title 18;

(3) the proceeds of forfeited appearance bonds, bail bonds, and collateral collected under section 3146 of Title 18;

(4) any money ordered to be paid into the Fund under section 3671(c)(2) of Title 18; and

(5) any gifts, bequests, or donations to the Fund from private entities or individuals, which the Director is hereby authorized to accept for deposit into the Fund, except that the Director is not hereby authorized to accept any such gift, bequest, or donation that –

(A) attaches conditions inconsistent with applicable laws or regulations; or

(B) is conditioned upon or would require the expenditure of appropriated funds that are not available to the Office for Victims of Crime.

(c) *Retention of sums in Fund; availability for expenditure without fiscal year limitation*
Sums deposited in the Fund shall remain in the Fund and be available for expenditure under this chapter for grants under this chapter without fiscal year limitation. Notwithstanding subsection (d)(5), all sums deposited in the Fund in any fiscal year that are not made available for obligation by Congress in the subsequent fiscal year shall remain in the Fund for obligation in future fiscal years, without fiscal year limitation.

(d) *Availability for judicial branch administrative costs; grant program percentages*
The Fund shall be available as follows:

(1) Repealed. P.L. 105-119, Title I, §109(a)(1), Nov. 26, 1997, 111 Stat. 2457

(2)

(A) Except as provided in subparagraph (B), the first $10,000,000 deposited in the Fund shall be available for grants under section 10603a of this title.

(B)

(i) For any fiscal year for which the amount deposited in the Fund is greater than the amount deposited in the Fund for fiscal year 1998, the $10,000,000 referred to in subparagraph (A) plus an amount equal to 50 percent of the increase in the amount from fiscal year 1998 shall be available for grants under section 10603a of this title.

(ii) Amounts available under this subparagraph for any fiscal year shall not exceed $20,000,000.

(3) Of the sums remaining in the Fund in any particular fiscal year after compliance with paragraph (2), such sums as may be necessary shall be available for the United States Attorneys Offices and the Federal Bureau of Investigation to

improve services for the benefit of crime victims in the Federal criminal justice system, and for a Victim Notification System.

(4) Of the remaining amount to be distributed from the Fund in a particular fiscal year –

(A) 47.5 percent shall be available for grants under section 10602 of this title;

(B) 47.5 percent shall be available for grants under section 10603(a) of this title; and

(C) 5 percent shall be available for grants under section 10603(c) of this title.

(5)

(A) In addition to the amounts distributed under paragraphs (2), (3), and (4), the Director may set aside up to $50,000,000 from the amounts transferred to the Fund in response to the airplane hijackings and terrorist acts that occurred on September 11, 2001, as an antiterrorism emergency reserve. The Director may replenish any amounts obligated from such reserve in subsequent fiscal years by setting aside up to 5 percent of the amounts remaining in the Fund in any fiscal year after distributing amounts under paragraphs (2), (3) and (4). Such reserve shall not exceed $50,000,000.

(B) The antiterrorism emergency reserve referred to in subparagraph (A) may be used for supplemental grants under section 10603b of this title and to provide compensation to victims of international terrorism under section 10603c of this title.

(C) Amounts in the antiterrorism emergency reserve established pursuant to subparagraph (A) may be carried over from fiscal year to fiscal year. Notwithstanding subsection (c) and section 619 of the Departments of Commerce, Justice, and State, the Judiciary, and Related Agencies Appropriations Act, 2001 (and any similar limitation on Fund obligations in any future Act, unless the same should expressly refer to this section), any such amounts carried over shall not be subject to any limitation on obligations from amounts deposited to or available in the Fund.

(e) *Amounts awarded and unspent*

Any amount awarded as part of a grant under this chapter that remains unspent at the end of a fiscal year in which the grant is made may be expended for the purpose for which the grant is made at any time during the 3 succeeding fiscal years, at the end of which period, any remaining unobligated sums shall be available for deposit into the emergency reserve fund referred to in subsection (d)(5) at the discretion of the Director. Any remaining unobligated sums shall be returned to the Fund.

(f) *"Offenses against the United States" as excluding*

As used in this section, the term "offenses against the United States" does not include –

(1) a criminal violation of the Uniform Code of Military Justice (10 U.S.C. 801 et seq.);

(2) an offense against the laws of the District of Columbia; and

(3) an offense triable by an Indian tribal court or Court of Indian Offenses.

(g) *Grants for Indian tribes; child abuse cases*

(1) The Attorney General shall use 15 percent of the funds available under subsection (d)(2) of this section to make grants for the purpose of assisting

Native American Indian tribes in developing, establishing, and operating programs designed to improve –

(A) the handling of child abuse cases, particularly cases of child sexual abuse, in a manner which limits additional trauma to the child victim; and

(B) the investigation and prosecution of cases of child abuse, particularly child sexual abuse.

(2) The Attorney General may use 5 percent of the funds available under subsection (d)(2) of this section (prior to distribution) for grants to Indian tribes to establish child victim assistance programs, as appropriate.

(3) As used in this subsection, the term "tribe" has the meaning given that term in section 450b(b) of Title 25.

Federal Forfeiture Statutes (Citations) [217]

7 U.S.C. 1595 violation of the Federal Seed Act (seed)

7 U.S.C. 2024(g), (h) misuse of food stamp coupons or authorization cards (nonfood items, money, negotiable instruments, securities, things of value furnished in exchange of coupons)

7 U.S.C. 2024 Food Stamp Act felonies (property traceable to proceeds)*

7 U.S.C. 2156 animal fighting violations (animals)

8 U.S.C. 1324(b) bringing in or harboring aliens (conveyances)

8 U.S.C. 1324 bringing in and harboring aliens for profit (property traceable to proceeds)*

8 U.S.C. 1327 aiding or assisting aliens to enter the U.S. for profit (property traceable to proceeds)*

8 U.S.C. 1328 importing aliens for immoral purpose for profit (property traceable to proceeds)*

11 U.S.C. 1 et seq. bankruptcy fraud (except 11 U.S.C. 157 cases)(property traceable to proceeds)*

15 U.S.C. 6 restraint of interstate or foreign trade (property in transit and involved in restraint)

15 U.S.C. 11 restraint of trade (property in transit)

15 U.S.C. 77 unauthorized departure of vessel detained in time of war in the interests of American neutrality (vessel)

15 U.S.C. 77q fraud in the sale of securities (property traceable to proceeds)*

15 U.S.C. 78dd-2 Foreign Corrupt Practices Act felonies (property traceable to proceeds)*

15 U.S.C. 292 falsely stamped gold or silver (gold, silver, gold goods, silver goods)

15 U.S.C. 715f hot oil (illegally transported contraband oil)

15 U.S.C. 1177 illegally transporting gambling devices (gambling devices)

15 U.S.C. 1195 making, moving or dealing in materials without complying with the Flammable Fabrics Act (material)

15 U.S.C. 1265 Federal Hazardous Substances Act violations (misbranded and banned substances)

15 U.S.C. 2071(b) consumer product safety violations (prohibited products and those which fail to comply with an applicable consumer product safety rule)

15 U.S.C. 2104 political or numismatic items violations (imported products)

16 U.S.C. 26 hunting or fishing in Yellowstone National Park (guns, traps, beasts of burden, means of transportation)

16 U.S.C. 65 hunting or fishing in Sequoia or Yosemite National Parks (guns, teams, horses, means of transportation, and traps)

16 U.S.C. 99 hunting or fishing in Mt. Rainier National Park (guns, traps, beasts of burden, means of transportation)

16 U.S.C. 117d hunting or fishing in Mesa Verde National Park (guns, traps, beasts of burden, means of transportation)

16 U.S.C. 128 hunting or fishing in Crater Lake National Park (guns, traps, beasts of burden, means of transportation)

16 U.S.C. 171 hunting or fishing in Glacier National Park (guns, traps, beasts of burden, means of transportation)

16 U.S.C. 198d hunting or fishing in Rocky Mountain National Park (guns, traps, beasts of burden, means of transportation)

16 U.S.C. 204d hunting or fishing in Lassen Volcanic National Park (guns, traps, beasts of burden, means of transportation)

16 U.S.C. 256c hunting or fishing in Olympic Volcanic National Park (guns, bows, traps, nets, seines, fishing tackle, clothing, beasts of burden, machinery, logging equipment, motor vehicles, aircraft, boats or means of transportation)

16 U.S.C. 395d hunting or fishing in Hawaii National Park (guns, traps, beasts of burden, means of transportation)

16 U.S.C. 403c-4 hunting or fishing in the Shenandoah National Park (guns, traps, nets, seines, teams, horses, means of transportation)

16 U.S.C. 403h-4 hunting or fishing in Great Smoky Mountains National Park (guns, traps, nets, seines, fishing tackle, beasts of burden, means of transportation)

16 U.S.C. 404c-4 hunting or fishing in Mammoth Cave National Park (guns, traps, nets, seines, fishing tackle, beasts of burden, means of transportation)

16 U.S.C. 408l hunting or fishing in Isle Royale National Park (guns, traps, nets, seines, fishing tackle, beasts of burden, means of transportation)

16 U.S.C. 470gg(b) excavation of and dealing in archaeological resources (archaeological resources, vehicles and equipment used)

16 U.S.C. 470aaa-7 unlawfully acquired paleontological resources (paleontological resources)

16 U.S.C. 668b Bald and Golden Eagle protection violations (products, guns, traps, nets, equipment, vessels, vehicles, aircraft, means of transportation)

16 U.S.C. 668dd endangered species violations (species members)

16 U.S.C. 670j hunting or fishing on wetlands (guns, traps, nets, equipment, vessels, vehicles and other means of transportation)

16 U.S.C. 690e hunting in Bear River Migratory Bird Refuge (game)

16 U.S.C. 957 violations of the Tuna conventions (fish)

16 U.S.C. 707 migratory bird hunting violations (guns, traps, nets, equipment, vessels, vehicles, means of transportation)

16 U.S.C. 727 hunting and fishing in Upper Mississippi River Wild Life and Fish Refuge (guns, fishing equipment, boats, other paraphernalia)

16 U.S.C. 742j-1 hunting or harassing game from a plane (game, guns, plane, equipment)

16 U.S.C. 773h Northern Pacific Halibut Act violations (vessel, fishing gear, furniture, appurtenances, stores, cargo, fish of fishing boat)

16 U.S.C. 916f Whaling Convention violations (whales, whale products)

16 U.S.C. 959 Tuna Convention violations (fish)

16 U.S.C. 971e Atlantic Tuna Convention violations (fish)

16 U.S.C. 972f Eastern Pacific Tuna Convention violations (fish)

16 U.S.C. 1171 North Pacific Fur Seal violations (vessel, gear, furniture, appurtenances, stores, cargo, furs)

16 U.S.C. 1376 marine mammal violations (vessel and cargo)

16 U.S.C. 1417 sell or transport tuna not taken in compliance with a International Dolphin Conservation program (vessel, equipment and fish)

16 U.S.C. 1418(c) global moratorium on certain tuna harvesting practices (vessels (including fishing gear, appurtenances, stores, and cargo) used and fish taken in violation)

16 U.S.C. 1437 marine sanctuary violations (vessel, equipment, stores, cargo, item used in violation, sanctuary resources)

16 U.S.C. 1540 endangered species violations (species, guns, traps, nets, equipment, vessels, vehicles, aircraft, means of transportation)

16 U.S.C. 1860 Fishery Conservation and Management Act violations (fishing vessels, their gear, furniture, appurtenances, stores, cargo, and fish)

16 U.S.C. 2409 Antarctic conservation violations (game, guns, traps, nets, equipment, vessels, vehicles, aircraft, other means of transportation)

16 U.S.C. 2439 Antarctic Marine Living Resources Convention violations (guns, traps, nets, other equipment, vessels, their gear, furniture, appurtenances, stoves, and cargo, vessels, vehicles, aircraft, and other means of transportation)

16 U.S.C. 3374 transporting fish, wildlife or plants contrary to law (fish, wildlife, plants, vessels, vehicles, aircraft, and other means of transportation)

16 U.S.C. 3606 North Atlantic salmon violations (vessels and fish)

16 U.S.C. 3637 Pacific salmon violations (fish and vessels, their gear, furniture, appurtenances, stores, and cargo)

16 U.S.C. 5010 North Pacific anadromous fish violations (fish and vessels including fishing gear, furniture, appurtenances, stores and cargo)

16 U.S.C. 5106 Atlantic coastal fisheries moratorium violations (fish, vessels, gear, equipment, appurtenances, stores and cargo)

16 U.S.C. 5305a rhinoceros and tiger conservation violations (derivative products)

16 U.S.C. 5154 violations of Atlantic striped bass moratorium (vessel, equipment, cargo, fish)

16 U.S.C. 5158 violations relating to striped base in the exclusive economic zone (vessel, equipment, cargo, fish)

16 U.S.C. 5509 high seas fish conservation offenses (fish, vessels, gear, equipment, furniture, appurtenances, stores, and cargo)

16 U.S.C. 5606 Northwest Atlantic Fisheries Convention offenses (fishing vessels, their gear, furniture, appurtenances, stores, cargo, and fish)

17 U.S.C. 506 copyright infringement (copies, and copying implements, devices, and equipment)

17 U.S.C. 509 copyright infringement of phonorecords (copies, copying implements, devices, and equipment)

17 U.S.C. 603 importation of items infringing on copyright (copies)

17 U.S.C. 1328 infringement on copyrighted original design (articles imported)

18 U.S.C. 32 destruction of aircraft (property traceable to proceeds)*

18 U.S.C. 37 violence at international airports (property traceable to proceeds)*

18 U.S.C. 38 fraud involving aircraft or spacecraft parts (proceeds and property used to facilitate offenses)

18 U.S.C. 81 arson within U.S. special maritime and territorial jurisdiction (property traceable to proceeds)*

18 U.S.C. 115 influencing, impeding, or retaliating against a Federal official by threatening or injuring a family member (property traceable to proceeds)*

18 U.S.C. 152 concealment of assets; false oaths and claims; bribery (property traceable to proceeds)*

18 U.S.C. 175 biological weapons offenses (property traceable to proceeds)*

18 U.S.C. 175b unlawful possession of biological materials (property traceable to proceeds)*

18 U.S.C. 175c unlawful possession of smallpox materials (property traceable to proceeds)*

18 U.S.C. 176 Biological Weapons Act violations (biological agent, toxin and delivery system)

18 U.S.C. 201 bribery of U.S. officials (property traceable to proceeds)*

18 U.S.C. 215 commissions or gifts for procuring loans (property traceable to proceeds)*

18 U.S.C. 224 sports bribery (property traceable to proceeds)*

18 U.S.C. 229 chemical weapons offenses (property traceable to proceeds)*

18 U.S.C. 229B Chemical Weapons Act offenses (property used in, constituting the proceeds from, or facilitating offenses)

18 U.S.C. 287 false claims involving health care benefits (property traceable to proceeds)*

18 U.S.C. 351 congressional or Cabinet officer assassination (property traceable to proceeds)*

18 U.S.C. 371 conspiracy to defraud health care programs (property traceable to proceeds)*

18 U.S.C. 438 unlawful Indian contracts for services (proceeds)

18 U.S.C. 471 counterfeiting obligations or securities of the United States (property traceable to proceeds)*

18 U.S.C. 472 uttering counterfeit obligations or securities (property traceable to proceeds)*

18 U.S.C. 473 dealing in counterfeit obligations or securities (property traceable to proceeds)*

18 U.S.C. 474 possession of plates or stones for counterfeit obligations or securities (property traceable to proceeds)*

18 U.S.C. 476 taking impressions of tools used for obligations or securities (property traceable to proceeds)*

18 U.S.C. 477 sale or possession of impressions of tools used for obligations or securities (property traceable to proceeds)*

18 U.S.C. 478 counterfeiting foreign obligations or securities (property traceable to proceeds)*

18 U.S.C. 479 uttering counterfeit foreign obligations or securities (property traceable to proceeds)*

18 U.S.C. 480 possessing counterfeit foreign obligations or securities (property traceable to proceeds)*

18 U.S.C. 481 possession of plates or stones for counterfeit foreign obligations or securities (property traceable to proceeds)*

18 U.S.C. 485 counterfeiting U.S. coins (property traceable to proceeds)*

18 U.S.C. 486 uttering counterfeit coins (property traceable to proceeds)*

18 U.S.C. 487 possession of counterfeit dies for U.S. coins (property traceable to proceeds)*

18 U.S.C. 488 possession of counterfeit dies for foreign coins (property traceable to proceeds)*

18 U.S.C. 492 counterfeiting U.S. or foreign government coins, obligations or securities (counterfeits, and any articles, devices, and things used to counterfeit)

18 U.S.C. 500 counterfeiting U.S. postal money orders (property traceable to proceeds)*

18 U.S.C. 501 counterfeiting U.S. postage stamps (property traceable to proceeds)*

18 U.S.C. 502 counterfeiting foreign postage stamps (property traceable to proceeds)*

18 U.S.C. 503 counterfeiting U.S. postmarking stamps (property traceable to proceeds)*

18 U.S.C. 510 forging U.S. checks, bonds or securities (property traceable to proceeds)*

18 U.S.C. 511 altering motor vehicle identification numbers (property traceable to proceeds)*

18 U.S.C. 512 removing or changing motor vehicle identifications numbers (vehicle or part with altered or removed id. number)

18 U.S.C. 513 counterfeiting securities of States and private entities (property traceable to proceeds)*

18 U.S.C. 541 entry of falsely classified goods (property traceable to proceeds)*

18 U.S.C. 542 entry of goods by means of false statements (property traceable to proceeds)*

18 U.S.C. 544 relanding goods(goods)

18 U.S.C. 545 smuggling (goods smuggled)

18 U.S.C. 545 smuggling goods into the United States (property traceable to proceeds)*

18 U.S.C. 548 removing or repacking goods stored in customs warehouses (goods)

18 U.S.C. 549 removing goods from Customs custody (property traceable to proceeds)*

18 U.S.C. 550 false claims for refund of duties (merchandise)

18 U.S.C. 553 (importing/exporting stolen motor vehicles (property traceable to proceeds)*

18 U.S.C. 554 (smuggling goods from the United States (property traceable to proceeds)*

18 U.S.C. 641 theft of public money, property, or records (property traceable to proceeds)*

18 U.S.C. 656 theft, embezzlement, or misapplication by bank officer or employee (property traceable to proceeds)*

18 U.S.C. 657 theft from lending, credit, and insurance institutions (property traceable to proceeds)*

18 U.S.C. 658 property mortgaged or pledged to farm credit agencies (property traceable to proceeds)*

18 U.S.C. 659 felonious theft from interstate shipments (property traceable to proceeds)*

18 U.S.C. 664 pension fund embezzlement (property traceable to proceeds)*

18 U.S.C. 666 theft or bribery concerning programs receiving Federal funds (property traceable to proceeds)*

18 U.S.C. 669 health care theft or embezzlement (property traceable to proceeds)*

18 U.S.C. 793 espionage (property derived from payments from foreign sources)

18 U.S.C. 793 espionage (property traceable to proceeds)*

18 U.S.C. 794 serious espionage (property derived from or used in commission of violation)

18 U.S.C. 794 serious espionage (property traceable to proceeds)*

18 U.S.C. 798 disclosure of classified information (property derived from or used in violation)*

18 U.S.C. 798 disclosure of classified information (property traceable to proceeds)*

18 U.S.C. 831 transactions involving nuclear materials (property traceable to proceeds)*

18 U.S.C. 832 participation in foreign terrorist production of weapons of mass destruction (property traceable to proceeds)*

18 U.S.C. 842 explosives offenses (property traceable to proceeds)*

18 U.S.C. 844 explosives offenses (property traceable to proceeds)*

18 U.S.C. 844 explosives violations (explosives)

18 U.S.C. 875 threats in interstate communications (property traceable to proceeds)*

18 U.S.C. 892 loansharking (property traceable to proceeds)*

18 U.S.C. 893 financing a loansharking operation (property traceable to proceeds)*

18 U.S.C. 894 collecting extortionate loans (property traceable to proceeds)*

18 U.S.C. 922(l) unlawfully importing firearms (property traceable to proceeds)*

18 U.S.C. 924(n) gun running (property traceable to proceeds)*

18 U.S.C. 924 firearms violations (guns and ammunition)

18 U.S.C. 930(c) armed violence at federal facility (property traceable to proceeds)*

18 U.S.C. 956 conspiracy to kill, kidnap, maim, or injure certain property in a foreign country (property traceable to proceeds)*

18 U.S.C. 962 arming vessel against friendly nation (vessel, its tackle, apparel, furniture, arms, materials, ammunition and stores)

18 U.S.C. 963 departure of detained vessel in violation of neutrality (vessel, its tackle, apparel, furniture, equipment and cargo)

18 U.S.C. 964 delivery of armed vessel to belligerent (vessel, its tackle, apparel, furniture, equipment and cargo)

18 U.S.C. 965 departure without filing verification statements (vessel, its tackle, apparel, furniture, equipment and cargo)

18 U.S.C. 966 departure after filing falsified statements (vessel, its tackle, apparel, furniture, equipment and cargo)

18 U.S.C. 967 departure without clearance (vessel, its tackle, apparel, furniture, equipment and cargo)

18 U.S.C. 981 money laundering, civil forfeiture (all property, real or personal, constituting, derived from, or traceable to a violation)

18 U.S.C. 982 money laundering, criminal forfeiture (all property, real or personal involved in or traceable to a violation)

18 U.S.C. 984 fungible property involved in money laundering (fungible property)

18 U.S.C. 1001 false statements in a matter with the jurisdiction of a federal agency with respect to health care benefits (property traceable to proceeds)*

18 U.S.C. 1005 fraudulent bank entries (property traceable to proceeds)*

18 U.S.C. 1006 fraudulent Federal credit institution entries (property traceable to proceeds)*

18 U.S.C. 1007 fraudulent Federal Deposit Insurance transactions) (property traceable to proceeds)*

18 U.S.C. 1014 fraudulent loan or credit applications (property traceable to proceeds)*

18 U.S.C. 1027 ERISA fraud involving health care benefits (property traceable to proceeds)*

18 U.S.C. 1028 identification fraud (property traceable to proceeds)*

18 U.S.C. 1028 fraud with respect to identification documents (property used)

18 U.S.C. 1029 access device fraud (property traceable to proceeds)*

18 U.S.C. 1029 fraud with respect to access devices (property used)

18 U.S.C. 1030 computer fraud and abuse (property traceable to proceeds)*

18 U.S.C. 1031 major fraud against the U.S. involving the assets of a financial institution (property traceable to proceeds)*

18 U.S.C. 1032 concealment of assets from conservator, receiver, or liquidating agent of financial institution) (property traceable to proceeds)*

18 U.S.C. 1035 false statements in health care matters (property traceable to proceeds)*

18 U.S.C. 1037 fraud relating to electronic mail (property traceable to or used facilitate the offense)

18 U.S.C. 1082 gambling ships (vessel, its tackle, apparel, and furniture)

18 U.S.C. 1084 interstate transmission of gambling information (property traceable to proceeds)*

18 U.S.C. 1111 murder in the special maritime and territorial jurisdiction of the United States (property traceable to proceeds)*

18 U.S.C. 1114 federal officers or employees (property traceable to proceeds)*

18 U.S.C. 1116 murder of foreign officials, official guests, or internationally protected persons (property traceable to proceeds)*

18 U.S.C. 1165 hunting, trapping or fishing on Indian land (game, pelts, and fish)

18 U.S.C. 1201 kidnaping (property traceable to proceeds)*

18 U.S.C. 1203 hostage taking (property traceable to proceeds)*

18 U.S.C. 1341 mail fraud (property traceable to proceeds)*

18 U.S.C. 1343 wire fraud (property traceable to proceeds)*

18 U.S.C. 1344 bank fraud (property traceable to proceeds)*

18 U.S.C. 1347 health care fraud (property traceable to proceeds)*

18 U.S.C. 1361 willful injury of Government property (property traceable to proceeds)*

18 U.S.C. 1362 destruction of communications facilities (property traceable to proceeds)*

18 U.S.C. 1363 destruction of property within U.S. special maritime and territorial jurisdiction (property traceable to proceeds)*

18 U.S.C. 1336 destruction of energy facilities (property traceable to proceeds)*

18 U.S.C. 1425 procuring citizenship unlawfully (property traceable to proceeds)*

18 U.S.C. 1426 reproducing of citizenship papers (property traceable to proceeds)*

18 U.S.C. 1427 sale of citizenship papers (property traceable to proceeds)*

18 U.S.C. 1461 mailing obscene material (property traceable to proceeds)*

18 U.S.C. 1462 importing/exporting obscene material (property traceable to proceeds)*

18 U.S.C. 1463 mailing indecent material (property traceable to proceeds)*

18 U.S.C. 1464 broadcasting obscene language (property traceable to proceeds)*

18 U.S.C. 1465 transporting obscene material for sale (property traceable to proceeds)*

18 U.S.C. 1467 obscene material (material, real and personal property derived from, traceable to, or used to commit a violation)

18 U.S.C. 1503 obstruction of justice (property traceable to proceeds)*

18 U.S.C. 1510 obstructing criminal investigations (property traceable to proceeds)*

18 U.S.C. 1511 obstructing state law enforcement (property traceable to proceeds)*

18 U.S.C. 1512 tampering with federal witnesses (property traceable to proceeds)*

18 U.S.C. 1513 retaliating against federal witnesses (property traceable to proceeds)*

18 U.S.C. 1518 obstruction of health care crime investigations (property traceable to proceeds)*

18 U.S.C. 1542 false statement in a passport application (property traceable to proceeds)*

18 U.S.C. 1543 passport forgery (property traceable to proceeds)*

18 U.S.C. 1544 passport misuse (property traceable to proceeds)*

18 U.S.C. 1546 visa fraud (property traceable to proceeds)*

18 U.S.C. 1581 peonage (property traceable to proceeds)*

18 U.S.C. 1582 vessels in the slave trade (property traceable to proceeds)*

18 U.S.C. 1583 enticing another into slavery (property traceable to proceeds)*

18 U.S.C. 1584 selling another into slavery (property traceable to proceeds)*

18 U.S.C. 1585 slave trading (property traceable to proceeds)*

18 U.S.C. 1586 service on a slave ship (property traceable to proceeds)*

18 U.S.C. 1587 possession of slaves aboard ship (property traceable to proceeds)*

18 U.S.C. 1588 transportation of slaves to the United States (property traceable to proceeds)*

18 U.S.C. 1589 forced labor (property traceable to proceeds)*

18 U.S.C. 1590 trafficking relating to peonage, slavery, involuntary servitude or forced labor (property traceable to proceeds)*

18 U.S.C. 1591 sex trafficking in children (property traceable to proceeds)*

18 U.S.C. 1592 false statements relating to peonage (property traceable to proceeds)*

18 U.S.C. 1594 peonage, slavery, and forced labor violations (property derived from or used to facilitate the offense)

18 U.S.C. 1708 theft from the mail (property traceable to proceeds)*

18 U.S.C. 1751 Presidential assassination (property traceable to proceeds)*

18 U.S.C. 1762 illicit transportation of prisoner-made goods (goods)

18 U.S.C. 1834 trade secret offenses (proceeds and property used to facilitate offenses)

18 U.S.C. 1951 robbery or violence affecting interstate commerce (Hobbs Act) (property traceable to proceeds)*

18 U.S.C. 1952 use of interstate commerce to facilitate unlawful activity (Travel Act) (property traceable to proceeds)*

18 U.S.C. 1953 interstate transportation of wagering paraphernalia (property traceable to proceeds)*

18 U.S.C. 1954 corruption of employee benefit plans (property traceable to proceeds)*

18 U.S.C. 1955 illegal gambling business (property traceable to proceeds)*

18 U.S.C. 1955 illegal gambling business (any property including money used in violation)

18 U.S.C. 1956 money laundering (property traceable to proceeds)*

18 U.S.C. 1957 unlawful monetary transactions (property traceable to proceeds)*

18 U.S.C. 1958 interstate murder for hire (property traceable to proceeds)*

18 U.S.C. 1960 unlawful money transmission business (property involved or traceable to proceeds)*

18 U.S.C. 1963 Racketeer Influenced and Corrupt Organizations (RICO) (property derived from and interest acquired and maintained in violation)

18 U.S.C. 1992 terrorist attacks on mass transit (property traceable to proceeds)*

18 U.S.C. 2113 bank robbery (property traceable to proceeds)*

18 U.S.C. 2114 postal robbery and theft (property traceable to proceeds)*

18 U.S.C. 2119 carjacking (property traceable to proceeds)*

18 U.S.C. 2155 destruction of national defense material (property traceable to proceeds)*

18 U.S.C. 2156 product of defective national defense material (property traceable to proceeds)*

18 U.S.C. 2241 aggravated sexual abuse (property traceable to proceeds)

18 U.S.C. 2242 sexual abuse (property traceable to proceeds)

18 U.S.C. 2243 sexual abuse of a minor or ward (property traceable to proceeds)

18 U.S.C. 2244 abusive sexual contact (property traceable to proceeds)

18 U.S.C. 2251 sexual exploitation of children (property traceable to proceeds)*

18 U.S.C. 2251A selling children (property traceable to proceeds)*

18 U.S.C. 2252 material involving sexual exploitation of children (property traceable to proceeds)*

18 U.S.C. 2252A activities relating to child pornography (property traceable to proceeds)

18 U.S.C. 2252B misleading internet domain names (property traceable to proceeds)

18 U.S.C. 2253 sexual exploitation of children, criminal forfeiture (product, real and personal property derived from, traceable to, and used in violation)

18 U.S.C. 2254 sexual exploitation of children, civil forfeiture (product, real and personal property derived from, traceable to, and used in violation)

18 U.S.C. 2260 production of sexual exploitative material for importation (property traceable to proceeds)*

18 U.S.C. 2274 destruction or misuse of vessel by owner (vessel, its tackle, apparel, furniture and equipment)

18 U.S.C. 2280 violence against maritime navigation (property traceable to proceeds)*

18 U.S.C. 2281 violence against maritime fixed platforms (property traceable to proceeds)*

18 U.S.C. 2312 interstate transportation of stolen motor vehicles (property traceable to proceeds)*

18 U.S.C. 2313 receipt of a stolen motor vehicle transported interstate (property traceable to proceeds)*

18 U.S.C. 2314 interstate transportation of stolen property (property traceable to proceeds)*

18 U.S.C. 2315 receipt of a stolen property transported interstate (property traceable to proceeds)*

18 U.S.C. 2318 trafficking in counterfeit labels affixed or to be affixed to phonograph records, motion pictures or other audiovisual works (counterfeit labels and articles to which they are affixed)

18 U.S.C. 2318 same (property traceable to proceeds)*

18 U.S.C. 2319 copyright infringement (property traceable to proceeds)*

18 U.S.C. 2319A unauthorized commercial exploitation of sound recordings (property traceable to proceeds)*

18 U.S.C. 2319A same (recordings and phonorecords)

18 U.S.C. 2320 trafficking in counterfeit goods and services (property traceable to proceeds)*

18 U.S.C. 2321 chop shop offenses (property traceable to proceeds)*

18 U.S.C. 2332 terrorist acts abroad against United States nationals (property traceable to proceeds)*

18 U.S.C. 2332a weapons of mass destruction (property traceable to proceeds)*

18 U.S.C. 2332b international terrorist acts transcending national boundaries (property traceable to proceeds)*

18 U.S.C. 2332f bombing public places and facilities (property traceable to proceeds)*

18 U.S.C. 2332g anti-aircraft missile offenses (property traceable to proceeds)*

18 U.S.C. 2332h radiological dispersal device offenses (property traceable to proceeds)*

18 U.S.C. 2339 harboring terrorists (property traceable to proceeds)*

18 U.S.C. 2339A providing material support to terrorists (property traceable to proceeds)*

18 U.S.C. 2339B providing material support to terrorist organizations (property traceable to proceeds)*

18 U.S.C. 2339C financing terrorism (property traceable to proceeds)*

18 U.S.C. 2339D receipt of military training from a foreign terrorist organization (property traceable to proceeds)*

18 U.S.C. 2340A torture (property traceable to proceeds)*

18 U.S.C. 2342 trafficking in untaxed cigarettes (property traceable to proceeds)*

18 U.S.C. 2344 same (cigarettes)

18 U.S.C. 2421 interstate transportation for sexual purposes (property traceable to proceeds)*

18 U.S.C. 2422 coercing or enticing another to travel interstate for sexual purposes (property traceable to proceeds)*

18 U.S.C. 2423 interstate transportation of minors for sexual purposes (property traceable to proceeds)*

18 U.S.C. 2424 keeping a house of alien prostitution without registering with immigration officials (property traceable to proceeds)*

18 U.S.C. 2513 interception of wire, oral or electronic communications (wiretapping and bugging devices)

18 U.S.C. 3113 liquor violations in Indian country (unlawful liquor and the conveyances and packages in which it is found)

18 U.S.C. 3665 firearms possessed by convicted felons (firearms and ammunition unlawfully possessed)

18 U.S.C. 3667 liquors involved in violations of 18 U.S.C. 1261-1265 relating to tax and transportation of liquor (liquor and conveyances)

18 U.S.C. 3669 using conveyances to unlawful transport liquor into Indian country (conveyances)

18 U.S.C. 4012 prison contraband (contraband)

19 U.S.C. 130 importing goods in certain foreign owned ships (goods, vessels, and their cargo, tackle, apparel, and furniture)

19 U.S.C. 467 unstamped imported distilled spirits (spirits)

19 U.S.C. 469 dealing in empty stamped imported liquor containers (containers)

19 U.S.C. 1305 importation of immoral materials (contents of packages in which immoral materials are found)

19 U.S.C. 1322 rescue and relief equipment imported contrary to regulations for admission pursuant to treaty with Mexico (equipment)

19 U.S.C. 1338 foreign discrimination against American commerce (articles imported in violation)

19 U.S.C. 1436 failure to comply with Customs entry requirements (conveyance and goods)

19 U.S.C. 1453 unloading without meeting Customs requirements (goods and, if their value exceeds $500, the importing vessel)

19 U.S.C. 1462 refusal to allow customs inspection of container or vehicle (container or vehicle and its contents)

19 U.S.C. 1464 failure to comply with Customs requirements for sealed conveyances (conveyances and contents)

19 U.S.C. 1466 avoiding duty on repairs made overseas (vessel)

19 U.S.C. 1497 failure to declare goods upon entry (goods)

19 U.S.C. 1526 import of foreign made goods with American labels (goods)

19 U.S.C. 1527 import of animals and birds contrary to foreign law (animals and birds)

19 U.S.C. 1584 failure to describe goods in a manifest (goods)

19 U.S.C. 1586 unlawful unloading or shipment (vessel and cargo)

19 U.S.C. 1587 smuggled goods discovered on inspection (vessel and cargo)

19 U.S.C. 1588 transportation of goods between U.S. ports via foreign ports (goods)

19 U.S.C. 1590 aviation smuggling (plane or vessel)

19 U.S.C. 1590 same (property traceable to proceeds)*

19 U.S.C. 1592 false or incomplete statements to customs (goods)

19 U.S.C. 1594 smuggling (conveyances)

19 U.S.C. 1595a use of conveyances for smuggling (conveyances and merchandise)

19 U.S.C. 1627a importing or exporting stolen conveyances (conveyances)

19 U.S.C. 1703 smuggling (vessel and cargo)

19 U.S.C. 1706 importation in unlicensed planes and small boats (planes, small boats and goods)

19 U.S.C. 1707 importing liquor without vessel certificate (liquor)

19 U.S.C. 2093 unlawfully imported pre-Columbian art (art)

19 U.S.C. 2609 theft or unlawfully importing archaeological or ethnological material or articles (material or articles)

21 U.S.C. 134a Livestock and Poultry threatening the introduction or dissemination of communicable diseases (livestock and poultry)

21 U.S.C. 334 misbranded or adulterated foods, drugs and cosmetics (products, counterfeit drugs, their containers, manufacturing equipment)

21 U.S.C. 467b processing, transporting or distributing diseased poultry and poultry products (poultry and poultry products)

21 U.S.C. 673 processing, transporting or distributing diseased meat (meat)

21 U.S.C. 841 controlled substance trafficking (property traceable to proceeds)*

21 U.S.C. 842 controlled substance regulatory offenses (property traceable to proceeds)*

21 U.S.C. 843 unlawful conduct relating to controlled substance (property traceable to proceeds)*

21 U.S.C. 846 attempt or conspiracy to a commit controlled substance offense (property traceable to proceeds)*

21 U.S.C. 848 drug kingpin offenses (property traceable to proceeds)*

21 U.S.C. 853 controlled substance violations, criminal forfeiture (property derived from, traceable to, used to facilitate violation)

21 U.S.C. 854 investment of controlled substance offense proceeds (property traceable to proceeds)*

21 U.S.C. 856 maintaining drug-involved premises (property traceable to proceeds)*

21 U.S.C. 858 endangerment in the illicit production of controlled substances (property traceable to proceeds)*

21 U.S.C. 859 drug trafficking to minors (property traceable to proceeds)*

21 U.S.C. 860 drug trafficking near schools and similar facilities (property traceable to proceeds)*

21 U.S.C. 861 drug trafficking using minors (property traceable to proceeds)*

21 U.S.C. 863 transportation of drug paraphernalia (property traceable to proceeds)*

21 U.S.C. 863 same (property traceable to proceeds)*

21 U.S.C. 881 controlled substance violations, civil forfeiture (substance, raw materials, precursor chemicals, records, containers, conveyances, property including real property traceable to, derived from or used to facilitate violations)

21 U.S.C. 952 unlawfully importing controlled substances (property traceable to proceeds)*

21 U.S.C. 953 unlawfully exporting controlled substances (property traceable to proceeds)*

21 U.S.C. 957 unlicensed exporting or importing controlled substances (property traceable to proceeds)*

21 U.S.C. 959 overseas controlled substance offenses (property traceable to proceeds)*

21 U.S.C. 960 violations of 21 U.S.C. 952, 953, 957, 959 (property traceable to proceeds)*

21 U.S.C. 960A narcoterrorism (property traceable to proceeds)*

21 U.S.C. 961 regulatory import/export offenses (property traceable to proceeds)*

21 U.S.C. 963 attempt or conspiracy to commit controlled substance import/export offenses (property traceable to proceeds)*

21 U.S.C. 970 controlled substance importing and exporting violations (property derived from, traceable to, used to facilitate violation)

21 U.S.C. 1049 processing, transporting or distributing contaminated eggs (eggs)

22 U.S.C. 287c violation of import restrictions on Rhodesian chromium (property, funds, securities, papers, vessel (with tackle, apparel, furniture and equipment, vehicle, aircraft concerned in violation)

22 U.S.C. 401 illegal exportation of war materials (arms, munitions of war and other articles, vessels, vehicles, and aircraft)

22 U.S.C. 611 et seq. felonious violations of the Foreign Agents Registration Act (property traceable to proceeds)*

22 U.S.C. 1978 importing fish and wildlife from countries threatening endangered species (fish and wildlife)

22 U.S.C. 2778 Arms Export Control Act offenses (property traceable to proceeds)*

22 U.S.C. 6744 disclosure trade secrets acquired through Chemical Weapons Convention implementation (property used in, constituting the proceeds from, or facilitating offenses)

25 U.S.C. 264 trading in Indian country without a license (merchandise)

26 U.S.C. 5607 unlawful use, recovery or concealment of denatured distilled spirits (all personal property used, buildings and grounds constituting business premises on which violations occurred)

26 U.S.C. 5608 smuggling liquor (liquor, vessels, vehicles and planes)

26 U.S.C. 5612 mingling taxed and untaxed liquor in distilling plants (liquor)

26 U.S.C. 5613 improperly marked liquor (liquor)

26 U.S.C. 5615 bootlegging (unregistered stills, distilling apparatus, products, land used or facilitating, personal property proximate)

26 U.S.C. 5661 wine tax evasion (property used)

26 U.S.C. 5671 beer tax evasion (beer, vessels, utensils, and apparatus)

26 U.S.C. 5673 evading beer tax (lands and buildings holding brewery)

26 U.S.C. 5681 transporting liquor or raw materials to plants or warehouses with insufficient signs (vehicles, planes, and vessels used)

26 U.S.C. 5683 transporting liquor under improper brands (liquor)

26 U.S.C. 5685 possession of illegal firearms (firearms)

26 U.S.C. 5763 tobacco tax violations (all property, real and personal, used in violation, property of illicit operators used to defraud, tobacco and tobacco products)

26 U.S.C. 5872 firearms tax violations (firearms)

26 U.S.C. 7301 tax avoidance (property subject to taxation, and associated raw material, equipment, containers, conveyances)

26 U.S.C. 7302 possession of property to be used to violate the tax laws (property intended to such use)

26 U.S.C. 7303 use of counterfeit tax stamps and documents (counterfeit stamps, falsely stamped containers and their contents, fraudulent permits and like documents)

27 U.S.C. 206 violation of bulk intoxicating liquor sales regulations (liquor)

29 U.S.C. 186 restrictions on payments and loans to labor organizations (property traceable to proceeds)*

29 U.S.C. 501(c) embezzlement from union funds (property traceable to proceeds)*

30 U.S.C. 1466 Deep Seabed Hard Mineral Resource Act violations (minerals, vessel and its gear, furniture, appurtenances, stores and cargo)

31 U.S.C. 5111 U.S. coins exported, melted or treated contrary to regulation (coins)

31 U.S.C. 5137 crossing a U.S. border with more than $10,000 in unreported cash (cash)

33 U.S.C. 384 piracy (vessels)

33 U.S.C. 1251 et seq. Federal Water Pollution Control Act felonies (property traceable to proceeds)*

33 U.S.C. 1401 et seq. Ocean Dumping Act felonies (property traceable to proceeds)*

33 U.S.C. 1415 ocean dumping (proceeds of, property used in, property facilitate violation)

33 U.S.C. 1901 et seq. Act to Prevent Pollution from Ships felonies (property traceable to proceeds)*

33 U.S.C. 2236 failure pay harbor dues (cargo)

33 U.S.C. 2716 oil tankers failure to maintain evidence of financial responsibility (vessel)

42 U.S.C. 300f et seq. Safe Drinking Water Act felonies (property traceable to proceeds)*

42 U.S.C. 1490s equity skimming (property traceable to proceeds)*

42 U.S.C. 2122 atom weapons offenses (property traceable to proceeds)*

42 U.S.C. 2284 sabotage of nuclear facilities (property traceable to proceeds)*

42 U.S.C. 6901 et seq. Resources Conservation and Recovery Act felonies (property traceable to proceeds)*

46 U.S.C. 12118 unlawful foreign shipping in domestic commerce (vessel)

46 U.S.C. 12122 vessel documentation offenses (vessel and its equipment)

46 U.S.C. 12151 failure to report foreign rebuilding (vessel, tackle, apparel, equipment and furniture)

46 U.S.C. 12507 vessel identification offenses (vessel and its equipment)

46 U.S.C. 31330 violation of restrictions on sale of mortgaged vessels (vessel)

46 U.S.C. 55109 use of unlicensed foreign built dredges (dredge)

46 U.S.C. 55118 unlawful salvage operations by foreign vessels (vessel)

46 U.S.C. 56101 improper transfer of a U.S. registered vessel to foreign registry (vessel)

46 U.S.C. 56102 violation of restrictions on transfer of shipping facilities (vessel, shipyard, drydock, ship building or repairing facilities, or interest therein)

46 U.S.C. 60505 retaliatory suspension of commercial privileges to foreign vessels (vessel and goods)

46 U.S.C. 80103 carrying property from ship wrecks to foreign ports (vessel, its tackle, apparel and furniture)

46 U.S.C. 70507 manufacture, distribution or possession of controlled substances in violation of the Maritime Drug Enforcement Act (controlled substances and other property used or intended for use in violation of Act)

47 U.S.C. 510 broadcasting without a license (radio equipment)

49 U.S.C. 46306 aircraft registration violations (plane)

49 U.S.C. 46502 chemical trafficking offenses (property traceable to proceeds)*

49 U.S.C. 46504 assault of aircraft flight crew with a dangerous weapons (property traceable to proceeds)*

49 U.S.C. 46505 placing explosives aboard an aircraft (property traceable to proceeds)*

49 U.S.C. 46506 homicide or attempted homicide aboard an aircraft (property traceable to proceeds)*

49 U.S.C. 80303 contraband in the Guam and the North Marianas (conveyances)

49 U.S.C. 60123 destruction of interstate gas pipeline facilities (property traceable to proceeds)*

50 U.S.C. 192 failure to comply with regulations during a national emergency (vessel, tackle, apparel, furniture and equipment)

50 U.S.C. 205 suspension of commercial intercourse with State in insurrection (goods, vessels or vehicles entering or departing after suspension)

50 U.S.C. 212 property employed in aid of insurrection (property used)

50 U.S.C. 216 transportation of goods in aid of insurrection (goods)

50 U.S.C. 221 entering ports of entry closed due to insurrection (vessel and its tackle, apparel, furniture and cargo)

50 U.S.C. 223 states in insurrection (vessels)

50 U.S.C. 224 unauthorized departure during time of insurrection (vessel and its tackle, apparel, furniture and cargo)

50 U.S.C. 783 unlawful communication of classified information (proceeds from, property used, or property facilitating offense)

50 U.S.C. 1705 International Emergency Economic Powers Act offenses (property traceable to proceeds)*

50 U.S.C.App. 16 Trading With the Enemy Act violations (property and vessels that is the subject of a violation)

50 U.S.C. App. 16 Trading With the Enemy Act offenses (property traceable to proceeds)*

50 U.S.C.App. 2410 export regulation violations (resulting property interests and proceeds)

State Forfeiture Statutes (citations)

State Drug Forfeiture Acts

Alabama: Ala.Code §20-2-93;
Alaska: Alaska Stat. §§17.30.100 to 17.30.126;
Arizona: Ariz.Rev.Stat.Ann. §§13-4301 to 13-4315;
Arkansas: Ark.Code §§5-64-505 to 5-64-508;
California: Cal.Health & Safety Code §§ 11469 to 11495;
Colorado: Colo.Rev.Stat. §§16-13-501 to 16-13-702;
Connecticut: Conn.Gen.Stat.Ann. §§54-36a to 54-36n;
Delaware: Del.Code tit.16 §4784;
Florida: Fla.Stat.Ann. §§893.12, 932.701 to 932.706;
Georgia: Ga.Code Ann. §16-13-49;
Hawaii: Hawaii Rev.Stat. §329-55;
Idaho: Idaho Code §§37-2744 to 37-2744B, 37-2801 to 37-2815;
Illinois: Ill.Stat.Ann. ch.720 §§550/12, 570/505, ch.725 §§175/1 to 175/5.2;
Indiana: Ind.Code Ann. §§34-24-1-1 to 34-24-1-8;
Iowa: Iowa Code Ann. §§809A.1 to 809A.25;

Kansas: Kan.Stat.Ann. §§60-4101 to 60-4126;
Kentucky: Ky.Rev.Stat. §§218A.405 to 218A.460;
Louisiana: La.Rev.Stat.Ann. §§40:2601 to 40:2622;
Maine: Me.Rev.Stat.Ann. ch.15 §§5821 to 5827;
Maryland: Md.Crim. Pro.Code §§12-101 to 13-206;
Massachusetts: Mass.Gen.Laws Ann. ch. 94C §§47, 47A;
Michigan: Mich.Comp.Laws Ann. §§333.7521 to 333.7524a;
Minnesota: Minn.Stat.Ann. 609.531 to 609.5319;
Mississippi: Miss.Code §41-29-176 to 41-29-187;
Missouri: Mo.Ann.Stat. §§195.130 to 195.146;
Montana: Mont.Code Ann. §§44-12-101 to 44-12-206;
Nebraska: Neb.Rev.Stat. §28-431;
Nevada: Nev.Rev.Stat. §§453.301 to 453. 311;
New Hampshire: N.H.Rev.Stat.Ann. §§318-B:17 to 318-B:17-f;
New Jersey: N.J.Stat.Ann. §§2C:64-1 to 2C:64-9;
New Mexico: N.M.Stat.Ann. §§30-31-34 to 30-31-36;
New York: N.Y.Pub.Health Law §§3387, 3388; N.Y.Civil Practice Law §§1310 to 1352;
North Carolina: N.C.Gen.Stat. §§90-112, 112.1;
North Dakota: N.D.Cent.Code §§19-03.1-36 to 19-03.1-36.7;
Ohio: Ohio Rev.Code §§2925.41 to 2925.45;
Oklahoma: Okla.Stat.Ann. tit.63 §§2-501 to 2-508;
Oregon: Ore.Rev.Stat. §§475A.005 to 475A.160;
Pennsylvania: Pa.Stat.Ann. tit.42 §§6801, 6802;
Rhode Island: R.I.Gen.Laws §§21-28-5.0 to 21-28-5.07.5;
South Carolina: S.C.Code §§44-53-520 to 44-53-590;
South Dakota: S.D.Comp.Laws §§34-20B-70 to 34-20B-101;
Tennessee: Tenn.Code Ann. §§53-11-201 to 53-11-204; 53-11-451, 53-11-452;
Texas: Tex.Code of Crim.Pro. Arts. 59.01 to 59.14;
Utah: Utah Code Ann. §§58-37-13 to 58-37-20;
Vermont: Vt.Stat.Ann. tit.18 §§4241 to 4248;
Virginia: Va.Code §19.2-386.1 to 19.2-386.27;
Washington: Wash.Rev.Code Ann. §§69.50.505 to 69.50. 509, 69.50.520;
West Virginia: W.Va.Code §§60A-7-701 to 60A-7-707;
Wisconsin: Wis.Stat.Ann. §§961.55, 961.555;
Wyoming: Wyo.Stat. §35-7-1049.

State RICO Forfeiture Acts

Arizona: Ariz.Rev.Stat.Ann. §§13-2314 to 13-2314.04;
California: Cal.Penal Code §§186 to 186.8;
Colorado: Colo.Rev.Stat. §§18-17-101 to 18-17-109;
Connecticut: Conn.Gen.Stat.Ann. §§53-393 to 53-403;
Delaware: Del.Code tit.11 §§1501 to 1511;
Florida: Fla.Stat.Ann. §§895.01 to 895.09;

Georgia: Ga.Code Ann. §§16-14-1 to 16-14-15;
Hawaii: Haw.Rev.Stat. §§842-1 to 842-12;
Idaho: Idaho Code §§18-7801 to 18-7805;
Indiana: Ind.Code Ann. §§34-24-2-1 to 34-24-2-8;
Iowa: Iowa Code Ann. §706A.3;
Louisiana: La.Rev.Stat.Ann. §§15:1351 to 15:1356;
Michigan: Mich.Comp.Laws Ann. §§750.159f to 750.159x;
Minnesota: Minn.Stat.Ann. §§609.901 to 609.912;
Mississippi: Miss.Code §§97-43-1 to 97-43-11;
Missouri: Mo.Ann.Stat. §§513.600 to 513.653;
Nevada: Nev.Rev.Stat. §§207.350 to 207.520;
New Jersey: N.J.Stat.Ann. §§2C:41-1 to 2C:41-6.2;
New Mexico: N.M.Stat.Ann. §§30-42-1 to 30-42-6;
New York: N.Y.Penal Law §§460.00 to 460.80;
North Carolina: N.C.Gen.Stat. §§75D-1 to 75D-14;
North Dakota: N.D.Cent.Code §§12.1-06.1-01 to 12.1-06.1-08;
Ohio: Ohio Rev.Code §§2923.31 to 2923.36;
Oklahoma: Okla.Stat.Ann. tit.22 §§1401 to 1419;
Oregon: Ore.Rev.Stat. §§166.715 to 166.735;
Pennsylvania: Pa.Stat.Ann. tit.18 §911;
Rhode Island: R.I.Gen.Laws §§7-15-1 to 7-15-11;
Tennessee: Tenn.Code Ann. §§39-12-201 to 39-12-210;
Texas: Tex.Penal Code §§71.01 to 71.05;
Utah: Utah Code Ann. §§76-10-1601 to 76-10-1610;
Virginia: Va.Code §§18.2-512 to 18.2-517;
Washington: Wash.Rev.Code Ann. §§9A.82.010 to 9A.82.170;
Wisconsin: Wis.Stat.Ann. §§946.80 to 946.88.

End Notes

[1] Forfeiture is the loss of any right—ordinarily a property right—as a consequence of a breach of some legal obligation, BLACK'S LAW DICTIONARY, 667 (8th ed. 2004). Discussion inthis chapter is limited to forfeitures associated with criminal conduct, other than the forfeiture of bail. Throughoutthis chapter, the terms "forfeiture" and "confiscation" will be used interchangeably.

[2] *Austin v. United States*, 509 U.S. 602, 611-13 (1993); *Calero-Toledo v. Pearson Yacht Leasing Co.*, 416 U.S. 663, 680-82 (1974); *Bane of American Forfeiture Law—Banished at Last?* 62 CORNELL LAW REVIEW 768, 770 (1977).

[3] *Goldsmith-Grant Co. v. United States*, 254 U.S. 505 (1921); 1 HALE,HISTORY OF THE PLEAS OF THE CROWN 419 (1778); 2 POLLOCK &MAITLAND,THE HISTORY OF ENGLISH LAW 473 (2d ed. 1923); Finklestein, *The Goring Ox: Some Historical Perspective on Deodands, Forfeiture, Wrongful Death and the Western Notion of Sovereignty*, 46 TEMPLE LAW QUARTERLY 169 (1973).

[4] 1 HALE, HISTORY OF THE PLEAS OF THE CROWN, 419 (1778); 1 BLACKSTONE,COMMENTARIES, 290 (1765-69). The value of the offending object or animal had to be determined because the owner was permitted to recover his property as long as he paid the Crown its value, *id.*

[5] *Id.* Originally, the proceeds were used to pay for a Mass to be said for the repose of the soul of the deceased, hence the name—giving ("dand") to God ("deo").

[6] GOEBEL, LAW ENFORCEMENT IN COLONIAL NEW YORK 717 (1944); SEMMES, CRIME AND PUNISHMENT IN EARLY MARYLAND 136 (1938); SCOTT,CRIMINAL LAW IN COLONIAL VIRGINIA 52 (1930).

[7] BISHOP,COMMENTARIES ON THE CRIMINAL LAW §827 (7th ed. 1882); N.J. Const. Art.XVII (1776); Vt. Const. ch.2, §35 (1777); N.H. Const. pt.2, Art.89 (1783); Del. Const. Art.I, §15 (1792).

[8] *United States v. United States Coin & Currency*, 401 U.S. 715, 720-21 (1971); *Calero-Toledo v. Pearson Yacht Leasing Co.*, 416 U.S. at 680-81; *Goldsmith-Grant Co. v. United States*, 254 U.S. at 510-11.

[9] 1 HALE, HISTORY OF THE PLEAS OF THE CROWN 354-67 (1778); 1 CHITTY, APRACTICAL TREATISE ON CRIMINAL LAW 727-39 (1816); 1 STEPHENS,AHISTORY OF THE CRIMINAL LAW OF ENGLAND 468-88 (1883); 4 BLACKSTONE, COMMENTARIES 376-81 (1765-69).

[10] *Id.* at 373-74. Attainder not only resulted in forfeiture but in corruption of the blood as well, "so that an attained person can neither inherit lands or hereditaments from his ancestors, nor retain those he is already in possession of, nor transmit them by descent to any heir; but the same shall escheat to the lord of the fee, subject to the king's superior right of forfeiture; and the person attained shall also obstruct all descents of his posterity, wherever they are obliged to derive a title through him to a remoter ancestor." *Id.* at 381.

[11] SEMMES,CRIME AND PUNISHMENT IN EARLY MARYLAND 107-10 (1938); GOEBEL, LAW ENFORCEMENT IN COLONIAL NEW YORK 717 (1944). During the Revolution, some of the states enacted provisions forfeiting the land and goods of those considered sympathetic to the Crown, see e.g., 5 Mass.Acts & Resolves 1769-1780, 966-67 (1779); 9 Hening's (Va.) Stat. at Large 1775-1778, ch.9 (1777); 1 N.H. Laws 22 (1778).

[12] "The Congress shall have power to declare the punishment of treason, but no attainder to treason shall work corruption of blood, or forfeiture except during the life of the person attainted." U.S.Const. Art.III, §3. "[N]o conviction or judgment for any of the offenses aforesaid, shall work corruption of blood, or any forfeiture of estate." 1 Stat. 177 (1790). This provision and its successors remained in force until 1984, Rev. Stat. §5326; 35 Stat. 1151 (1909); 62 Stat. 837 (1948); 18 U.S.C. 3563 (1982 ed.); 98 Stat. 1987 (1984).

[13] 1 MADDOX,HISTORY AND ANTIQUITIES OF THE EXCHEQUER 781-82 (1769); HARPER,THE ENGLISH NAVIGATION LAWS 109-10 (1964); Currency, *The Courts in the American Colonies* 11 AMERICAN JOURNAL OF LEGAL HISTORY 253, 357 (1967). Admiralty jurisdiction extended to piracy, spoils of war, and ship registration offenses, all of which called for confiscation, 1 HOLDSWORTH,HISTORY OF ENGLISH LAW 328 (1903 ED.); II SELDON SOCIETY, SELECT PLEAS OF THE COURT OF ADMIRALTY,A.D.1517-1602 (Vol.II) xvi-xxii (Marsden ed. 1897). The Exchequer dealt with customs duties and other revenue matters.

[14] HARPER,THE ENGLISH NAVIGATION LAWS 109-11 (1964); Currency, *The Courts in the American Colonies*, 11 AMERICAN JOURNAL OF LEGAL HISTORY 253, 357 (1967).

[15] *E.g.*, 18 Stat. 186, 188 (1874) (smuggling); 41 Stat. 305, 315 (1919) (prohibition); 18 U.S.C. 3665 (unlawful firearms possession).

[16] The Supreme Court in *Calero-Toledo* summarized the relative contributions of the three English procedures with the observation that:
Deodands did not become part of the common law tradition of this country. Nor has forfeiture of estate as a consequence of a federal criminal conviction been permitted. Forfeiture of estate resulting from a conviction for treason has been constitutionally proscribed by Art.III, §3 though forfeitures of estate for the lifetime of a traitor have been sanctioned. But "[l]ong before the adoption of the Constitution the common law courts in the Colonies—and later in the states during the period of Confederation—were exercising jurisdiction *in rem* in the enforcement of [English and local] forfeiture statutes" which provided for the forfeiture of commodities and vessels used in violation of the customs and revenue laws. And almost immediately after adoption of the Constitution, ships and cargoes involved in customs offenses were made subject to forfeiture under federal law, as were vessels used to deliver slaves to foreign countries, and somewhat later those used to deliver slaves to this country. The enactment of forfeiture statutes has not abated; contemporary federal and state forfeiture statutes reach virtually any type of property that might be used in the conduct of a criminal enterprise. 416 U.S. at 682-83 (citations and footnotes omitted). *Calero-Toledo*, however, was written prior to legislation apparently authorizing forfeiture of the estates of certain terrorists, 18 U.S.C. 981(a)(1)(G)(i)("The following property is subject to forfeiture to the United States . . .(G) All assets, foreign or domestic—(i) of any individual . . . engaged in planning or perpetrating any Federal crime of terrorism (as defined in section 2332b(g)(5)) against the United States, citizens or residents of the United States, or their property. . . "); see also, 50 U.S.C. 1702(a)(1)(C). At least to date, this authority has rarely, if ever, been used.

[17] A list of federal forfeiture laws, along with the type of property whose confiscation they permit or require, is attached, as are the citations to state RICO and drug forfeiture statutes.

[18] *E.g.*, 21 U.S.C. 853(b); 18 U.S.C. 1963(b)("[p]roperty subject to criminal forfeiture under this section includes—(1) real property, including things growing on, affixed to, and found in land; and (2) tangible and intangible personal property, including rights, privileges, interests, claims and securities");*United States v. Dicter*, 198 F.3d 1284, 1290 (11th Cir. 1999) (a physician's license to practice medicine is forfeitable under section 853); the text of 18 U.S.C. 1963 is attached.

[19] *E.g.*, 18 U.S.C. 2513 (wiretapping equipment), 18 U.S.C. 844 (unlawful explosives); 19 U.S.C. 467 (distilled spirits without a tax stamp).

[20] *E.g.*, 19 U.S.C. 1595a (conveyances used for smuggling); 18 U.S.C. 492 (counterfeiting paraphernalia); 16 U.S.C. 128 (guns and traps used in violation of hunting and trapping restrictions); 18 U.S.C. 229B("any person convicted under section 229A(a)[relating to chemical weapons] shall forfeit to the United States . . . any of the property used in any manner or part, to commit, or to facilitate the commission of such violation").

[21] *E.g.*, 18 U.S.C. 1963(a)(3) (racketeer influenced and corrupt organizations (RICO)); 21 U.S.C. 881(a)(6) (drug trafficking).

[22] "If the property described in subsection (a) [listing the types of property forfeitable], as a result of any act or omission of the defendant—(1) cannot be located upon the exercise of due diligence; (2) has been transferred or sold to, or deposited with, a third party; (3) has been placed beyond the jurisdiction of the court; (4) has been substantially diminished in value; or (5) has been commingled with other property which cannot be divided without difficulty; the court shall order the forfeiture of any other property of the defendant up to the value of any property described in paragraphs (1) through (5)." 18 U.S.C. 1963(m); 21 U.S.C. 853(p); see also, 18 U.S.C. 984(a)(1)("In any forfeiture action in rem in which the subject property is cash, monetary instruments in bearer form, funds deposited in an account in a financial institution (as defined in section 20 of this title), or precious metals—(A) it shall not be necessary for the Government to identify the specific property involved in the offense that is the basis for the forfeiture; and (B) it shall not be a defense that the property involved in such an offense has been removed and replaced by identical property").

[23] 18 U.S.C. 981, 982 (money laundering); 18 U.S.C. 1963 (RICO).

[24] P.L. 106-185, 114 Stat. 202 (2000).

[25] 18 U.S.C. 981(a)(1)(C)("the following property is subject to forfeiture to the United States . . . (C) Any property , real or personal, which constitutes or is derived from proceeds traceable to . . . any offense constituting 'specified unlawful activity' (as defined in section 1956(c)(7) of this title)[*i.e.*, the list of predicate offenses form money laundering (18 U.S.C. 1956) which list includes by cross reference all the predicate offenses for a RICO prosecution)], or a conspiracy to commit such offense").
As one court noted, this trend could have unfortunate consequences, *United States v. Funds Held in the Name or for the Benefit of Wetterer*, 210 F.3d 96, 110 (2d Cir. 2000)("We have previously observed the government's virtually unchecked use of the civil forfeiture statutes and the disregard for due process that is buried in those statutes. Another source of potential abuse is that the forfeited funds are kept by the Department of Justice as a supplement to its budget. Thus the agency that conceives the jurisdiction and ground for seizures, and executes them, also absorbs their proceeds. This arrangement creates incentives that evidently require a more-than-human judgment and restraint. The Supreme Court has politely remarked on the Department of Justice's direct pecuniary interest in maximizing drug forfeitures to meet the Department's budget target. *See United States v. James Daniel Good Real Property*, 510 U.S. 43, 56 n.2 (1993)(quoting 1990 memo of the Attorney General: 'We must significantly increase production to reach our budget target. . . . Every effort must be made to increase forfeiture income during the remaining three months of fiscal year 1990.'). The bare financial facts of this case shine a light on the corrupting incentives of this arrangement: we see aggressive but marginal claims asserted on dubious jurisdiction to seize charitable funds raised for the relief of abject orphans in an impoverished country, so that the money can be diverted for expenditure by the Department of Justice"). Sensitive to such criticism, CAFRA sought to balance increased procedural efficiency with additional procedural safeguards.

[26] 50 U.S.C. 1702(a)(1)(C)(". . .the President may. . . when the United States is engaged in armed hostilities or has been attacked by a foreign country or foreign nationals, confiscate any property, subject to the jurisdiction of the United States, of any foreign person, foreign organization, or foreign country that he determines has planned, authorized, aided, or engaged in such hostilities or attacks against the United States . . ."); see also, 18 U.S.C. 981(a)(1)(G)(i)(text at footnote 16, *supra*). At first glance, the two seem to resemble common law forfeiture of estate.

[27] 18 U.S.C. 981(a)(1)(B)("(a)(1) The following property is subject to forfeiture to the United States. . . (B) Any property, real or personal, within the jurisdiction of the United States, constituting, derived from, or traceable to, any proceeds obtained directly or indirectly from an offense against a foreign nation, or any property used to facilitate such an offense, if the offense—(i) involves trafficking in nuclear, chemical, biological, or radiological weapons technology or material, or the manufacture, importation, sale, or distribution of a controlled substance (as that term is defined for purposes of the Controlled Substances Act), or any other conduct described in section 1956(c)(7)(B); (ii) would be punishable within the jurisdiction of the foreign nation by death or imprisonment for a term exceeding 1 year; and (iii) would be punishable under the laws of the United States by imprisonment for a term exceeding 1 year, if the act or activity constituting the offense had occurred within the jurisdiction of the United States"); see *e.g., United States v. $125,938.62 (Cardenal)*, 537 F.3d 1287, 1288 (11th Cir. 2008).

[28] More precisely, ". . . an offense against a foreign nation involving—(i) the manufacture, importation, sale, or distribution of a controlled substance (as such term is defined for the purposes of the Controlled Substances Act); (ii) murder, kidnapping, robbery, extortion, destruction of property by means of explosive or fire, or a crime of violence (as defined in section 16); (iii) fraud, or any scheme or attempt to defraud, by or against a foreign bank (as defined in paragraph 7 of section 1(b) of the International Banking Act of 1978); (iv) bribery of a public official, or the misappropriation, theft, or embezzlement of public funds by or for the benefit of a public official; (v) smuggling or export control violations involving—(I) an item controlled on the United States Munitions List established under section 38 of the Arms Export Control Act (22 U.S.C. 2778); or (II) an item controlled under regulations under the Export Administration Regulations (15 C.F.R. Parts 730-774); (vi)

an offense with respect to which the United States would be obligated by a multilateral treaty, either to extradite the alleged offender or to submit the case for prosecution, if the offender were found within the territory of the United States; or (vii) trafficking in persons, selling or buying children, sexual exploitation of children, or transporting, recruiting or harboring a person, including a child, for commercial sex acts, " 18 U.S.C. 1956(c)(7)(B).

[29] "This [civil] 'forfeiture proceeding . . . is in rem. It is the property which is proceeded against, and by resort to a legal fiction, held guilty and condemned as though it were conscious instead of inanimate and insentient,'" *United States v. Ursery*, 518 U.S. 267, 275 (1996), quoting *Various Items of Personal Property v. United States*, 282 U.S. 577, 284 (1931); see also, *United States v. Cherry*, 330 F.3d 658, 669 n.16 (4th Cir. 2003); *United States v. Nava*, 404 F.3d 1119, 1123-124 (9th Cir. 2005); *United States v. Timley*, 443 F.3d 615, 627-28 (8th Cir. 2006); *von Hofe v. United States*, 492 F.3d 175, 184 (2d Cir. 2007); *United States v. Fleet*, 498 F.3d 1225, 1231 (11th Cir. 2007).

[30] *Bennis v. Michigan*, 516 U.S. 442, 453 (1996); *United States v. One "Piper" Aztec "F" DeLuxe Model 250 PA 23 Aircraft*, 321 F.3d 355, 360 (3d Cir. 2003); *United States v. Funds in the Amount of Thirty Thousand Six Hundred Seventy Dollars (Calhoun)*, 403 F.3d 448, 469 (7th Cir. 2005); *von Hofe v. United States*, 492 F.3d at 185.

[31] *United States v. Lazarenko*, 476 F.3d 642, 647 (9th Cir. 2007); *United States v. Totaro*, 345 F.3d 989, 993 (8th Cir. 2003); *cf., United States v. Ferrario-Pozzi*, 368 F.3d 5, 8 (1st Cir. 2004).

[32] *E.g.*, 21 U.S.C. 853(a); 18 U.S.C. 982, 1963(a); *United States v. Nava*, 404 F.3d 1119, 1124 (9th Cir. 2005).

[33] 18 U.S.C. 981(d); 21 U.S.C. 881(d).

[34] 18 U.S.C. 983; the new procedural framework, however, does not apply to forfeitures that originate under the customs laws, the tax laws, and several others, 18 U.S.C. 983(i)("In this section, the term 'civil forfeiture statute'—(1) means any provision of Federal law providing for the forfeiture of property other than as a sentence imposed upon conviction of a criminal offense; and (2) does not include—(A) the Tariff Act of 1930 or any other provision of law codified in title 19 [(the customs laws)]; (B) the Internal Revenue Code of 1986 [(federal tax laws)]; (C) the Federal Food, Drug, and Cosmetic Act (21 U.S.C. 301 et seq.)[(relating to misbranded, adulterated and other unhealthy or unsafe food, drugs, or cosmetics)]; (D) the Trading with the Enemy Act (50 U.S.C. App. 1 et seq.) or the International Emergency Economic Powers Act (IEEPA)(50 U.S.C. 1701 et seq.); or (E) section 1 of title VI of the Act of June 15, 1917 (40 Stat. 233; 22 U.S.C. 401)[relating to the export of war materials in violation of the Neutrality Act"); see also, 18 U.S.C. 985 (civil forfeiture of real property), 986 (subpoena of bank records) which contain additional provisions applicable to "all civil forfeitures" and to "any civil forfeiture" respectively.

[35] *United States v. Ursery*, 518 U.S. 267, 289 (1996)("'In contrast to the in personam nature of criminal actions, [forfeiture] actions in rem have traditionally been viewed as civil proceedings, with jurisdiction dependent upon seizure of a physical object'")(quoting *United States v. One Assortment of 89 Firearms*, 465 U.S. 354, 363 (1984); *Calero-Toledo v. Pearson Yacht Leasing Co.*, 416 U.S. 663, 684 (1974)); see also, *Dobbin's Distillery v. United States*, 96 U.S. 395, 396 (1877); *United States v. $506,231 (Lombardo)*, 125 F.3d 442, 447-49 (7th Cir. 1997); *United States v. All Funds Distributed to Weiss*, 345 F.3d 49, 55 (2d Cir. 2003); *United States v. All Funds in Account Banco Espanol de Credito, Spain*, 295 F.3d 23, 27 n* (D.C. Cir. 2002); *United States v. Real Property Located at 475 Martin Lane*, 545 F.3d 1134, 1144 (9th Cir. 2008); but see *Contents of Account Number 03001288 (Jalal) v. United States*, 344 F.3d 399, 404-405 (3d Cir. 2003).

In fact, until the Supreme Court's decision in *Republic National Bank v. United States*, 506 U.S. 80 (1992), confirmed that initial rather than continued control was ordinarily sufficient to support jurisdiction, some believed that a court's continued jurisdiction depended upon its continued control over the res, and that its power to proceed disappeared if the property were released other than by accident, fraud or some other improper or inequitable means, *United States v. $1,322,242.58 (Road Atlanta, Inc.)*, 938 F.2d 433, 437 (3d Cir. 1991); *United States v. $84,740.00 (Potter)*, 900 F.2d 1402, 1404 (9th Cir. 1990); *United States v. Four Parcels of Real Property*, 941 F.2d 1428, 1435-436 (11th Cir. 1991); *Appellate Jurisdiction for Civil Forfeiture: The Case for the Continuation of Jurisdiction Beyond the Release of the Res*, 65 FORDHAM LAW REVIEW 679 (1991).

When the property is located overseas, three of the circuits have concluded that as long as the court has subject matter jurisdiction, in person jurisdiction over the res is only necessary after the fact, if at all, *United States v. Approximately $1.67 Million (US) in Cash, Stock, and Other Valuable Assets(Hartog)*, 513 F.3d 991, 997 (9th Cir. 2008)("'Spain's compliance and cooperation determines only the effectiveness of the forfeiture orders of the district courts, not their jurisdiction to issue those orders"), quoting *United States v. All Funds in Accounts Nos. 747.034/278 (Banco Espanol de Credito)*, 295 F.3d 23, 27 (D.C.Cir. 2002); accord, *Contents of Account Number 03001288 (Jalal) v. United States*, 344 F.3d 399, 405 (3d Cir. 2003); contra, *United States v. All Funds on Deposit in Any Accounts Maintained in the names of Meza*, 63 F.3d 148, 151-54 (2d Cir. 1995). Congress provided an alternative mechanism in 18 U.S.C. 981(k) under which permits the confiscation of funds in interbank accounts of a foreign bank held in this country when the foreign banks holds forfeitable assets on account overseas, *United States v. Union Bank for Savings & Investment (Jordan)*, 487 F.3d 8, 15-6 (1st Cir. 2007).

[36] 18 U.S.C. 981(b); *United States v. $29,828 in United States Currency (Braddy)*, 536 F.3d 1234, 1237 (11th Cir. 2008). Although the court may permit the pretrial sale of perishable property seized under the Supplemental Rules, it may refuse to do so in the interest of public safety, *United States v. Approximately 81,454 Cans of Baby Formula*, 560 F.3d 638, 641-42 (7th Cir. 2009).

[37] *United States v. James Daniel Good Real Property*, 510 U.S. 43, 48 (1993).

[38] 18 U.S.C. 985.

[39] 18 U.S.C. 983(f)("(1) A claimant under subsection (a) is entitled to immediate release of seized property if—(A) the claimant has a possessory interest in the property; (B) the claimant has sufficient ties to the community to provide assurance that the property will be available at the time of the trial; (C) the continued possession by the Government pending the final disposition of forfeiture proceedings will cause substantial hardship to the claimant, such as preventing the functioning of a business, preventing an individual from working, or leaving an individual homeless; (D) the claimant's likely hardship from the continued possession by the Government of the seized property outweighs the risk that the property will be destroyed, damaged, lost, concealed, or transferred if it is returned to the claimant during the pendency of the proceeding; and (E) none of the conditions set forth in paragraph (8) applies. . . .(8) This subsection shall not apply if the seized property—(A) is contraband, currency, or other monetary instrument, or electronic funds unless such currency or other monetary instrument or electronic funds constitutes the assets of a legitimate business which has been seized; (B) is to be used as evidence of a violation of the law; (C) by reason of design or other characteristic, is particularly suited for use in illegal activities; or (D) is likely to be used to commit additional criminal acts if returned to the claimant"); *United States v. Undetermined Amount of U.S. Currency (Warren)*, 376 F.3d 260, 263-69 (4th Cir. 2004)(petition for release seized funds in order to pay attorneys' fees without incurring undue hardship denied on the grounds the funds would likely be dissipated before the completion of forfeiture proceedings). In a similar vein perhaps conscious of the fact that the seizure of vessel may cause economic hardship greater than its market value, the customs laws authorize the release of seized property upon the posting of an amount equal to its value, 19 U.S.C. 1614.

[40] 18 U.S.C. 983(j); *United States v. Melrose East Subdivision*, 357 F.3d 493, 498-500 (5th Cir. 2004)(recognizing the government's right to seek a restraining order, but acknowledging that in such cases due process may require a post-restraint, pretrial hearing on the forfeitability of the encumbered property).

[41] Under CAFRA and the customs laws, administrative forfeiture may be used if the property to be forfeited is cash; or if the property is worth less than $500,000; or is a boat, plane or car used to carry or store drugs, 19 U.S.C. 1607; 21 U.S.C. 881(d); 18 U.S.C. 981(d). Under the tax laws, the procedure is available with respect to personal property valued at $100,000 or less, 26 U.S.C. 7325. One commentator has estimated that each year administrative forfeitures account for 80 to 85 percent of the 30,000 federal forfeitures, Rabiej, *Proposed Supplemental Rule G Governing Pretrial Procedures in Forfeiture in Rem Actions*, 51 FEDERAL LAWYER 41, 42 (Sept. 2004).

[42] 18 U.S.C. 983(a); 19 U.S.C. 1607, 1608; *Dusenbery v. United States*, 534 U.S. 161, 167 (2002); *United States v. James Daniel Good Real Property*, 510 U.S. 43, 48 (1993).

At any point after seizure, an owner or anyone else with a property interest in the res may petition for remission or mitigation. Remission is a petition for return of all of the property seized or its entire value; mitigation for return of only a portion, *see e.g.*, 28 C.F.R. pt. 9; *Malladi Drugs & Pharmaceuticals, Ltd. v. Tandy*, 552 F.3d 885, 887-88 (D.C.Cir. 2009). The authority to grant remission or mitigation is ordinarily a matter of discretion vested in the executive official whose agency is responsible for enforcement of the law under which the property was confiscated and is subject to only limited review. Courts will not review a decision to grant or withhold remission or mitigation, although they will grant relief upon a showing of refusal to consider a remission petition, *In re $67,470.00 (Averhart)*, 901 F.2d 1540, 1543-545 (11th Cir. 1990); *Yskamp v. DEA*, 163 F.3d 767, 770 (3d Cir. 1998); *Vereda, Ltda v. United States*, 271 F.3d 1367, 1371 (Fed. Cir. 2001); Congress, of course, may provide otherwise, *e.g.*, 18 U.S.C. 3668 (permitting judicial remission or mitigation for forfeitures under federal liquor laws).

[43] *United States v. One Star Class Sloop Sailboat (Flash II)*, 458 F.3d 16, 22 (1st Cir. 2006).

[44] 19 U.S.C. 1609; 26 U.S.C. 7325.

[45] "(1) Any person entitled to written notice in any nonjudicial civil forfeiture proceeding under a civil forfeiture statute who does not receive such notice may file a motion to set aside a declaration of forfeiture with respect to that person's interest in the property, which motion shall be granted if—(A) the Government knew, or reasonably should have known, of the moving party's interest and failed to take reasonable steps to provide such party with notice; and (B) the moving party did not know or have reason to know of the seizure within sufficient time to file a timely claim. (2)(A) Notwithstanding the expiration of any applicable statute of limitations, if the court grants a motion under paragraph (1), the court shall set aside the declaration of forfeiture as to the interest of the moving party without prejudice to the right of the Government to commence a subsequent forfeiture proceeding as to the interest of the moving party. (B) Any proceeding described in subparagraph (A) shall be commenced—(i) if nonjudicial, within 60 days of the entry of the order granting the motion; or (ii) if judicial, within 6 months of the entry of the order granting the motion. (3) A motion under paragraph (1) may be filed not later than 5 years after the date of final publication of notice of seizure of the

property. (4) If, at the time a motion made under paragraph (1) is granted, the forfeited property has been disposed of by the Government in accordance with law, the Government may institute proceedings against a substitute sum of money equal to the value of the moving party's interest in the property at the time the property was disposed of. (5) A motion filed under this subsection shall be the exclusive remedy for seeking to set aside a declaration of forfeiture under a civil forfeiture statute," 18 U.S.C. 983(e). Otherwise, "[o]nce an administrative forfeiture is complete, a district court may review only whether the forfeiture comported with constitutional due process guarantees," *Taylor v. United States*, 483 F.3d 385, 388 (5th Cir. 2007); *Mesa Valderrama v. United States*, 417 F.3d 1189, 1194 (11th Cir. 2005).

[46] This resolved an earlier conflict among the circuits over whether the statute of limitations barred further forfeiture proceedings in cases where an administrative forfeiture was set aside after the period of limitations had run. *United States v. Dusenbery*, 201 F.3d 763, 768 (6th Cir. 2000); *cf.,Boero v. Drug Enforcement Administration*, 111 F.3d 301, 306 (2d Cir. 1997); contra, *United States v. Marolf*, 173 F.3d 1213, 1216-217 (9th Cir. 1999); *Clymore v. United States*, 164 F.3d 569, 572-74 (10th Cir. 1999); *Kadonsky v. United States,* 216 F.3d 499, 505-6 (5th Cir. 2000); *cf.,United States v. One Toshiba Color Television (McGlory)*, 213 F.3d 147, 158-59 (3d Cir. 2000).

[47] 18 U.S.C. 983(a)(1). The timetables of 18 U.S.C. 983 apply to the noncustoms forfeiture statutes that once relied extensive upon customs procedure, *e.g.*, 18 U.S.C. 981 (money laundering) and 21 U.S.C. 881 (controlled substances), they do not apply to forfeitures arising under the customs laws, 18 U.S.C. 983(i).

[48] 18 U.S.C. 983(a)(2)(the deadline is set in the notice but must give the claimant at least 35 days from the mailing of personal notice; 30 days from the final publication notice, if personal notice is not received).

[49] 18 U.S.C. 983(a)(3).

[50] *United States v. Robinson*, 434 F.3d 357, 364 (5th Cir. 2005); *see discussion infra*, at footnote 191 and accompanying text; *Delay Between Seizure of Personal Property by Federal Government and Institution of Proceedings for Forfeiture Thereof as Violative of Fifth Amendment Due Process Requirements*, 69 ALR Fed. 373.

[51] 18 U.S.C. 983(a)(3); 19 U.S.C. 1608.

[52] 18 U.S.C. 983(a)(4)(A); 20 days in customs cases, F.R.Civ.P.Supp.Rule C(6).

[53] 18 U.S.C. 983(a)(4)(B); F.R.Civ.P.Supp. Rule C(6).

[54] *United States v. Clark*, 84 F.3d 378, 380 (10th Cir. 1996)("Due process thus requires 'notice reasonably calculated, under all the circumstances to apprise interested parties of the pendency of the act and afford them an opportunity to present their objects'")(quoting *Mennonite Bd. of Missions v. Adams*, 462 U.S. 791, 800 (1983)); *Armendariz-Mata v. U.S. Dept. of Justice*, 82 F.3d 679, 683 (5th Cir. 1996); *United States v. Marolf*, 173 F.3d 1213, 1216 (9th Cir. 1999); *Clymore v. United States*, 164 F.3d 569, 572-74 (10th Cir. 1999); *Ikelionwu v. United States*, 150 F.3d 233, 238-39 (2d Cir. 1998).

[55] *E.g., United States v. DEA*, 92 F.3d 648, 654 (8th Cir. 1996)("Should the citizen prove inept, the government may keep the property, without having to explain its actions"); *United States v. Lot 65 Pine Meadow*, 976 F.2d 1155, 1156-157 (8th Cir. 1992)(upholding a decree of forfeiture by default for filing a verified claim and answer on August 26, 1991 instead of on August 13 when the claim should have been filed and on August 20 when the answer was due); *Sarit v. U.S. Drug Enforcement Administration*, 987 F.2d 10, 15-7 (1st Cir. 1993); *United States v. Commodity Account No. 549 54930 (Lindstrom)*, 219 F.3d 595, 597-98 (7th Cir. 2000); cf., *Malladi Drugs & Pharmaceuticals, Ltd. v. Tandy*, 552 F.3d 885, 887-88 (D.C.Cir. 2009)("If no interested party files a claim, then the DEA adminsitratively forfeits the property by default and the only option remaining for an interested party is to file a petition for remission or mitigation of the forfeiture with the DEA").

[56] 18 U.S.C. 983(c); *United States v. 5208 Los Franciscos Way*, 385 F.3d 1187, 1191 (9th Cir. 2004); *United States v. 6 Fox Street*, 480 F.3d 38, 42 (1st Cir. 2007); *United States v. 3234 Washington Avenue North*, 480 F.3d 841, 843 (8th Cir. 2007); *von Hofe v. United States*, 492 F.3d 175, 179 (2d Cir. 2007); *United States v. $92,203 in United States Currency (Garcia-Baeza),* 537 F.3d 504, 507 (5th Cir. 2008); *United States v. $125,938.62 (Cardenal)*, 537 F.3d 1287, 1288-289 (11th Cir. 2008); *Malladi Drugs & Pharmaceuticals, Ltd. v. Tandy*, 552 F.3d 885, 887 (D.C.Cir. 2009). The government may not rely on hearsay evidence to meet its burden under section 983(c), *United States v. $92,203 in United States Currency (Garcia-Baeza)*, 537 F.3d 504, 510 (5th Cir. 2008).

[57] 19 U.S.C. 1615; *United States v. 3234 Washington Avenue North*,480 F.3d 841, 843 (8th Cir. 2007); *United States v. One Harrington and Richardson Rifle, Model M-14, 7.62 Caliber*, 378 F.3d 533, 534 (6th Cir. 2004); *United States v. Collado*, 348 F.3d 323, 326-327 (2d Cir. 2003); *United States v. One "Piper" Aztec "F" DeLuxe Model 250 PA 23 Aircraft*, 321 F.3d 355, 359-60 (3d Cir. 2003); *Kadonsky v. United States*, 216 F.3d 499, 503 (5th Cir. 2000); *United States v. United States Currency Deposited for Active Trade Co.*, 176 F.3d 941, 944 (7th Cir. 1999); *United States v. 22249 Dolorosa St.*, 167 F.3d 509, 513 (9th Cir. 1999); *United States v. $141,770 (Moreno-Pena)*, 157 F.3d 600, 603 (8th Cir. 1998).

"The standard for probable cause in forfeiture proceedings resembles that required to support a search warrant. The determination of probable cause is based upon a totality of the circumstances test, and the government's evidence must be more than that which gives rise to a mere suspicion, although it need not rise to the level of prima facie proof," *United States v. One 1978 Piper Cherokee Aircraft*, 91 F.3d 1204, 1207 (9th Cir. 1996); *United States v. $39,873 (Armfield)*, 80 F.3d 317, 318 (8th Cir. 1996); *United States v. United States Currency Deposited for Active Trade Co.*, 176 F.3d 941, 944 (7th Cir. 1999); *United States v. $9,041,598.68 (Massieu)*, 163 F.3d 238, 246 (5th Cir. 1999); *United States v. $141,770 (Moreno-Pena)*, 157 F.3d 600, 603 (8th Cir. 1998).

CAFRA does not apply retroactively; proceedings initiated prior to August 23, 2000 are governed by earlier law, *United States v. $100,348 (Mayzel)*, 354 F.3d 1110, 1116 (9th Cir. 2004); *United States v. Collado*, 348 F.3d 323, 326 (2d Cir. 2003); *United States v. One "Piper" Aztec "F" DeLuxe Model 250 PA 23 Aircraft*, 321 F.3d 355, 357-58 (3d Cir. 2003); *United States v. $174,206 (Ricard)*, 320 F.3d 658, 661-62 (6th Cir. 2003); *United States v. Wagoner County Real Estate*, 278 F.3d 1091, 1097 n.5 (10th Cir. 2002).

[58] The claimant must demonstrate some legal or equitable interest in the res, *United States v. Various Computers*, 82 F.3d 582, 585 (3d Cir. 1996); *United States v. $9,041,598.68 (Massieu)*, 163 F.3d 238, 245 (5th Cir. 1999); *United States v. One Parcel of Property Located at RR2*, 959 F.2d 101, 103-104 (8th Cir. 1992); *United States v. 5208 Los Franciscos Way*, 385 F.3d 1187, 1191 (9th Cir. 2004); *Via Mat International South America Ltd. v. United States*, 446 F.3d 1258, 1262 (11th Cir. 2006). Several courts have held that possession or mere legal title may be insufficient to establish standing if the claimant is only a nominal or straw owner who does not have dominion and control over the property, *United States v. Bridwell's Grocery*, 195 F.3d 819, 821-22 (6th Cir. 1999); *United States v. Ford 250 Pickup*, 980 F.2d 1242, 1246 (9th Cir. 1992); *United States v. Cambio Exacto, S.A.*, 166 F.3d 522, 526-27 (2d Cir. 1999). Standing is a threshold requirement for any claim, but at least one court has suggested that such a view constitutes a merger of the less demanding entry requirements with the subsequent more stringent requirements for recovery as an "innocent owner," *United States v. One Lincoln Navigator*, 328 F.3d 1011, 1013-1014 (8th Cir. 2003); *cf.*, *United States v. $557,933.89 More or Less (Mercado-Filpo)*, 287 F.3d 66, 77-79 (2d Cir. 2002) (explaining the absence of conflict between the lower court's finding of standing and the jury's conclusion that the claimant had no ownership interest in the res); *United States v. Real Property Located at 475 Martin Lane*, 545 F.3d 1134, 1140 (9th Cir. 2008)("To demonstrate Article III standing in a civil forfeiture action, a claimant must have a sufficient interest in the property create a case or controversy. This burden s is not a heavy one, *at least at the initial stages* of a forfeiture suit")(emphasis added); *United States v. $148,840 in United States Currency (Austin)*, 521 F.3d 1268, 1273-275 (10th Cir. 2008)("At the pleading stage, a claimant satisfies this burden by alleging a sufficient interest in the seized property, such as an ownership interest, some type of lawful possessory interest, or a security interest. In contrast, at the summary judgment stage, a claimant must prove by a preponderance of the evidence that he has a facially colorable interest in the res such that he would be injured if the property were forfeited to the United States. . . As our sister circuits have recognized in other forfeiture cases, there is an important difference, for standing purposes, between one who claims to be the owner of property and one who claims to be a mere possessor of it. . . . In cases in which a person has asserted an ownership interest, our sister courts have not required the claimant to present the type of explanatory evidence urged by the government to establish his or her standing").

[59] *United States v. Approximately $1.67 Million (US) in Cash, Stock, and Other Valuable Assets (Hartog)*, 513 F.3d 991, 1000 (9th Cir. 2008); *United States v. 5208 Los Franciscos Way*, 385 F.3d 1187, 1193 (9th Cir. 2004); *United States v. Funds Held in the Name or for the Benefit of Wetterer*, 210 F.3d 96, 104 (2d Cir. 2000); *United States v. United States Currency Deposited for Active Trade Co.*, 176 F.3d 941, 945 (7th Cir. 1999); *United States v. $39,873 (Armfield)*, 80 F.3d 317, 318 (8th Cir. 1996).

[60] *United States v. $39,873*, 80 F.3d 317, 318 (8th Cir. 1996); *United States v. All Assets of G.P.S. Automotive Corp.*, 66 F.3d 483, 487 (2d Cir. 1996); *United States v. 22249 Dolorosa St.*, 167 F.3d 509, 511 (9th Cir. 1999).

[61] 18 U.S.C. 983(c)(3); *United States v. 3234 Washington Avenue North*, 480 F.3d 841, 843 (8th Cir. 2007); *United States v. 6 Fox Street*, 480 F.3d 38, 42 (1st Cir. 2007).

[62] *Austin v. United States*, 509 U.S. 602, 617 (1993). The Supreme Court has observed that due process only precludes forfeiture either (1) where the property has "been taken from [its owner] without his privity or consent" and used in a manner which would ordinarily give rise to confiscation, or (2) where the owner was "not only. . . uninvolved in and unaware of the wrongful activity, but also that he had done all that reasonably could be expected to prevent the proscribed use of the property," *Calero-Toledo v. Pearson Yacht Leasing Co.*, 416 U.S. 663, 689(1974). Although some argue that the splintered nature of the majority in *Bennis v. Michigan*, 516 U.S. 442 (1996), erodes the support for this view, it remains the law until modified or rejected by the Court.

[63] Outside of CAFRA, statutory "innocent owner" defenses in civil forfeiture, more generous than due process requires, are relatively rare.

[64] 18 U.S.C. 983(d).

[65] 18 U.S.C. 983(d)(2)(A); *United States v. $493,850 in U.S. Currency (Bruno)*, 518 F.3d 1159, 1170 (9th Cir. 2008); *von Hofe v. United States*, 492 F.3d 175, 180 (2d Cir. 2007); *United States v. 45 Claremont St.*, 395 F.3d 1, 4-5 (1st Cir. 2004); *United States v. One Lincoln Navigator*, 328 F.3d 1011, 1014 (8th Cir. 2003); *United States v. 16328 South 43rd East Avenue*, 275 F.3d 1281, 1284 n.1 (10th Cir. 2002).

[66] 18 U.S.C. 983(d)(3)(A). The defense may also be available to claimants who acquire an interest in their primary residence through inheritance or divorce rather than by purchase, 18 U.S.C. 983(d)(3)(B); *United States v. 221 Dana Avenue*, 261 F.3d 65, 74 (1st Cir. 2001); *United States v. $125,938.62 (Cardenal)*, 537 F.3d 1287, 1293 n.3 (11th Cir. 2008).

[67] 28 U.S.C. 2465 (text *infra*, footnote 70); *Republic National Bank v. United States*, 506 U.S. 80, 95 (1992); *United States v. Seifuddin*, 820 F.2d 1074, 1078-79 (9th Cir. 1987); *cf., Lee v. City of Chicago*, 330 F.3d 456, 466 (7th Cir. 2003)("the government should not, by virtue of its authority to seize, effect *de facto* forfeitures of property by retaining items indefinitely. But we know that due process guarantees would prevent this. . ."); but see, *Synagogue v. United States*, 482 F.3d 1058, 1064 (9th Cir. 2007)(a property owner is not entitled interest, attorney fees or costs when the government seizes his property but later returns it without initiating forfeiture proceedings).

A property owner may petition the court for return of his property under Rule 41(g) of the Federal Rules of Criminal Procedure, *Jackson v. United States*, 526 F.3d 394, 396-97 (8th Cir. 2008). An owner, however, is not entitled to the return of property that cannot be lawfully possessed, *Boggs v. Rubin*, 161 F.3d 37, 40 (D.C. Cir. 1998); *United States v. Felici*, 208 F.3d 667, 670 (8th Cir. 2000); *United States v. Vanhorn*, 296 F.3d 713, 719 (8th Cir. 2002).

[68] 28 U.S.C. 2680(c)("The provisions of this chapter and section 1346(b) of this title [relating to federal tort claims] shall not apply to . . . (c) Any claim arising in respect of the assessment or collection of any tax or customs duty, or the detention of any goods, merchandise, or other property by any officer of customs or excise or any other law enforcement officer, except that the provisions of this chapter and section 1346(b) of this title apply to any claim based on injury or loss of goods, merchandise, or other property, while in the possession of any officer of customs or excise or any other law enforcement officer, if—(1) the property was seized for the purpose of forfeiture under any provision of Federal law providing for the forfeiture of property other than as a sentence imposed upon conviction of a criminal offense; (2) the interest of the claimant was not forfeited; (3) the interest of the claimant was not remitted or mitigated (if the property was subject to forfeiture); and (4) the claimant was not convicted of a crime for which the interest of the claimant in the property was subject to forfeiture under a Federal criminal forfeiture law").

[69] Attorneys' fees are available for civil forfeiture costs but not for related criminal proceedings, even though the result may permit the government to first press weak criminal charges and thus ensure that the lion's share of the cost of related civil forfeiture attorneys' services are beyond recovery, *United States v. Certain Real Property, Located at 317 Nick Fitchard Rd, N.W.*, 579 F.3d 1315, 1318-319 (11th Cir. 2009)("The district court added that 'if [it] were to find that fees incurred defending the criminal case were not recoverable under CAFRA, then the government would be allowed to avoid CAFRA, as it has tried to in this case, by moving for a stay in the civil case and prosecuting the criminal case'"), quoting 566 F.Supp.2d 1252, 1261 (N.D.Ala. 2008). Moreover, an award of attorneys' fees may be adjusted to reflect the prevailing party's level of success as well as the reasonableness of the level of litigation effort, although not for failure to overcome lack of notice, *United States v. One Star Class Sloop Sailboat Named Flash II*, 546 F.3d 26, 38-43 (1st Cir. 2008).

[70] "(a) Upon the entry of a judgment for the claimant in any proceeding to condemn or forfeit property seized or arrested under any provision of Federal law—(1) such property shall be returned forthwith to the claimant or his agent; and (2) if it appears that there was reasonable cause for the seizure or arrest, the court shall cause a proper certificate thereof to be entered and, in such case, neither the person who made the seizure or arrest nor the prosecutor shall be liable to suit or judgment on account of such suit or prosecution, nor shall the claimant be entitled to costs, except as provided in subsection (b).

"(b)(1) Except as provided in paragraph (2), in any civil proceeding to forfeit property under any provision of Federal law in which the claimant substantially prevails, the United States shall be liable for—(A) reasonable attorney fees and other litigation costs reasonably incurred by the claimant; (B) post-judgment interest, as set forth in section 1961 of this title; and (C) in cases involving currency, other negotiable instruments, or the proceeds of an interlocutory sale—(i) interest actually paid to the United States from the date of seizure or arrest of the property that resulted from the investment of the property in an interest-bearing account or instrument; and (ii) an imputed amount of interest that such currency, instruments, or proceeds would have earned at the rate applicable to the 30-day Treasury Bill, for any period during which no interest was paid (not including any period when the property reasonably was in use as evidence in an official proceeding or in conducting scientific tests for the purpose of collecting evidence), commencing 15 days after the property was seized by a Federal law enforcement agency, or was turned over to a Federal law enforcement agency by a State or local law enforcement agency. (2)(A) The United States shall not be required to disgorge the value of any intangible benefits nor make any other payments to the claimant not specifically authorized by this subsection. (B) The provisions of paragraph (1) shall not apply if the claimant is convicted of a crime for which the interest of the claimant in the property was subject to forfeiture under a Federal criminal forfeiture law. (C) If there are multiple claims to the same property, the United States shall not be liable for costs and attorneys fees associated with any such claim if the United States—(i) promptly recognizes such claim; (ii) promptly returns the interest of the claimant in the property to the claimant, if the property can be divided without difficulty and there are no competing claims to that portion of the property; (iii) does not cause the claimant to incur additional, reasonable costs or fees; and (iv) prevails in obtaining forfeiture with respect to one or more of the other claims. (D) If the court enters judgment in part for the claimant and in part for the Government, the court shall reduce the award of costs and attorney fees accordingly," 28 U.S.C. 2465.

[71] 18 U.S.C. 981(d), 881(d), 853(h)-(j).

[72] "(1) The Secretary of the Treasury may apply property forfeited under this chapter in accordance with subparagraph (A) or (B), or both: (A) Retain any of the property for official use. (B) Transfer any of the property to—(i) any other Federal agency; (ii) any State or local law enforcement agency that participated directly or indirectly in the seizure or forfeiture of the property; or (iii) the Civil Air Patrol.

"(2) The Secretary may transfer any forfeited personal property or the proceeds of the sale of any forfeited personal or real property to any foreign country which participated directly or indirectly in the seizure or forfeiture of the property, if such a transfer—A) has been agreed to by the Secretary of State; (B) is authorized in an international agreement between the United States and the foreign country; and (C) is made to a country which, if applicable, has been certified under section 2291j(b) of Title 22.

"(3) Aircraft may be transferred to the Civil Air Patrol under paragraph (1)(B)(iii) in support of air search and rescue and other emergency services and, pursuant to a memorandum of understanding entered into with a Federal agency, illegal drug traffic surveillance. Jet-powered aircraft may not be transferred to the Civil Air Patrol under the authority of paragraph (1)(B)(iii)," 19 U.S.C. 1616a(c). The Attorney General enjoys similar authority under 21 U.S.C. 881(e) and 18 U.S.C. 981(e), (*i*).

[73] "The Attorney General shall assure that any property transferred to a State or local law enforcement agency under [21 U.S.C. 881(e)(1)(A)]—(A) has a value that bears a reasonable relationship to the degree of direct participation of the State or local agency in the law enforcement effort resulting in the forfeiture, taking into account the total value of all property forfeited and the total law enforcement effort with respect to the violation of law on which the forfeiture is based; and (B) will serve to encourage further cooperation between the recipient State or local agency and Federal law enforcement agencies," 21 U.S.C. 881(e)(3); see also, 31 U.S.C. 9703(b)(4).

[74] *In re U.S. Currency, $844,520 (Cole)*, 136 F.3d 581, 582 (8th Cir. 1998)(Loken, J., concurring) ("But the underlying facts of this case should prompt Congress and the Department of Justice to investigate whether federal law enforcement officials are using their extensive forfeiture powers to frustrate the fiscal policy of States such as Missouri"); *United States v. Winston-Salem/Forsyth County Bd. of Education*, 902 F.2d 267, 267(4th Cir. 1990))("Practice of local officials of allowing federal officials to adopt seizures made by the local law enforcement official and to federally forfeit the property, with a portion returned to the local law enforcement agency, does not violate federal law, even though the practice assertedly allows state officials to avoid following [a] state constitutional provision that all forfeited monies be used to maintain the public schools").

[75] Executive Office for Asset Forfeiture, United States Department of the Treasury, *Guide to Equitable Sharing for Foreign Countries and Federal, State, and Local Law Enforcement Agencies*, 16, 22 (April 2009), http://www.treas.gov/offices/enforcement/teoaf/guidelines/greenbook.pdf; United States Department of Justice, *United States Attorneys' Manual*, §9-118.510, *http://www.usdoj.gov/usao/eousa/foia_reading_room/usam/title9/title9.htm*. Recipients may, however, use assets acquired through an equitable sharing program for matching purposes with respect to any COPS (Community Policing) grants they receive, 42 U.S.C. 3796dd-3(b)(1). The Department of Justice expected to shared $412 million with state, local and foreign law enforcement agencies in fiscal year 2009, U.S. Department of Justice, *Asset Forfeiture Fund: FY 2009 Performance Budget*, at 16 (2008), http://www.usdoj.gov/jmd/2009justifications/pdf/fy09-aff.pdf; the Treasury Department made equitable sharing payments of $130 million in fiscal year 2008, *United States Department of the Treasury, Treasury Forfeiture Fund: Accountability Report: Fiscal Year 2008*, 29 (2008), http://www.treas.gov/officers/enforcement/teoaf/ publications/TFF-Final%20-Accountability_Report_2008.pdf.

[76] The number of criminal forfeiture judgments has surpassed the number of civil forfeiture judgments every year since fiscal 1995, U.S. Department of Justice, Executive Office for United States Attorneys, *United States Attorneys' Annual Statistical Report: Fiscal Year 2005 & 2008*, AF Chart 1, *http://www.usdoj.gov* /usao/reading_room/foiamanuals.html.

[77] 18 U.S.C. 982(a)(1)("The court, in imposing sentence on a person convicted of an offense in violation of section . . . 1960 of this title, shall order that the person forfeit to the United States any property, real or personal, involved in such offense, or any property traceable to such property").

[78] 18 U.S.C. 982(a)(2) ("The court, in imposing sentence on a person convicted of a violation of, or a conspiracy to violate . . . (B) section 471, 472, 473, 474, 476, 477, 478, 479, 480, 481, 485, 486, 487, 488, 501, 502, 510, 542, 545, 842, 844. . . of this title, shall order that the person forfeit to the United States any property constituting, or derived from, proceeds the person obtained directly or indirectly, as the result of such violation").

[79] 18 U.S.C. 982(a)(2)("The court, in imposing sentence on a person convicted of a violation of, or a conspiracy to violate . . . (B) section . . . 1028 . . . of this title, shall order that the person forfeit to the United States any

property constituting, or derived from, proceeds the person obtained directly or indirectly, as the result of such violation").

80 18 U.S.C. 982(a)(2)("The court, in imposing sentence on a person convicted of a violation of, or a conspiracy to violate . . . (B) section . . . 1029 . . . of this title, shall order that the person forfeit to the United States any property constituting, or derived from, proceeds the person obtained directly or indirectly, as the result of such violation").

81 18 U.S.C. 982(a)(2)("The court, in imposing sentence on a person convicted of a violation of, or a conspiracy to violate . . . (B) section . . . 1030 of this title, shall order that the person forfeit to the United States any property constituting, or derived from, proceeds the person obtained directly or indirectly, as the result of such violation").

82 18 U.S.C. 982(a)(5)("The court, in imposing sentence on a person convicted of a violation or conspiracy to violate—(A) section 511 (altering or removing motor vehicle identification numbers); (B) section 553 (importing or exporting stolen motor vehicles); (C) section 2119 (armed robbery of automobiles); (D) section 2312 (transporting stolen motor vehicles in interstate commerce); or (E) section 2313 (possessing or selling a stolen motor vehicle that has moved in interstate commerce); shall order that the person forfeit to the United States any property, real or personal, which represents or is traceable to the gross proceeds obtained, directly or indirectly, as a result of such violation").

83 18 U.S.C. 982(a)(7)("The court, in imposing sentence on a person convicted of a Federal health care offense, shall order the person to forfeit property, real or personal, that constitutes or is derived, directly or indirectly, from gross proceeds traceable to the commission of the offense").

84 18 U.S.C. 982(a)(8)("The court, in sentencing a defendant convicted of an offense under section 1028, 1029, 1341, 1342, 1343, or 1344, or of a conspiracy to commit such an offense, if the offense involves telemarketing (as that term is defined in section 2325), shall order that the defendant forfeit to the United States any real or personal property—(A) used or intended to be used to commit, to facilitate, or to promote the commission of such offense; and (B) constituting, derived from, or traceable to the gross proceeds that the defendant obtained directly or indirectly as a result of the offense").

85 18 U.S.C. 982(a)(2), (3), (4)("(2) The court, in imposing sentence on a person convicted of a violation of, or a conspiracy to violate—(A) section 215, 656, 657, 1005, 1006, 1007, 1014, 1341, 1343, or 1344 of this title, affecting a financial institution, . . .shall order that the person forfeit to the United States any property constituting, or derived from, proceeds the person obtained directly or indirectly, as the result of such violation.

"(3) The court, in imposing a sentence on a person convicted of an offense under—(A) section 666(a)(1) (relating to Federal program fraud); (B) section 1001 (relating to fraud and false statements); (C) section 1031 (relating to major fraud against the United States); (D) section 1032 (relating to concealment of assets from conservator, receiver, or liquidating agent of insured financial institution); (E) section 1341 (relating to mail fraud); or (F) section 1343 (relating to wire fraud), involving the sale of assets acquired or held by the Resolution Trust Corporation, the Federal Deposit Insurance Corporation, as conservator or receiver for a financial institution or any other conservator for a financial institution appointed by the Office of the Comptroller of the Currency or the Office of Thrift Supervision, or the National Credit Union Administration, as conservator or liquidating agent for a financial institution, shall order that the person forfeit to the United States any property, real or personal, which represents or is traceable to the gross receipts obtained, directly or indirectly, as a result of such violation.

"(4) With respect to an offense listed in subsection (a)(3) committed for the purpose of executing or attempting to execute any scheme or artifice to defraud, or for obtaining money or property by means of false or fraudulent statements, pretenses, representations, or promises, the gross receipts of such an offense shall include any property, real or personal, tangible or intangible, which is obtained, directly or indirectly, as a result of such offense").

86 18 U.S.C. 982(a)(6)("The court, in imposing sentence on a person convicted of a violation of, or conspiracy to violate, section 274(a), 274A(a)(1), or 274A(a)(2) of the Immigration and Nationality Act or section 554, 1425, 1426, 1427, 1541, 1542, 1543, 1544, or 1546 of this title, or a violation of, or conspiracy to violate, section 1028 of this title if committed in connection with passport or visa issuance or use, shall order that the person forfeit to the United States, regardless of any provision of State law—(i) any conveyance, including any vessel, vehicle, or aircraft used in the commission of the offense of which the person is convicted; and (ii) any property real or personal—(I) that constitutes, or is derived from or is traceable to the proceeds obtained directly or indirectly from the commission of the offense of which the person is convicted; or (II) that is used to facilitate, or is intended to be used to facilitate, the commission of the offense of which the person is convicted. (B) The court, in imposing sentence on a person described in subparagraph (A), shall order that the person forfeit to the United States all property described in that subparagraph").

87 "If a person is charged in a criminal case with a violation of an Act of Congress for which the civil or criminal forfeiture of property is authorized, the Government may include notice of the forfeiture in the indictment or information pursuant to the Federal Rules of Criminal Procedure. If the defendant is convicted of the offense giving rise to the forfeiture, the court shall order the forfeiture of the property as part of the sentence in the

criminal case pursuant to the Federal Rules of Criminal Procedure and section 3554 of title 18, United States Code. The procedures in section 413 of the Controlled Substances Act (21 U.S.C. 853) apply to all stages of a criminal forfeiture proceeding, except that subsection (d) of such section applies only in cases in which the defendant is convicted of a violation of such Act," 28 U.S.C. 2461(c).

Originally, the bridge statute only applied if "no specific statutory provision is made for criminal forfeiture," 28 U.S.C. 2461(c)(2000 ed.). Some questioned whether the bridge statute might be used in general mail and wire fraud cases. True, tainted property was subject to civil forfeiture in mail and wire fraud cases as a general rule, but it was also subject to criminal forfeiture as long as the fraud was committed against a financial institution, 18 U.S.C. 982(a)(2) (A)(2000 ed.). Nevertheless, federal appellate courts read section 2461 to permit criminal forfeiture in mail and wire fraud cases in which a financial institution was not the victim, *United States v. Day*, 524 F.3d 1361, 1374-377 (D.C.Cir. 2008); *United States v. Schlesinger*, 514 F.3d 277, 278 (2d Cir. 2008); *United States v. Foley*, 508 F.3d 627, 635 (11th Cir. 2007). Congress changed the language to its present form to eliminate any uncertainty.

[88] *E.g.*, 18 U.S.C. 982 (money laundering); 18 U.S.C. 1963 (RICO); 21 U.S.C. 853 (drug dealing).

[89] The federal Racketeer Influenced and Corrupt Organization (RICO) forfeiture statute, for example, is designed not only to sever the offender from the organization he or she has corrupted but to confiscate any property right which affords a source of influence over the enterprise, 18 U.S.C. 1963(a)(2)(D).

[90] 21 U.S.C. 853(n)(6); *United States v. Fleet*, 498 F.3d 1225, 1232 (11th Cir. 2007); *United States v. Vampire Nation*, 451 F.3d 189, 202 (3d Cir. 2006)("criminal forfeiture is a sanction against the individual defendant rather than against the property itself"); *United States v. Saccoccia*, 354 F.3d 9, 15 (1st Cir. 2003)("[T]he government may reach only the defendant's substitute assets and not those of a third party").

[91] *United States v. Juluke*, 426 F.3d 323, 327-28 (5th Cir. 2005). When a defendant is convicted of racketeering under RICO, 18 U.S.C. 1961-1963, he need not have personally committed each of the enterprise's predicate offenses and consequently his property derived from those offenses is subject to criminal forfeiture under RICO, *United States v. Hively*, 437 F.3d 752, 765 (11th Cir. 2006).

[92] "(2) In any case described in any of subparagraphs (A) through (E) of paragraph (1) [below], the court shall order the forfeiture of any other property of the defendant, up to the value of any property described in subparagraphs (A) through (E) of paragraph (1), as applicable. "(1) Paragraph (2) of this subsection shall apply, if any property described in subsection (a), as a result of any act or omission of the defendant—(A) cannot be located upon the exercise of due diligence; (B) has been transferred or sold to, or deposited with, a third party; (C) has been placed beyond the jurisdiction of the court; (D) has been substantially diminished in value; or (E) has been commingled with other property which cannot be divided without difficulty," 21 U.S.C. 853(p)(2),(1); see also, 18 U.S.C. 1963(m).

[93] F.R.Crim.P. 7(c), 32.2(a).

[94] F.R.Crim.P. 32.2(b)(4).

[95] Rule 32.2 permits the Attorney General to seize the property upon the court's entry of a preliminary forfeiture order, F.R.Crim.P. 32.2(b)(3).

[96] *E.g.*, 21 U.S.C. 853(e)(1), (2). A defendant may have a due process right to a pre-trial, post-restraint hearing as to whether the government has probable cause to believe that the restrained property is subject to confiscation, if the property is the only means available to the defendant with which to retain private counsel or provide for the defendant and his or her family, *United States v. Jones*, 160 F.3d 641, 647-48 (10th Cir. 1998); *United States v. E-Gold, Ltd.*, 521 F.3d 411, 415-21 (D.C.Cir. 2008)(citing cases in accord from other circuits); *United States v. Kaley*, 579 F.3d 1246, 1259 (11th Cir. 2009). At least one circuit has held that pretrial restraining orders may not be had when government opts for a criminal forfeiture by merging a civil forfeiture authorization with a criminal prosecution under the auspices of 28 U.S.C. 2461(c), *United States v. Razmilovic*, 419 F.3d 134, 137-41 (2d Cir. 2005).

[97] Substitute assets may become subject to forfeiture if the tainted property has become unavailable, but most courts have refused to permit pre-trial restraint orders on substitute assets, *United States v. Parrett*, 530 F.3d 422, 429 (6th Cir. 2008); *United States v. Patelidis*, 335 F.3d 226, 234 (3d Cir. 2003); *United States v. Gotti*, 155 F.3d 144, 147-49 (2d Cir. 1998); *United States v. Riley*, 78 F.3d 367, 371 (8th Cir. 1996); *In re Assets of Martin*, 1 F.3d 1351, 1359 (3d Cir. 1993); *United States v. Floyd*, 992 F.2d 498, 502 (5th Cir. 1993); *cf., United States v. Farmer*, 274 F.3d 800, 802 (4th Cir. 2001)(emphasis added)("Furthermore, in *Caplin's* companion case, the Court held that the pre-trial restraint of a criminal defendant's assets does not violate the constitution *as long as the assets are restrained based upon a finding of probable cause that they are subject to forfeiture. United States v. Monsanto*, 491 U.S. 600, 615-16 (1989)"). In some instances, the government may reach the same end by recording a notice of *lis pendens* under applicable state law, thereby providing public notice that the property is the subject of pending forfeiture litigation and precluding disposal to a good faith purchaser in the interim, *United States v. Parrett*, 530 F.3d at 431-32; *United States v. Grossman*, 501 F.3d 846, 849-51(7th Cir. 2007).

[98] 28 U.S.C. 2461.

[99] 28 U.S.C. 2461(c)(2000 ed.)("If a forfeiture of property is authorized in connection with a violation of an Act of Congress, and any person is charged in an indictment or information with such violation but no specific

statutory provision is made for criminal forfeiture upon conviction, the Government may include the forfeiture in the indictment or information in accordance with the Federal Rules of Criminal Procedure, and upon conviction, the court shall order the forfeiture of the property in accordance with the procedures set forth in section 413 of the Controlled Substances Act (21 U.S.C. 853), other than subsection (d) of that section").

[100] *United States v. Razmilovic*, 419 F.3d 134, 137-41 (2d Cir. 2005).

[101] *Id.* at 139, quoting 18 U.S.C. 982(b)(emphasis of the Court).

[102] *Id.* at 139, quoting 28 U.S.C. 2461(c)(2000 ed.)(emphasis added).

[103] H.Rept. 109-333 at 56. The new language which appears in the Act under the caption "uniform procedures for criminal forfeiture," is not mentioned in the report's Joint Explanatory Statement of the Committee of Conference where the Act's other sections are briefly described.

[104] "If a person is charged in a criminal case with a violation of an Act of Congress for which the civil or criminal forfeiture of property is authorized, the Government may include notice of the forfeiture in the indictment or information pursuant to the Federal Rules of Criminal Procedure. If the defendant is convicted of the offense giving rise to the forfeiture, the court shall order the forfeiture of the property as part of the sentence in the criminal case pursuant to the Federal Rules of Criminal Procedure and section 3554 of title 18, United States Code. The procedures in section 413 of the Controlled Substances Act (21 U.S.C. 853) apply to all stages of a criminal forfeiture proceeding, except that subsection (d) of such section [(rebuttable presumption of forfeitability)]]applies only in cases in which the defendant is convicted of a violation of such Act," 18 U.S.C. 2461(c)).

[105] But it may do more. The Deputy Chief of the Justice Department's asset forfeiture section has written that the new language also overturns *Razmilovic*, and authorizes the issuance of pretrial restraining orders in section 2461(c) cases, Cassella, *Criminal Forfeiture Procedure in 2006: A Survey of Developments in the case Law*, 42 CRIMINAL LAW BULLETIN 515, 523 (2006). The difficulty is that the new language is not that of section 982 which the Second Circuit indicated would authorize such pretrial restraining orders. Quite the contrary, the new language appears to follow the same linguistic path that the Court found led to the opposite result in the earlier version: application of the Federal Rules before conviction, confiscation order of the court upon conviction, and application of section 853 thereafter. On the other hand, the new language does end with the statement that section 853 is to apply "to all stages of a criminal forfeiture proceeding." Some might argue that if Congress intended to overturn the result in *Razmilovic* with its amendment, it selected a particularly cryptic way of doing so.

[106] Perhaps the best known of these are found in the RICO and the drug trafficking criminal forfeiture provisions, ". . . . [a]ny such property that is subsequently transferred to a person other than the defendant may be the subject of a special verdict of forfeiture and thereafter shall be ordered forfeited to the United States, unless the transferee establishes in a hearing pursuant to subsection (*l*) that he is a bona fide purchaser for value of such property who at the time of purchase was reasonably without cause to believe that the property was subject to forfeiture under this section." 18 U.S.C. 1963(c); 21 U.S.C. 853(c).

[107] F.R.Crim.P. 32.2(b)(1).

[108] Id.

[109] F.R.Crim.P. 32.2(b)(4)

[110] F.R.Crim.P. 32.2(b)(1).

[111] F.R.Crim.P. 32.2(b)(2); *United States v. Lazarenko*, 476 F.3d 642, 648 (9th Cir. 2007).

[112] 21 U.S.C. 853(n)(1).

[113] F.R.Crim.P. 32.2(c)

[114] 21 U.S.C. 853(n)(2). The petition must be filed within 30 days or the claimant's interest is lost, 21 U.S.C. 853(n)(7); *United States v. Marion*, 562 F.3d 1330, 1341 (11th Cir. 2009); *United States v. Grossman*, 501 F.3d 846, 848-49 (7th Cir. 2007).

[115] 18 U.S.C. 982(b)(1); 21 U.S.C. 853(n)(6); 18 U.S.C. 1963(*l*)(6); *United States v.* Cox, 575 F.3d 352, 355 (4th Cir. 2009); *United States v. Huntington National Bank*, 574 F.3d 329, 331 (6th Cir. 2009); *United States v. Soreide*, 461 F.3d 1351, 1354-355 (11th Cir. 2006). Under 21 U.S.C. 853(k) third parties are barred from intervening in earlier or other separate proceedings to contest the forfeiture of property in which they have an interest, *United States v. Cox*, 575 F.3d at 358; *United States v. Porchay*, 533 F.3d 704, 710 (8th Cir. 2008); *DSI Associates LLC v. United States*, 496 F.3d 175, 183 (2d Cir. 2007); *United States v. Lazarenko*, 476 F.3d at 648.

[116] *United States v. Cox*, 575 F.3d at 356; *DSI Associates LLC v. United States*, 496 F.3d at 184.

[117] *United States v. Shefton*, 548 F.3d 1360, 1364 (11th Cir. 2008); *United States v. Andrews*, 530 F.3d 1232, 1238 (10th Cir. 2008). The courts are divided over the question of whether a recognized constructive trust for the benefit of a victim is sufficient to establish a superior interest under section 853(n), compare, *United States v. Shefton*, 548 F.3d at 1364-366; *United States v. $4,224,958.57(Boylan)*, 392 F.3d 1002, 1004-1005 (9th Cir. 2004); *United States v. Schwimmer*, 968 F.2d 1570, 1582 (2d Cir. 1992), with, *United States v. Andrews*, 530 F.3d at 1238-239; *United States v. BCCI Holdings (Luxembourg), S.A.*, 46 F.3d 1185, 1190-191(D.C.Cir. 1995).

[118] 21 U.S.C. 853(n)(6); *United States v. Lazarenko*, 476 F.3d at 648.

[119] *United States v. Misla-Aldarondo*, 478 F.3d 52, 73-4 (1st Cir. 2007); *United States v. Casey*, 444 F.3d 1071, 1077 (9th Cir. 2006)("money judgments are appropriate under §853, even in cases of insolvent defendants. . . . the government is entitled to a money judgment in criminal forfeiture cases, even when a defendant has no assets. . .").

[120] *United States v. Hall*, 434 F.3d 42, 59 (1st Cir. 2006)("A money judgment permits the government to collect on the forfeiture order in the same way that a successful plaintiff collects a money judgment from a civil defendant"); *United States v. Casey*, 444 F.3d at 1074; contra, *United States v. Vampire Nation*, 451 F.3d 189, 202 (3d Cir. 2006)("The judgment *in personam* here is one in forfeiture and is limited by the provisions of 21 U.S.C. 853(a) to [forfeitable assets]. In the event that property traceable to the crime is not available, the Court may direct forfeiture of substitute property subject to the conditions set out in 21 U.S.C. 853(p)").

[121] *E.g.*, 21 U.S.C. 881(f), 853(i).

[122] *E.g.*, 21 U.S.C. 881(e), 853(i).

[123] "(1) The Secretary of the Treasury may apply property forfeited under this chapter in accordance with subparagraph (A) or (B), or both: (A) Retain any of the property for official use. (B) Transfer any of the property to—(i) any other Federal agency; (ii) any State or local law enforcement agency that participated directly or indirectly in the seizure or forfeiture of the property; or (iii) the Civil Air Patrol.

"(2) The Secretary may transfer any forfeited personal property or the proceeds of the sale of any forfeited personal or real property to any foreign country which participated directly or indirectly in the seizure or forfeiture of the property, if such a transfer—(A) has been agreed to by the Secretary of State; (B) is authorized in an international agreement between the United States and the foreign country; and (C) is made to a country which, if applicable, has been certified under section 2291j(b) of Title 22.

"(3) Aircraft may be transferred to the Civil Air Patrol under paragraph (1)(B)(iii) in support of air search and rescue and other emergency services and, pursuant to a memorandum of understanding entered into with a Federal agency, illegal drug traffic surveillance. Jet-powered aircraft may not be transferred to the Civil Air Patrol under the authority of paragraph (1)(B)(iii)," 19 U.S.C. 1616a(c). The Attorney General enjoys similar authority under 21 U.S.C. 881(e) and 18 U.S.C. 981(e), (*i*).

[124] 28 U.S.C. 524(c).

[125] 31 U.S.C. 9703.

[126] Creation of the forfeiture funds and other forfeiture adjustments can be traced to criticisms, beginning in the 96th Congress, that the drug and racketeering forfeiture provisions enacted in 1970 were being underutilized, were difficult to enforce, and that the proceeds from such confiscations should be used more directly for law enforcement purposes. *E.g.*, *Forfeiture of Narcotics Proceeds: Hearings Before the Subcomm. on Criminal Justice of the Senate Comm. on the Judiciary*, 96th Cong., 2d Sess. (1980); *Forfeiture in Drug Cases: Hearings Before the Subcomm. on Crime of the House Comm. on the Judiciary*, 97th Cong., 1st & 2d Sess. (1982); *DEA Oversight and Budget Authority: Hearing Before the Subcomm. on Security and Terrorism of the Senate Comm. on the Judiciary*, 97th Cong., 2d Sess. (1982); General Accounting Office, *Asset Forfeiture–A Seldom Used Tool in Combating Drug Trafficking*, GGD 81-5 (April 10, 1981).

[127] The Constitution requires that "[n]o money shall be drawn from the Treasury, but in consequence of appropriations made by law," U.S.Const. Art.I, §9, cl.7, and so "no money can be paid out of the Treasury unless it has been appropriated by an act of Congress," *OPM v. Richmond*, 496 U.S. 414, 424 (1990). Congress ordinarily authorizes an appropriation before it makes an appropriation. An authorization of appropriation is little more than a prediction of future appropriations; it is not an appropriation nor is Congress bound by it. Most appropriations are made on an annual basis, but Congress may enact an appropriation measure covering several years or making a "permanent" appropriation. Sometimes Congress requires that money appropriated be spent within a particular time period such as during a particular fiscal year; other times such as here it gives its permission "without fiscal year limitation." *See generally,* General Accounting Office [Government Accountability Office], I *Principles of Federal Appropriations Law*, 2-13 to 2-14, 2-40 to 2-42 (2004), http://www.gao.gov/special.pubs/d04261sp.pdf.

[128] The Department of Justice realized receipts of over $1.1 billion during fiscal year 2008, U.S. Department of Justice, Executive Office for United States Attorneys, *United States Attorneys' Annual Statistical Report: Fiscal Year 2008*, http://www.usdoj.gov/usao/reading_room/reports/asr2008/08statrpt.pdf; the Treasury Department reports receipts of $557 million in the Treasury Forfeiture Fund for FY' 2008, Office of Management and Budget, *Budget of the U.S. Government, Fiscal Year 2010: Appendix*, at 973 (2009).

A third fund, the Special Forfeiture Fund at one time used to fund the drug czar's office, no longer receives forfeiture proceeds. A fourth, the Crime Victims Fund, which technically is fed by federal "Son of Sam" and espionage forfeitures, in fact is supported primarily by receipts from a source other than forfeiture—the proceeds from the collections of criminal fines—which are used to support a grant program for the relief of victims of crime. References to the Postal Service Fund, 39 U.S.C. 2003, which might be considered a fifth forfeiture fund, have been omitted as general matter for several reasons. Although it receives the Postal Service's share of equitably distributed forfeitures, it was not created solely or even primarily for that purpose. It is instead a general operational fund into which all or virtually all Postal Service receipts are deposited and which is available, not merely for law enforcement or related purposes, but for the general operational needs of the Postal Service, 39 U.S.C. 2003(e)(1)("The Fund shall be available for the payment of all expenses incurred by the Postal Service in carrying out its functions as provided by law . . ."). As a practical matter it is much more closely analogous to the general fund than to any of the forfeiture funds under discussion.

[129] 28 U.S.C. 524(c).

[130] 98 Stat. 2052, 2193.

[131] 28 U.S.C. 524(c)(4). The proceeds from three forfeiture provisions are expressly excluded from the Fund, those pursuant to: (1) section 11(d) of the Endangered Species Act (16 U.S.C. 1540(d)), (2) section 6(d) of the Lacey Act Amendments of 1981(16 U.S.C. 3375(d)), and (3) section 2003(b)(7) of title 39 of the United States Code dealing with the Postal Service, *id.*

[132] *E.g.*, 21 U.S.C. 881(e); 19 U.S.C. 1616a; 21 U.S.C. 853(i); 18 U.S.C. 981(d),(e); 18 U.S.C. 982(b); 18 U.S.C. 1963(g).

[133] Rewards may not exceed $500,000, 28 U.S.C. 524(c)((2).

[134] Rewards may not exceed the lesser of $500,000 or 25% of the amount realized from the confiscation without the personal approval of the Attorney General and notification of the chairmen and ranking minority members of the Appropriations and Judiciary Committees, *id.*

[135] The amount paid here may not exceed $100,000 without the approval of the agency head, 28 U.S.C. 524(c)(3).

[136] The "drug czar's" office was originally supported by the Special Forfeiture Fund, and the Fund continued in existence even after the office secured a more regular, more reliable source of support. Deposits in the Special Forfeiture Fund extended only through Fiscal Year 1997, 28 U.S.C. 524(c)(8).

[137] The Department of Justice's annual forfeiture fund report anticipated fy 2009 expenditures of:

$48.4 million for management seized assets;
$300.3 million to settle liens, mortgages, and petitions for remission and mitigation;
$88.9 million for automation-related contract costs;
$18.2 million for automation;
$13.8 million for training and printing;
$9.7 million for information leading to forfeiture;
$19.529 million for the purchase of evidence;
$15 million for contract to identify assets;
$1.461 million to equip cars, boats and planes for law enforcement use;
$25.8 million for investigative costs leading to seizure;
$62.7 million for joint state, local and federal cooperative law enforcement operations;
$412 million was transferred to state, local and tribal entities;
$4.11 million for storage, protection, and destruction of controlled substances; and
$23.5 million for other program management expenses.

U.S. Department of Justice, *Asset Forfeiture Fund: FY 2009 Performance Budget*, at 13-7, http://www.usdoj.gov/ jmd/2009justification/pdf/fy09-aff.pdf.

[138] *E.g.*, 28 U.S.C. 524(c)(1)(I)(2000 ed.) making the Fund available during fiscal year 1989 to pay expenses related to prison construction; Anti-Drug Abuse Act, §9310, P.L. 100-690, 102 Stat. 4540 (1988) granting access to the Fund to pay U.S. Attorney salaries and expenses during fiscal year 1989 for purposes authorized in the Omnibus Drug Initiative Act.

[139] ". . .[A]ny excess unobligated balances remaining in the Fund on September 30, 1997, and thereafter shall be available to the Attorney General, without fiscal year limitation, for any federal law enforcement, litigative/prosecutive, and correctional activities, or any other authorized purpose of the Department of Justice. . ." 28 U.S.C. 524(c)(8)(E).

In the fiscal year 2008, the Attorney General authorized recourse to the super surplus in the Fund in the amount of $57.149 million; recipients included the Bureau of Alcohol, Tobacco, Firearms and Explosives ($105,000); the Civil Division ($338,000); the Criminal Division's Office of the Organized Crime Drug Enforcement Task Force ($138,000); the Drug Enforcement Administration ($118,000); the Executive Office of United States Attorneys ($330,000); the National Security Division ($6.120 million); the Bureau of Prisons ($30 million); and the Office of the Federal Detention Trustee ($20 million), U.S. Department of Justice, Office of the Inspector General, Audit Division, *Asset Forfeiture Fund and Sized Assets Deposit Fund Annual Financial Statement Fiscal Year 2008*, Audit Report 097-19, at 72 (Mar. 2009), *http://www.us* doj.gov/jmd/afp/01progamaudit/fy2008/fy2008_afs_report.pdf.

[140] 28 U.S.C. 524(c)(1).

[141] Id.

[142] Criminal Division, United States Department of Justice, *Asset Forfeiture: Law and Practice Manual*, 10-26 n.115 (June, 1998); *Department of Commerce, Justice, and State, the Judiciary, and Related Agencies Appropriations: Hearings Before a Subcomm. of the House Comm. on Appropriations*, 100th Cong., 2d Sess. 734-35 (1988) (Marshals Service response to questions submitted for the record); Executive Office of Asset Forfeiture, United States Department of Justice, *The Attorney General's Guidelines on Seized and Forfeited Property*, 19 (July, 1990), reprinted in, U.S. Department of Justice, *U.S. Attorneys Manual*, tit.9, ch. 118, http://www.usdoj.gov/usao/eousa/foia_reading_room/ usam/title9/118mcrm.htm.

[143] P.L. 98-473, §§317, 2304, 98 Stat. 2054, 2193 (1984). In fact in the hectic days at the end of the Congress, the Fund was established twice, P.L. 98-573, §213(a)(11), 98 Stat. 2986 (1984), and continued its dual existence for a couple of years, see 19 U.S.C. 1613a, 1613b (Supp. II, 1984); (Supp. III. 1985). In 1986 and 1987, Congress repealed both and then revived one of the sections, P.L. 99-514, § 1888 (7), 100 Stat. 2925 (1986); P.L. 99-570, §1152(b)(1), 100 Stat. 3207-12 (1986); P.L. 100-71, 101 Stat. 438 (1987). The law appears in the United States Code as the second section 9703 of Title 31 (the first section 9703 and an accompanying section 9704 are unrelated to the forfeiture fund and address managerial flexibility generally).

[144] 31 U.S.C. 9703(d). Tax enforcement is exempted generally, 31 U.S.C. 9703(a), (d) and during fiscal year 1993, the transition period between the Customs Service and the Department of the Treasury Funds, deposits are those from laws administered or enforced by the Customs Service and equitable shares earned by the Customs Service rather than the entire Department, 31 U.S.C. 9703(d).

[145] *Budget of the U.S. Government, Fiscal Year 2004: Appendix*, 770 (2004); *Departments of Commerce, Justice, and State, the Judiciary, and Related Agencies Appropriations for 2005: Hearings Before a Subcomm. of the House Comm. on Appropriations (Pt.2)*, 108th Cong. 2d Sess. 937 (2004).

[146] 19 U.S.C. 1616a.

[147] "The Secretary shall make available to the United States Coast Guard, from funds appropriated under subsection (g)(2)* in excess of $10,000,000 for a fiscal year, an amount equal to the net proceeds in the Fund derived from seizures by the Coast Guard," 31 U.S.C. 9703(c).

* "There are authorized to be appropriated from the Fund to carry out the purposes set forth in subsections (a)(2) and (c) not to exceed—(A) $25,000,000 for fiscal year 1993; and (B) $50,000,000 for each fiscal year after fiscal year 1993." 31 U.S.C. 9703(g)(2).

[148] 31 U.S.C. 9703(c).

[149] Payments to settle liens or mortgages or in remission or mitigation may not exceed the value of the property at the time of seizure, 31 U.S.C. 9703(b)(1).

[150] The amount paid as a reward may not be more than 25% of the amount realized in the forfeiture, 19 U.S.C. 1619(a)(2).

[151] The offenses include money laundering, any of the money laundering predicate offenses, drug smuggling, credit card or computer fraud, counterfeiting, various firearms and explosives offenses, and fraud against certain financial institutions, 31 U.S.C. 9703(a)(2)(B).

[152] Equitable sharing payments may not exceed the value of the property at the time of disposal, 31 U.S.C. 9703(b)(2).

[153] 31 U.S.C. 9703(a), (g)(3).

[154] 31 U.S.C. 9703(g)(1).

[155] Congress established the Special Forfeiture Fund in the Anti-Drug Abuse Act of 1988, P.L. 100-690, §6073, 102 Stat. 4323.

[156] *E.g.*, P.L. 105-277, 112 Stat. 2681-496, 2681-497 (1998).

[157] See generally, CRS Report RL32579, *Victims of Crime Compensation and Assistance: Background and Funding*, by Celinda Franco.

[158] 42 U.S.C. 10601. It does not receive fines imposed under section 11(d) of the Endangered Species Act, 16 U.S.C. 1540(d); section 6(d) of the Lacey Act Amendments, 16 U.S.C. 3375(d); section 311 of the Federal Water Pollution Control Act, 33 U.S.C. 1321; or those deposited in the Postal Service Fund, 39 U.S.C. 2601(a)(2), 2003; or in the railroad unemployment insurance account, 45 U.S.C. 351 et seq., 42 U.S.C. 10601.

[159] 18 U.S.C. 794.

[160] 18 U.S.C. 3681. Section 3681 (special forfeiture of collateral profits of crime) establishes an escrow account within the Crime Victims Forfeiture Fund to receive the proceeds paid to those convicted of certain espionage or violent federal offenses for their literary efforts depicting their crimes. The account is available for five years to satisfy judgments in favor of the victims of such crimes, criminal fines, and, to a limited extent to pay for the defendant's attorneys' fees. After five years, the court may order the residue paid out of escrow and into the Fund. The section is not likely to have accounted for any substantial contributions to the Fund since the Fund could not have begun to receive unrestricted deposits under section 3681 until after the fifth anniversary of the section's enactment in November, 1991 and shortly thereafter the prospect of future receipts was clouded by the Supreme Court's opinion in *Simon & Schuster v. New York Crime Victims Bd.*, 502 U.S. 105 (1991), holding the New York State "Son of Sam" statute inconsistent with the First Amendment, Cohen, CRS Report 92-56, *The "Son of Sam" Case: First Amendment Analysis and Legislative Implications*.

[161] 42 U.S.C. 10601 to 10603a. In fiscal year 2010, the Fund is expected to receive $817 million, Office of Management and Budget, *Budget of the U.S. Government, Fiscal Year 2010: Appendix*, 762 (2009).

[162] *Austin v. United States*, 509 U.S. 602, 622 (1993); *Alexander v. United States*, 509 U.S. 544, 559 (1993)(holding eighth amendment excessive fines standards applicable to civil and criminal forfeitures respectively); *United States v. 92 Buena Vista Avenue*, 507 U.S. 111, 129 (1993)(a seemingly tortured statutory construction that could be read as driven by due process concerns for the property rights of innocent owners); *Republic National Bank v. United States*, 506 U.S. 80 (1992)(a case in which all nine members of the Court rejected application of the strict in rem legal fiction that the government sought to employ and in which one justice went so far as

to observe that "I am surprised that the Government would make such a transparently fallacious argument in support of its unconscionable position in this case," 506 U.S. at 99 (Stevens, J., concurring in part and concurring in the judgment)).

[163] *United States v. Ursery*, 518 U.S. 267, 270-71 (1996)(rejecting the suggestion that the double jeopardy clause preclude, consecutive forfeiture proceedings and criminal prosecutions); *Bennis v. Michigan*, 516 U.S. 442, 446 (1996) (refusing, at least under the facts before it, to find that due process bars the confiscation of the property of an innocent owner); *Libretti v. United States*, 516 U.S. 29, 48-51 (1995)(holding that neither the promise of a jury trial found in the Sixth Amendment nor that in the Federal Rules of Criminal Procedure extended to questions of fact in criminal forfeiture proceedings).

[164] *United States v. James Daniel Good Real Property*, 510 U.S. 43, 62 (1993)(generally requiring pre-seizure notice and hearing in real property cases); *United States v. Bajakajian*, 524 U.S. 321, 337 (1998)(holding criminal forfeitures to a grossly disproportionate standard under the excessive fines clause); see also, *Degen v. United States*, 517 U.S. 820, 828-29 (1996)(declining the request to extend the common law doctrine of fugitive disentitlement so as to bar fugitive claimants from contesting the forfeiture of their property)(CAFRA subsequently extended the doctrine as a matter of statute, 28 U.S.C. 2466).

[165] *United States v. Sarbello*, 985 F.2d 716, 722 (3d Cir. 1993); *United States v. Bucuvalas*, 970 F.2d 937, 945-46 (1st Cir. 1992); *United States v. Smith*, 966 F.2d 1045, 1056 (6th Cir. 1992).

[166] *E.g., United States v. Santoro*, 866 F.2d 1538, 1544 (4th Cir. 1989); *United States v. One 107.9 Acre Parcel of Land*, 898 F.2d 396, 400-1 (3d Cir. 1990).

[167] *Alexander v. United States*, 509 U.S. 544 (1993); *Austin v. United States*, 509 U.S. 602 (1993).

[168] *Austin v. United States*, 509 U.S. 602, 622 (1993); *Alexander v. United States*, 509 U.S. 544, 559 (1993).

[169] *United States v. Bajakajian*, 524 U.S. 321, 334 (1998). Bajakajian had tried to leave the United States with $357,144 in cash and pled guilty to willfully failing to accurately report the fact (as required by 31 U.S.C. 5316 and made punishable under 18 U.S.C. 5322). The cash was neither criminally acquired, used, nor destined. Bajakajian's "crime was solely a reporting offense," 524 U.S. at 337; one for which the applicable federal sentencing guidelines made him liable to a maximum term of imprisonment of six months and a maximum fine of $5,000. The harm . . . caused was also minimal. Failure to report this currency affected only one party, the Government and in a relatively minor way. There was no fraud on the United States, and [he] caused no loss to the public fisc. Had his crime gone undetected, the Government would have been deprived only of the information that $357,144 had left the country," 524 U.S. at 338-39. The Court was unpersuaded by the government's claim that early statutes which set the fine for various customs evasion offenses at twice the value of the goods demonstrated historic acceptance of proportional penalties. These "early monetary forfeitures . . . were considered not as punishment for an offense, but rather as serving the remedial purpose of reimbursing the government for the losses accruing from the evasion of customs duties," 524 U.S. at 342. Consistent with this observation, several lower federal courts have rejected Excessive Fines Clause arguments because the statutes in question were purely remedial rather than punitive, *e.g., United States v. Land [in] Winston Country (Wood)*, 221 F.3d 1194, 1199 (11th Cir. 2000);(18 U.S.C. 1955(d)); *United States v. $273,963.94 (Puzo)*, 164 F.3d 462, 466 (9th Cir. 1999)(19 U.S.C. 1497); *United States v. An Antique Platter of Gold (Stenhardt)*, 184 F.3d 131, 139-40 (2d Cir. 1999), and one did so because although arising under the same statute as *Austin* the court was convinced that the purpose of confiscation in the case before it was remedial and not punitive, *United States v. 1948 South Martin Luther King Drive (Locher)*, 270 F.3d 1102, 1114-115 (7th Cir. 2001); see also, *United States v. Betancourt*, 422 F.3d 240, 250 (5th Cir. 2005)("The forfeiture of drug proceeds [under criminal forfeiture provisions of 21 U.S.C. 853] does not constitute punishment, and thus neither the Eighth Amendment prohibition nor double jeopardy analysis is applicable").

[170] *United States v. Seher*, 562 F.3d 1344, 1371 (11th Cir. 2009)("A forfeiture order violates the Excessive Fines Clause if it is grossly disproportional to the gravity of a defendant's offense. To make this determination, we principally look at three factors (1) whether the defendant falls into the class of persons at whom the criminal statute was principally directed; (2) other penalties authorized by the legislature (or the Sentencing Commission); and (3) the harm caused by the defendant. . . In addition, if the value of forfeited property is within the range of fines prescribed by Congress, a strong presumption arises that the forfeiture is constitutional")(internal quotations and citations omitted); *United States v. Jose*, 499 F.3d 105, 111 (1st Cir. 2007)(same); *United States v. Varrone*, 554 F.3d 327, 331 (2d Cir. 2009)("In applying *Bajakajian*, we have noted that among the factors the *Bajakajian* Court considered in determining whether the forfeiture was excessive were [1] the essence of the crime of the defendant and its relating to other criminal activity, [2] whether the defendant fit into the class of persons for whom the statute was principally designed, [3] the maximum sentence and fine that could have been imposed, and [4] the nature of the harm caused by the defendant's conduct")(internal quotations and bracketing omitted); *United States v. $100,348 (Mayzel)*, 354 F.3d 1110, 1122 (9th Cir. 2004)("In *Bajakajian*, the Supreme Court considered four factors in weighing the gravity of the defendant's offense: (1) the nature and extent of the crime, (2) whether the violation was related to other illegal activities, (3) the other penalties that may be imposed for the violation, and (4) the extent of the harm caused").

[171] *United States v. Segal*, 495 F.3d 826, 840 (7th Cir. 2007)("It is true that the forfeiture is large. It is only excessive, however, if it is disproportional to the offense. We cannot say that it was. This was massive fraud. When a defendant commits a multimillion-dollar crime, he can be required to forfeit assets also running into the millions"); *United States v. Ortiz-Cintron*, 461 F.3d 78, 81-2 (1st Cir. 2006)(confiscation of property in drug dealing case with a relatively low value compared to the authorized fine); *United States v. Bollin*, 264 F.3d 391, 418-19 (4th Cir. 2001)(money laundering over an extended period of time in connection with a harmful securities fraud scheme contrasted with *Bajakajian*'s onetime reporting violation).

[172] *United States v. Elfgeeh*, 515 F.3d 100, 139 (2d Cir. 2008)("The order for a forfeiture of $22,435,467 is not disproportional. The essence of defendants' offenses was the unlicensed transmission of money, and neither defendant received the statutory maximum prison term allowed. . . . [T]he evidence showed that defendants in fact transmitted the moneys to 25 different countries. Plainly, defendants were persons at whom §1960(a) was aimed"); *United States v. Ely*, 468 F.3d 399, 403 (6th Cir. 2006)(noting in dicta that the amount confiscated was less than the advisory fine under the sentencing guidelines); *United States v. Dodge Caravan Grand SE/Sport Van (Clemons)*, 387 F.3d 758, 763 (8th Cir. 2004)("if the value of the property forfeited is within or near the permissible range of fines using the sentencing guidelines, the forfeiture almost certainly is not excessive"); *United States v. Puche*, 350 F.3d 1137, 1154 (11th Cir. 2003)("defendant's reliance on *Bajakajian* is misplaced as the defendant in that case was not a money launderer and was convicted only for a reporting offense"); *United States v. Collado*, 348 F.3d 323, 328 (2d Cir. 2003)(owner's conduct in allowing her property to be used for drug dealing constituted a serious, harmful crime (21 U.S.C. 856) subject to a fine in excessive of the value of the property); but see *von Hofe v. United States*, 492 F.3d 175, 191 (2d Cir. 2007)("Mrs. von Hofe's offensive conduct boils down to her joint ownership . . . and silence in the face of her husband's decision to grow marijuana in their basement almost thirty years into their marriage. And yet she is being punished as if she were distributing drugs, when the district court concluded as a matter of fact that she had no knowledge of any distribution or remuneration. The government cannot justify forfeiture of Mrs. von Hofe's interest in [the family home], for the punishment bears no reasonable correlation either to her minimal culpability or any harm she caused").

[173] The double jeopardy clause which declares that no one shall "be subject for the same offence to be twice put in jeopardy of life or limb, U.S.Const. Amend.V, prohibits both successive punishment and successive prosecutions of the same individual for the same criminal offense," *United States v. Dixon*, 509 U.S. 688, 696 (1993).

[174] *One Lot Emerald Cut Stones v. United States*, 409 U.S. 232, 235-37 (1972); *United States v. One Assortment of Firearms*, 465 U.S. 354, 366 (1984) ("We accordingly conclude that the forfeiture mechanism set forth in §924(d) is not an additional penalty for the commission of a criminal act, but rather a separate civil sanction, remedial in nature. Because the §924(d) forfeiture proceeding brought against Mulcahey's firearms is not a criminal proceeding, it is not barred by the Double Jeopardy Clause").

[175] *Austin v. United States*, 509 U.S. 602, 608 n.4 (1993).

[176] *United States v. Leyland*, 277 F.3d 628, 633 (2d Cir. 2002)(criminal prosecution following civil forfeiture does raise double jeopardy concerns); *United States v. 817 N.E. 29th Drive*, 175 F.3d 1304, 1311 (11th Cir. 1999) (civil forfeiture following conviction; "a forfeiture action cannot serve as the basis for a claim under the Double Jeopardy Clause"); *United States v. Candelaria-Silva*, 166 F.3d 19, 43-4 (1st Cir. 1999) (criminal forfeiture following initiation of civil forfeiture proceedings; "a completed civil forfeiture of property does not constitute 'jeopardy' under the Double Jeopardy Clause, and does not bar the subsequent criminal prosecution and punishment of the defendant whose property was forfeited").

[177] *United States v. $40,955 (el Fara)*, 554 F.3d 752, 758 (9th Cir. 2009), citing *United States v. Zucker*, 161 U.S. 475, 481 (1896).

[178] *Caplin & Drysdale v. United States*, 491 U.S. 617, 632 (1989); *United States v. Farmer*, 274 F.3d 800, 802 (4th Cir. 2001).

[179] *United States v. Monsanto*, 491 U.S. 600, 614-15 (1989); *United States v. Undetermined Amount of U.S. Currency (Warren)*, 376 F.3d 260, 269 (4th Cir. 2004); *United States v. Melrose East Subdivision*, 357 F.3d 493, 500 (5th Cir. 2004).

[180] *United States v. Saccoccia*, 564 F.3d 502, 505 (1st Cir. 2009).

[181] *United States v. 6 Fox Street*, 480 F.3d 38, 45 (1st Cir. 2007); *United States v. 817 N.E. 29th Drive*, 175 F.3d 1304, 1311 no.13 (11th Cir. 1999); *United States v. Michelle's Lounge*, 39 F.3d 684, 698 (7th Cir. 1994). CAFRA, however, permits the appointment of counsel for an indigent civil forfeiture claimant for whom counsel has already been appointed in connection with a related criminal case, 18 U.S.C. 983(b).

[182] *United States v. Saccoccia*, 564 F.3d 502, 507 (1st Cir. 2009)(bound by *Libretti)*; *United States v. Capoccia*, 503 F.3d 103, 116 n.18 (2d Cir. 2007); *United States v. Leahy*, 438 F.3d 328, (3d Cir. 2006)(refusing to apply *Apprendi*); *United States v. Tedder*, 403 F.3d 836, 841 (7th Cir. 2005)(same); *United States v. Hall*, 411 F.3d 651, 654 (6th Cir. 2005); *United States v. Shryock*, 342 F.3d 948, 991 (9th Cir. 2003)(same); *United States v. Gasanova*, 332 F.3d 297, 302-303 (5th Cir. 2003)(same); *United States v. Cabez*, 258 F.3d 1256, 1257 (11th Cir. 2001)(same); *United States v. Huber*, 462 F.3d 945, 949 (8th Cir. 2006)(upholding use of the preponderance standard); *United States v. Cherry*, 330 F.3d 658, 669-70 (4th Cir. 2003)(same).

[183] *United States v. James Daniel Good Real Property*, 510 U.S. 43, 48 (1993); *United States v. Ritchie*, 342 F.3d 903, 901-11 (9th Cir. 2003); *Helton v. Hunt*, 330 F.3d 242, 247 (4th Cir. 2003); *Krimstock v. Kelly*, 306 F.3d 40, 51 (2d Cir. 2002).

[184] *Dusenbery v. United States*, 534 U.S. 161, 173 (2002), quoting, *Mullane v. Central Hanover Bank & Trust Co.*, 339 U.S. 306, 314 (1950); see also, *Taylor v. United States*, 483 F.3d 385, 388-89 (5th Cir. 2007); *Nunley v. Department of Justice*, 425 F.3d 1132, 1135-136 (8th Cir. 2005); *Lobzun v. United States*, 422 F.3d 503, 507-508 (7th Cir. 2005); *Mesa Valderrama v. United States*, 417 F.3d 1189, 1196-197 (11th Cir. 2005).

[185] "*Fuentes* [*v. Shevin*, 407 U.S. 67 (1972)] reaffirmed, however, that, in limited circumstances, immediate seizure of a property interest, without an opportunity for prior hearing, is constitutionally permissible. Such circumstances are those in which the seizure has been directly necessary to secure an important governmental or general public interest. Second, there has been a special need for prompt action. Third, the State has kept strict control over its monopoly of legitimate force: the person initiating the seizure has been a government official responsible for determining, under standards of a narrowly drawn statute, that it was necessary and justified in the particular instance." [407 U.S.] at 91. . . "The considerations that justified postponement of notice and hearing in those cases are present here. First, seizure under the Puerto Rican statutes serves significant governmental purposes: Seizure permits Puerto Rico to assert *in rem* jurisdiction over the property in order to conduct forfeiture proceedings, thereby fostering the public interest in preventing continued illicit use of the property and in enforcing criminal sanctions. Second, preseizure notice and hearing might frustrate the interests served by the statutes, since the property seized—as here, a yacht—will often be of a sort that could be removed to another jurisdiction, destroyed, or concealed, if advance warning of confiscation were given. And finally, unlike the situation in *Fuentes*, seizure is not initiated by self-interested private parties; rather Commonwealth officials determine whether seizure is appropriate under the provisions of the Puerto Rico statutes." *Calero-Toledo v. Pearson Yacht Leasing Co.*, 416 U.S. at 678-79; see also, *United States v. Melrose East Subdivision*, 357 F.3d 493, 502 (5th Cir. 2004); *United States v. Any and All Radio Station Transmission Equipment (Perez)*, 218 F.3d 543, 550-51 (6th Cir. 2000); *Yskamp v. DEA*, 163 F.3d 767, 774 (3d Cir. 1998); *United States v. Lot 41, Berryhill Farm Estates*, 128 F.3d 1386, 1392 (10th Cir. 1997); *United States v. Down*, 68 F.3d 1030, 1038-39 (8th Cir. 1995).

[186] *United States v. James Daniel Good Real Property*, 510 U.S. 43 (1993).

[187] *United States v. Melrose East Subdivision*, 357 F.3d 493, 499-500 (5th Cir. 2004), *citing inter alia*, *United States v. Jones*, 160 F.3d 641, 645-48 (10th Cir. 1998); *United States v. Moya-Gomez*, 860 F.2d 760, 729-30 (7th Cir. 1988); *United States v. Farmer*, 274 F.3d 800, 805 (4th Cir. 2001); *United States v. Michelle's Lounge*, 39 F.3d 684, 700-01 (7th Cir. 1994).

[188] Due process bars forfeiture either (1) where the property has "been taken from [its owner] without his privity or consent" and used in a manner which would ordinarily give rise to confiscation, or (2) where the owner was "not only. . . uninvolved in and unaware of the wrongful activity, but also that he had done all that reasonably could be expected to prevent the proscribed use of the property," *Calero-Toledo v. Pearson Yacht Leasing Co.*, 416 U.S. at 689.

[189] *Bennis* also reaffirmed that the takings clause stands as no impediment to an otherwise valid forfeiture: "Petitioner also claims that the forfeiture in this case was a taking of private property for public use in violation of the Takings Clause of the Fifth Amendment, made applicable to the States by the Fourteenth Amendment. But if the forfeiture proceeding here in question did not violate the Fourteenth Amendment, the property in the automobile was transferred by virtue of that proceeding from petitioner to the State. The government may not be required to compensate an owner for property which it has already lawfully acquired under the exercise of governmental authority other than the power of eminent domain," *Bennis v. Michigan*, 516 U.S. at 452; see also, *United States v. $7,990 (Fiorentino)*, 170 F.3d 843, 845 (8th Cir. 1999).

[190] *Bennis v. Michigan*, 516 U.S. at 457-58 ("I join the opinion of the Court and highlight features of the case key to my judgment. . . . First, it bears emphasis that the car in question belonged to John Bennis as much as it did to Tina Bennis. . . . The sole question, then, is whether Tina Bennis is entitled not to the car, but to a portion of the proceeds (if any there be after deduction of police, prosecutorial, and court costs) as a matter of constitutional right. Second, it was 'critical' to the judgment of the Michigan Supreme Court that the nuisance abatement proceedings is an 'equitable action.'. . . That means the State's Supreme Court stands ready to police exorbitant applications of the statute. . . . Nor it is fair to charge the trial court with 'blatant unfairness' in the case at hand. . . . The court declined to order a division of sale proceeds. . . for two practical reasons: the Bennises have 'another automobile' and the age and value of the forfeited car . . . left practically nothing to divide after subtraction of costs. Michigan in short has not embarked on an experiment to punish innocent third parties. Nor do we conduct any such experiment. Michigan has decided to deter johns from using cars they own (or co-own) to contribute to neighborhood blight, and that abatement endeavor hardly warrants this Court's disapprobation").

[191] *United States v. $8,850 (Vasquez)*, 461 U.S. 555, 562-65 (1983); *United States v. Ninety Three Firearms*, 330 F.3d 414, 424-26 (6th Cir. 2003); (*United States v. $12,248 (Johnson)*, 957 F.2d 1513, 1518-519 (9th Cir. 1991); *United States v. Premises Located at Route 13*, 946 F.2d 749, 754-56 (11th Cir. 1991); but see *Smith v.*

City of Chicago, 524 F.3d 834, 836-39 (7th Cir. 2008), vac'd and rem'd sub nom., *Alvarez v. Smith*, 130 S.Ct. ____ (Dec. 8, 2009).

192 *United States v. Melrose East Subdivision*, 357 F.3d 493, 501 (5th Cir. 2004); *United States v. Property, Parcel of Aguilar*, 337 F.3d 225, 229-33 (2d Cir. 2003); *United States v. One "Piper" Aztec "F" DeLuxe Model 250 PA 23 Aircraft*, 321 F.3d 355, 360-61 (3d Cir. 2003); *United States v. Land [in] Winston County (Woods)*, 163 F.3d 1295, 1303 (11th Cir. 1998); *United States v. Santoro*, 866 F.2d 1538, 1544 (4th Cir. 1989).

193 *United States v. McHan*, 345 F.3d 262, 269-70 (4th Cir. 2003).

194 *Collazos v. United States*, 368 F.3d 190, 202 (2d Cir. 2004); *United States v. $6,976,934.65, Plus Intereset Deposited into Royal Bank of Scotland Int'l.*, 554 F.3d 123, 128 (D.C.Cir. 2009)("In *Collazos*, the Second Circuit distilled the statutory requirements for disentitlement into a five-element test: (1) a warrant or similar process has issued in a criminal case for the claimant's apprehension; (2) the claimant had notice or knowledge of the warrant or process; (3) the criminal case is related to the forfeiture action; (4) the claimant is not confined or otherwise held in custody in another jurisdiction; and (5) the claimant has deliberately avoided criminal prosecution by leaving the United States, declining to enter or renter the country, or to otherwise evading the criminal court's jurisdiction. These five elements track the statutory requirements, and we adopt the same test")(internal citations omitted); see also *United States v. Salti*, 579 F.3d 656, 663 (6th Cir. 2009); *United States v. $6,190 (Lum)*, 581 F.3d 881, 886-88 (9th Cir. 2009).

195 *United States v. Marolf*, 173 F.3d 1213, 1216-218 (9th Cir. 1999); *Clymore v. United States*, 164 F.3d 569, 574 (10th Cir. 1999); *Small v. United States*, 136 F.3d 1334, 1338 (D.C.Cir. 1998); *United States v. Girealdo*, 45 F.3d 509, 512 (1st Cir. 1995).

196 *Adames v. United States*, 171 F.3d 728, 732 (2d Cir. 1999).

197 *United States v. 1184 Drycreek Rd.*, 174 F.3d 720, 727-28 (6th Cir. 1999); *United States v. Land [in] Winston County (Woods)*, 163 F.3d 1295, 1301-302 (11th Cir. 1998); *United States v. Marsh*, 105 F.3d 927, 931 (4th Cir. 1997); *United States v. 51 Pieces of Real Property (Nitsua Management)*, 17 F.3d 1306, 1319 (10th Cir. 1994). Some circuits refuse to recognize the authority to permit such awards against the government, *United States v. $7,990 (Fiorentino)*, 170 F.3d 843, 844-46 (8th Cir. 1999); *Ikelionwu v. United States*, 150 F.3d 233, 238-39 (2d Cir. 1998).

198 18 U.S.C. 983(e).

199 *United States v. Monsanto*, 491 U.S. 600, 614-15 (1989); *Capplin & Drysdale v. United States*, 491 U.S. 617, 632-35 (1989).

200 *United States v. Monstanto*, 491 U.S. at 615 n.15.

201 *United States v. E-Gold, Ltd*, 521 F.3d 411, 416-19 (D.C.Cir. 2008), citing *inter alia, United States v. Property at 4492 S. Livonia Rd., Livonia*, 889 F.2d 1258, 1263 (2d Cir. 1989).

202 *Id.*

203 *United States v. Grande*, 620 F.2d 1026, 1038 (4th Cir. 1980) ("We would agree . . . that if [18 U.S.C.] §1963 [RICO criminal forfeiture] revives forfeiture of estate as that concept was expressed in the Constitution it is almost certainly invalid because of the irrationality of a ruling that forfeiture of estate cannot be imposed for treason but can be imposed for a pattern of lesser crimes").

204 The confusion apparently stems from the Congressional decision to authorize the use of criminal, in personam procedures rather than civil, in rem procedures to accomplish confiscation in RICO cases, see S.Rept. 617, 91st Cong., 1st Sess. 79 (1969). The character of the forfeiture, however, turns not upon the nature of the procedure selected but rather whether there is any required nexus between the property and the misconduct which provides the necessary predicate for confiscation.

205 *United States v. Grande*, 620 F.2d 1026, 1037-39 (4th Cir. 1980); *United States v. Thevis*, 474 F.Supp. 134, 140-41 (N.D.Ga. 1979), aff'd, 665 F.2d 616 (5th Cir. 1982); *United States v. Anderson*, 637 F.Supp. 632, 634 (N.D.Cal. 1986); *United States v. Pryba*, 674 F.Supp. 1504, 1517 (E.D.Va. 1987).

Under some interpretations, Article III or its due process shadow may limit the breadth or availability of the chemical weapons criminal forfeiture provisions and some of the terrorist civil forfeiture provisions, 18 U.S.C. 229B("Any person convicted under section 229A(a) shall forfeit to the United States . . . (1) any property, real or personal, owned . . . by a person involved in the offense") (note that like the forfeiture of estate condemned in Article III the only apparent nexus between the property and the crime is the property owner); 18 U.S.C. 981(a)(1)(G)(i); 50 U.S.C. 1702(a)(1)(C).

206 The Fourth Amendment guarantees that, "The right of the people to be secure in their persons, houses, papers and effects, against unreasonable searches and seizures shall not be violated, and no warrants shall issue but upon probable cause, supported by oath or affirmation, and particularly describing the place to be searched, and the persons or things to be seized."

207 "Warrantless searches [and seizures] are presumptively unreasonable, though the Court has recognized a few limited exceptions to this general rule. *E.g.*, *United States v. Ross*, 456 U.S. 798 (1982)(automobiles); *Schneckloth v. Bustamonte*, 412 U.S. 218 (1973) (consent); *Warden v. Hayden*, 387 U.S. 294 (1967)." *United States v. Karo*, 468 U.S. 705, 717 (1984). The Court noted some time ago that, "The seizure of stolen goods is authorized by the common law; and the seizure of goods forfeited for a breach of the revenue laws, or concealed to avoid the duties payable on them, has been authorized by English statutes for at least two

centuries past; and the like seizures have been authorized by our own revenue acts from the commencement of the government. The first statute passed by Congress to regulate the collection of duties, the act of July 31, 1789, 1 Stat. 19, 43, contains provisions to this effect. "As this act was passed by the same Congress which proposed for adoption the original amendments to the constitution, it is clear that the members of that body did not regard searches and seizures of this kind as unreasonable," and they are not embraced within the prohibitions of the [fourth] amendment." *Boyd v. United States*, 116 U.S. 616, 623 (1886), quoted in *United States v. Ramsey*, 431 U.S. 606, 617 (1977).

While the Court continues to recognize an exception to the warrant requirements in customs and other border entry cases, *United States v. Montoya de Hernandez*, 473 U.S. 531 (1985), it is less clear that it would find that the exception embraced purely domestic forfeiture seizures, *Fort Wayne Books, Inc. v. Indiana*, 489 U.S. 46, 63 (1989)(". . . the general rule under the Fourth Amendment is that any and all contraband, instrumentalities, and evidence of crimes may be seized on probable cause and even without a warrant in various circumstances. . . .").

[208] Compare *United States v. Salmon*, 944 F.2d 1106, 1119 (3d Cir. 1991), with, *United States v. Parcel of Land at 28 Emery Street*, 914 F.2d 1, 5 (1st Cir. 1990); *United States v. TWP 17 R4, Certain Real Property in Maine*, 970 F.2d 984, 987-89 (1st Cir. 1992); and *United States v. Any and All Radio Station Transmission Equipment (Perez)*, 218 F.3d 543, 550 (6th Cir. 2000)(forfeiture proceedings initiated under the Supplemental Rules do not require proof of wrongdoing for issuance of a warrant to seize the property).

The Court did little to clarify the question when it affirmed the traditional conveyance exception to the warrant requirement and held that police need not obtain a warrant before seizing a car from a public place when they have probable cause to believe the car is forfeitable, *Florida v. White*, 526 U.S. 559 (1999).

[209] Supplemental Rule G(3)(b)(emphasis added)("If the defendant is not real property: (i) *the clerk must issue a warrant to arrest the property if it is in the government's possession, custody, or control*; (ii) the court—on finding probable cause—must issue a warrant to arrest the property if it is not in the government's possession, custody, or control and is not subject to a judicial restraining order; and (iii) a warrant is not necessary if the property is subject to a judicial restraining order").

[210] *One 1958 Plymouth Sedan v. Pennsylvania*, 380 U.S. 693, 697-98 (1965); *United States v. $291,828 in United States Currency (Braddy)*, 536 F.3d 1234, 1237 (11th Cir. 2008); *United States v. $493,850 in U.S. Currency(Bruno)*, 518 F.3d 1159, 1165 (9th Cir. 2008); *United States v. Ninety-Two Thousand Four Hundred Twenty-Two Dollars and Fifty-Seven Cents (Kim's Warehouse)*, 307 F.3d 137, 142 (3d Cir. 2002); *United States v. $557,933.80 More or Less (Mercado-Filpo)*, 287 F.3d 66, 80 (2d Cir. 2002); *United States v. $404,905 (Alexander)*, 182 F.3d 643, 646 (8th Cir. 1999); *United States v. 9844 S.Titan Court*, 75 F.3d 1470, 1492 (10th Cir. 1996).

[211] *One 1958 Plymouth Sedan v. Pennsylvania*, 380 U.S. 693 (1965); *INS v. Lopez-Mendoza*, 468 U.S. 1032, 1039-40 (1984)("[T]he body or identity of a defendant or respondent in a criminal or civil proceeding is never itself suppressible as a fruit of an unlawful arrest, even if it is conceded that an unlawful arrest, search or interrogation occurred. *Gerstine v. Pugh*, 420 U.S. 103, 119 (1975); *Frisbie v. Collins*, 342 U.S. 519, 522 (1952). . . . [a] similar rule applies in forfeiture proceedings directed against contraband or forfeitable property"); *United States v. $291,828 in United States Currency (Braddy)*, 536 F.3d 1234, 1237 (11th Cir. 2008); *United States v. 51 Pieces of Real Property*, 17 F.3d 1306, 1315-316 (10th Cir. 1994); *United States v. $12,390.00 (Dorsey)*, 956 F.2d 801, 806 (8th Cir. 1992); *United States v. $277,000.00 (Montes)*, 941 F.2d 899, 902 (9th Cir. 1991); *United States v. 415 East Mitchell Ave.*, 149 F.3d 472, 476 (6th Cir. 1998); *Krimstock v. Kelly*, 306 F.3d 40, 50 (2d Cir. 2002)("[T]he seizure and forfeiture of property are two distinct events under the federal civil forfeiture laws. While both events require the government to have probable cause, the government is not required to demonstrate probable cause until the forfeiture trial unless a claimant challenges the validity of the seizure before trial. If the government, once challenged, cannot establish probable cause for the initial seizure or offer post-seizure evidence to justify continued impoundment, retention of the seized property runs afoul of the Fourth Amendment").

[212] U.S. Const. Art. I, §10, cl.1; Art. I, §9, cl.3.

[213] *California Dept. of Corrections v. Morales*, 514 U.S. 499, 504-505 (1995).

[214] *United States v. Valladares*, 544 F.3d 1257, 1270-271 (11th Cir. 2008)(the application of a forfeiture statute to conduct which began before the statute became effective and continued on past its effective date did not constitute an ex post facto violation); *United States v. Jennings*, 487 F.3d 564, (8th Cir. 2007)("In the case of continuing offenses . .. the Ex Post Facto clause is not violated by application of a statute to an enterprise that began prior to, but continued after the effective date of the statute" in this case a mail fraud scheme).

[215] *Alexander v. United States*, 509 U.S. 544, 552 (1993).

[216] *United States v. Any and All Radio Station Transmission Equipment (Perez)*, 218 F.3d 543, 549-60 (6th Cir. 2000).

[217] This list does not include statutes which are probably more accurately considered fines or penalties since they make no reference to specific property, i.e., "whoever violates this chapter shall forfeit an amount equal to three times the value of the goods." Nor does it include statutes where the forfeiture is essentially a lien against payment of a fine or penalty, e.g., 18 U.S.C. 3681. It does however include both criminal and civil forfeiture

statutes. It also includes statutes (marked an *) listed because CAFRA declared proceeds traceable to violation of their provisions subject to confiscation either by identified them individually or as predicate offenses for 18 U.S.C. 1956 (money laundering) or for 18 U.S.C. 1961 (RICO), 18 U.S.C. 981(a)(1).

In: Forfeiture, Conspiracy, Venue: Federal Crime Law
Editors: Ryan E. McGowan and Colin H. Grovsten
ISBN: 978-1-61209-315-4

Chapter 2

FEDERAL CONSPIRACY LAW: A BRIEF OVERVIEW

Charles Doyle

SUMMARY

Zacarias Moussaoui, members of the Colombian drug cartels, members of organized crime, and some of the former Enron executives have at least one thing in common: they all have federal conspiracy convictions. The essence of conspiracy is an agreement of two or more persons to engage in some form of prohibited misconduct. The crime is complete upon agreement, although some statutes require prosecutors to show that at least one of the conspirators has taken some concrete step or committed some overt act in furtherance of the scheme. There are dozens of federal conspiracy statutes. One, 18 U.S.C. 371, outlaws conspiracy to commit some other federal crime. The others outlaw conspiracy to engage in various specific forms of proscribed conduct. General Section 371 conspiracies are punishable by imprisonment for not more than five years; drug trafficking, terrorist, and racketeering conspiracies all carry the same penalties as their underlying substantive offenses, and thus are punished more severely than are Section 371 conspiracies. All are subject to fines of not more than $250,000 (not more than $500,000 for organizations), most may serve as the basis for a restitution order, and some for a forfeiture order.

The law makes several exceptions for conspiracy because of its unusual nature. Because many united in crime pose a greater danger than the isolated offender, conspirators may be punished for the conspiracy, any completed substantive offense which is the object of the plot, and any foreseeable other offenses which one of the conspirators commits in furtherance of the scheme. Since conspiracy is an omnipresent crime, it may be prosecuted wherever an overt act is committed in its furtherance. Because conspiracy is a continuing crime, its statute of limitations does not begin to run until the last overt act committed for its benefit. Since conspiracy is a separate crime, it may be prosecuted following conviction for the underlying substantive offense, without offending constitutional double jeopardy principles; because conspiracy is a continuing offense, it may be punished when it straddles enactment of the prohibiting statute, without offending constitutional ex post facto principles. Accused conspirators are likely to be tried together, and the statements of one may often be admitted in evidence against all.

In some respects, conspiracy is similar to attempt, to solicitation, and to aiding and abetting. Unlike aiding and abetting, however, it does not require commission of the underlying offense. Unlike attempt and solicitation, conspiracy does not merge with the substantive offense; a conspirator may be punished for both.

An abridged version ofthis chapter without footnotes and most citations to authority is available as CRS Report R41222, *Federal Conspiracy Law: A Sketch*, by Charles Doyle.

INTRODUCTION

Terrorists, drug traffickers, mafia members, and corrupt corporate executives have one thing in common: most are conspirators subject to federal prosecution.[1] Federal conspiracy laws rest on the belief that criminal schemes are equally or more reprehensible than are the substantive offenses to which they are devoted. The Supreme Court has explained that a "collective criminal agreement – [a] partnership in crime – presents a greater potential threat to the public than individual delicts. Concerted action both increases the likelihood that the criminal object will be successfully attained and decreases the probability that the individuals involved will depart from their path of criminality."[2] Moreover, observed the Court, "[g]roup association for criminal purposes often, if not normally, makes possible the attainment of ends more complex than those which one criminal could accomplish. Nor is the danger of a conspiratorial group limited to the particular end toward which it has embarked."[3] Finally, "[c]ombination in crime makes more likely the commission of crimes unrelated to the original purpose for which the group was formed."[4] In sum, "the danger which a conspiracy generates is not confined to the substantive offense which is the immediate aim of the enterprise."[5] Congress and the courts have fashioned federal conspiracy law accordingly.[6]

The United States Code contains dozens of criminal conspiracy statutes. One, 18 U.S.C. 371, outlaws conspiracy to commit any other federal crime. The others outlaw conspiracy to commit some specific form of misconduct, ranging from civil rights violations to drug trafficking.[7] Conspiracy is a separate offense under most of these statutes,[8] regardless of whether conspiracy accomplishes its objective.[9] The various conspiracy statutes, however, differ in several other respects. A few, including Section 371, require at least one conspirator to take some affirmative step in furtherance of the scheme. Most have no such overt act requirement.[10]

Section 371 has two prongs. One outlaws conspiracy to commit a federal offense; a second, conspiracy to defraud the United States. Conspiracy to commit a federal crime under Section 371 requires that the underlying misconduct be a federal crime. Conspiracy to defraud the United States under Section 371 and in several other instances has no such prerequisite.[11] Section 371 conspiracies are punishable by imprisonment for not more than five years. Elsewhere, conspirators often face more severe penalties.[12]

These differences aside, federal conspiracy statutes share much common ground because Congress decided they should. As the Court observed in *Salinas*, "When Congress uses well-settled terminology of criminal law, its words are presumed to have their ordinary meaning and definition. [When] [t]he relevant statutory phrase is 'to conspire,' [w]e presume Congress intended to use the term in its conventional sense, and certain well-established principles follow."[13]

These principles include the fact that regardless of its statutory setting, every conspiracy has at least two elements: (1) an agreement (2) between two or more persons.[14] Members of the conspiracy are also liable for the foreseeable crimes of their fellows committed in furtherance of the common plot.[15] Moreover, statements by one conspirator are admissible evidence against all.[16] Conspiracies are considered continuing offenses for purposes of the statute of limitations and venue.[17] They are also considered separate offenses for purposes of sentencing and of challenges under the Constitution's ex post facto and double jeopardy clauses.[18] This is a brief discussion of the common features of federal conspiracy law that evolved over the years, with passing references to some of the distinctive features of some of the statutory provisions.

BACKGROUND

Although it is not without common law antecedents, federal conspiracy law is largely of our own making. It is what Congress provided, and what the courts understood Congress intended. This is not to say that conspiracy was unknown in pre-colonial and colonial England,[19] but simply that it was a faint shadow of the crime we now know. Then, it was essentially a narrow form of malicious prosecution, subject to both a civil remedy and prosecution.[20] In the late 18th and early 19th centuries, state courts and legislatures recognized a rapidly expanding accumulation of narrowly described wrongs as "conspiracy." The patchwork reached a point where one commentator explained that there were "few things left so doubtful in the criminal law, as the point at which a combination of several persons in a common object becomes illegal."[21]

Congress, however, enacted few conspiracy statutes prior to the Civil War. It did pass a provision in 1790 that outlawed confining the master of a ship or endeavoring revolt on board.[22] This, Justice Story, sitting as a circuit judge, interpreted to include any conspiracy to confine the prerogatives of the master of ship to navigate, maintain, or police his ship.[23] The same year, 1825, Congress outlawed conspiracies to engage in maritime insurance fraud.[24] Otherwise, there were no federal conspiracy statutes until well after the mid-century mark.

During the War Between the States, however, Congress enacted four sweeping conspiracy provisions, creating federal crimes that have come down to us with little substantive change. The first, perhaps thought more pressing at the beginning of the war, was a seditious conspiracy statute.[25] Shortly thereafter, Congress outlawed conspiracies to defraud the United States through the submission of false claim,[26] and followed that four years later with a prohibition on conspiracies to violate federal law or to defraud the United States.[27]

Subsequent conspiracy statutes, though perhaps no less significant, were more topically focused. The Reconstruction civil rights conspiracy provisions,[28] the Sherman Act anti-trust provisions,[29] and the drug and racketeering statutes[30] may be the best known of these. All of them begin the same way—with an agreement by two or more persons.

Two or More Persons

There are no one-man conspiracies.[31] At common law where husband and wife were considered one, this meant that the two could not be guilty of conspiracy without the participation of some third person.[32] This is no longer the case.[33] In like manner at common law, corporations could not be charged with a crime.[34] This too is no longer the case. A corporation is criminally liable for the crimes, including conspiracy, committed at least in part for its benefit, by its employees and agents.[35] Moreover, a corporation may be criminally liable for intra-corporate conspiracies, as long as at least two of its officers, employees, or agents are parties to the plot.[36]

Notwithstanding the two-party requirement, no co-conspirator need have been tried or even identified, as long as the government produces evidence from which the conspiracy might be inferred.[37] Even the acquittal of a co-conspirator is no defense.[38] In fact, a person may conspire for the commission of a crime by a third person though he himself is legally incapable of committing the underlying offense.[39]

On the other hand, two people may not always be enough. The so-called Wharton's Rule placed a limitation on conspiracy prosecutions when the number of conspirators equaled the number of individuals necessary for the commission of the underlying offense.[40] Under federal law, the rule "stands as an exception to the general principle that a conspiracy and the substantive offense that is its immediate end do not merge upon proof of the latter."[41] And under federal law, the rule reaches no further than to the types of offenses that birth its recognition—dueling, adultery, bigamy, and incest.[42]

Agreement

It is not enough, however, to show that the defendant agreed only with an undercover officer to commit the underlying offense, for there is no agreement on a common purpose in such cases.[43] As has been said, the essence of conspiracy is an agreement, an agreement to commit some act condemned by law either as a separate federal offense or for purposes of the conspiracy statute.[44] The agreement may be evidenced by word or action; that is, the government may prove the existence of the agreement either by direct evidence or by circumstantial evidence from which the agreement may be inferred.[45] "Relevant circumstantial evidence [may] include[]: the joint appearance of defendants at transactions and negotiations in furtherance of the conspiracy; the relationship among codefendants; mutual representation of defendants to third parties; and other evidence suggesting unity of purpose or common design and understanding among conspirators to accomplish the objects of the conspiracy."[46]

The lower federal appellate courts have acknowledged that evidence of a mere buyer-seller relationship is insufficient to support a drug trafficking conspiracy charge. Some do so under the rationale that there is no singularity of purpose, no necessary agreement, in such cases: "the buyer's purpose is to buy; the seller's purpose is to sell."[47] Others do so to avoid sweeping mere customers into a large-scale trafficking operation.[48] Still others do so lest traffickers and their addicted customers face the same severe penalties.[49] All agree, however, that purchasers may be liable as conspirators when they are part of a large scheme.[50]

Again, in most cases the essence of conspiracy is agreement. "Nevertheless, mere association, standing alone, is inadequate; an individual does not become a member of a conspiracy merely associating with conspirators known to be involved in crime."[51]

One or Many Overlapping Conspiracies

The task of sifting agreement from mere association becomes more difficult and more important with the suggestion of overlapping conspiracies. Criminal enterprises may involve one or many conspiracies. Some time ago, the Supreme Court noted that "[t]hieves who dispose of their loot to a single receiver – a single 'fence' – do not by that fact alone become confederates: They may, but it takes more than knowledge that he is a 'fence' to make them such."[52] Whether it is a fence, or a drug dealer, or a money launderer, when several seemingly independent criminal groups share a common point of contact, the question becomes whether they present one overarching conspiracy or several separate conspiracies with a coincidental overlap. In the analogy suggested by the Court, when separate spokes meet at the common hub they can only function as a wheel if the spokes and hub are enclosed within a rim.[53] When several criminal enterprises overlap, they are one overarching conspiracy or several overlapping conspiracies depending upon whether they share a single unifying purpose and understanding—one common agreement.[54]

In determining whether they are faced with a single conspiracy or a rimless collection of overlapping schemes, the courts will look for "the existence of a common purpose ... (2) interdependence of various elements of the overall play; and (3) overlap among the participants."[55] "Interdependence is present if the activities of a defendant charged with conspiracy facilitated the endeavors of other alleged co-conspirators or facilitated the venture as a whole."[56]

If this common agreement exists, it is of no consequence that a particular conspirator joined the plot after its inception as long as he joined it knowingly and voluntarily.[57] Nor does it matter that a defendant does not know all of the details of a scheme or all of its participants, or that his role is relatively minor.[58]

Overt Acts

Conviction under 18 U.S.C. 371 for conspiracy to commit a substantive offense requires proof that one of the conspirators committed an overt act in furtherance of the conspiracy.[59] In the case of prosecution under other federal conspiracy statutes that have no such requirement, the existence of an overt act may be important for evidentiary and procedural reasons. The overt act need not be the substantive crime which is the object of the conspiracy, an element of that offense, nor even a crime in its own right.[60] Moreover, a single overt act by any of the conspirators in furtherance of plot will suffice.[61]

Conspiracy to Defraud the United States

Federal law contains several statutes that outlaw defrauding the United States. Two of the most commonly prosecuted are 18 U.S.C. 286, which outlaws conspiracy to defraud the United States through the submission of a false claim, and 18 U.S.C. 371, which in addition to conspiracies to violate federal law, outlaws conspiracies to defraud the United States of property or by obstructing the performance of its agencies. Section 371 has an overt act requirement;[62] section 286 does not.[63] The general principles of federal conspiracy law apply to both.[64]

The elements of conspiracy to defraud the United States under 18 U.S.C. 371 are (1) an agreement of two or more persons; (2) to defraud the United States; and (3) an overt act in furtherance of the conspiracy committed by one of the conspirators.[65] The "fraud covered by the statute reaches any conspiracy for the purpose of impairing, obstructing or defeating the lawful functions of any department of the Government"[66] by "deceit, craft or trickery, or at least by means that are dishonest."[67] The plot must be directed against the United States or some federal entity; a scheme to defraud the recipient of federal funds is not sufficient.[68] The scheme may be designed to deprive the United States of money or property, but it need not be so; a plot calculated to frustrate the functions of an entity of the United States will suffice.[69]

In contrast, a second federal statute, 18 U.S.C. 286, condemns conspiracies to defraud the United States of money or property through submission of a false claim.[70] The elements of a section 286 violation are that "the defendant entered into a conspiracy to obtain payment or allowance of a claim against a department or agency of the United States; (2) the claim was false, fictitious, or fraudulent; (3) the defendant knew or was deliberately ignorant of the claim's falsity, fictitiousness, or fraudulence; (4) the defendant knew of the conspiracy and intended to join it; and (5) the defendant voluntarily participated in the conspiracy."[71] Conviction does not require proof of an overt act in furtherance of the conspiracy.[72]

When Does it End

Conspiracy is a crime which begins with a scheme and may continue on until its objective is achieved or abandoned.[73] The liability of individual conspirators continues on from the time they joined the plot until it ends or until they withdraw.[74] The want of an individual's continued active participation is no defense as long as the underlying conspiracy lives and he has not withdrawn.[75] An individual who claims to have withdrawn bears the burden of establishing either that he took some action to make his departure clear to his co-conspirators or that he disclosed the scheme to the authorities.[76] As a general rule, overt acts of concealment do not extend the life of the conspiracy beyond the date of the accomplishment of its main objectives.[77] On the other hand, the rule does not apply when concealment is one of the main objectives of the conspiracy.[78]

Sanctions

Imprisonment and Fines

Section 371 felony conspiracies are punishable by imprisonment for not more than five years and a fine of not more than $250,000 (not more than $500,000 for organizations).[79] Most drug trafficking, terrorism, racketeering, and many white collar conspirators face the same penalties as those who committed the underlying substantive offense, e.g., 21 U.S.C. 846 ("Any person who ... conspires to commit any offense defined in [the Controlled Substances Act] shall be subject to the same penalties as those prescribed for the offense, the commission of which was the object of the ... conspiracy"); 18 U.S.C. 2339B ("Whoever knowingly provides material support or resources to a foreign terrorist organization ... . or conspires to do so, shall be fined under this title, or imprisoned not more than 15 years, or both"); 18 U.S.C. 1962(d), 1963(a)("(d) It shall be unlawful for any person to conspire to violate any of the [racketeering] provisions of subsection (a), (b), or (c) of this section.... (a) Whoever violates any provision of section 1962 ... shall be fined under this title, or imprisoned for not more than 20 years... or both"); 18 U.S.C. 1349 ("Any person who ... conspires to commit any offense under this chapter [relating to mail fraud, wire fraud, etc.] shall be subject to the same penalties as those prescribed for the offense, the commission of which was the object of ... the conspiracy").

The United States Sentencing Guidelines greatly influence the sentences for federal crimes. Federal courts are bound to impose a sentence within the statutory maximums and minimums. Their decision of what sentence to impose within those boundaries, however, must begin with a determination of the sentencing recommendation under the guidelines.[80] Reasonableness standards govern review of their sentencing decisions,[81] and a sentence within the Sentencing Guideline range is presumed reasonable.[82]

The Sentencing Guidelines system is essentially a scoring system. Federal crimes are each assigned a numerical base offense level and levels are added and subtracted to account for the various aggravating and mitigating factors in a particular case. Thus, for example, providing material support to a terrorist organization, 18 U.S.C. 2339B, has a base offense level of 26, which may be increased by 2 levels if the support comes in the form of explosives, U.S.S.G. §2M5.3(a), (b) and may be increased or decreased still further for other factors. The guidelines designate six sentencing ranges of each total offense level; the appropriate range within the six is determined by extent of the offender's criminal record. For instance, the sentencing range for a first-time offender with a total offense level of 28 would be imprisonment for between 78 and 97 months (Category I); while the range for an offender in the highest criminal history category (Category VI) would be imprisonment for between 140 and 175 months.[83]

The base offense level for conspiracy is generally the same as that for the underlying offense, either by operation of an individual guideline, for example, U.S.C. §2D1.1 (drug trafficking), or by operation of the general conspiracy guideline, U.S.S.C. §2X1.1. In any event, conspirators who play a leadership role in an enterprise are subject to an increase of from 2 to 4 levels, U.S.S.G. §3B1.1, and those who play a more subservient role may be entitled to reduction of from 2 to 4 levels, U.S.S.G. §3B1.2. In the case of terrorism offenses, conspirators may also be subject to a special enhancement which sets the minimum total offense level at 32 and the criminal history category at VI (regardless of the extent of the offender's criminal record), U.S.S.G. §3A1.4.[84]

The Sentencing Guidelines also address the imposition of fines below the statutory maximum. The total offense level dictates the recommended fine range for individual and organizational defendants. For instance, the fine range for an individual with a total offense level of 28 is $12,500 to $125,000, U.S.C. §5E1.2. The recommended fine range for an organization with a total offense level of 28 is $6,300,000 (assuming the loss or gain associated with the organization offense exceeds the usual $500,000 ceiling), U.S.S.G. §8C2.4.

Restitution

A conspirator's liability for restitution is a matter of circumstance. Most conspiracy statutes do not expressly provide for restitution, but in most instances restitution may be required or permitted under any number of grounds. As a general rule, federal law requires restitution for certain offenses and permits it for others. A sentencing court is generally required to order a defendant to make restitution following conviction for a crime of violence or for a crime against property (including fraud), 18 U.S.C. 366A(a), (c). Those entitled to restitution under Section 3663A include those "directly and proximately harmed" by the crime of conviction and "in the case of an offense that involves as an element a scheme, conspiracy, or pattern of criminal activity, any person directly harmed by the defendant's criminal conduct in the course of the scheme, conspiracy or pattern," 18 U.S.C. 3663A(b).[85]

Otherwise, a court is permitted to order restitution (a) following conviction for an offense prescribed under title 18 of the United States Code or for drug trafficking, 18 U.S.C. 3663;[86] (b) as a condition of probation or supervised release, 18 U.S.C. 3563(b)(2), 3583(d); or (c) pursuant to a plea agreement, 18 U.S.C. 3663(a)(3), 3663A(c)(2).[87]

Forfeiture

The treatment of forfeiture in conspiracy cases is perhaps even more individualistic than restitution in conspiracy cases. The general criminal forfeiture statute, 18 U.S.C. 982, authorizes confiscation for several classes of property as a consequence of a particular conspiracy conviction, for example, 18 U.S.C. 982(a)(2)(calling for the confiscation of proceeds realized from "a violation of, or a conspiracy to – (A) section ... 1341, 1343, 1344 of this title [relating to mail, wire and bank fraud], affecting a financial institution"); 18 U.S.C. 982(a)(8)(calling for the confiscation of proceeds from, and property used to facilitate or promote, "an offense under section ... 1341, or 1343, or of a conspiracy to commit such an offense, if the offense involves telemarketing").

In the case of drug trafficking, forfeiture turns on the fact that it is authorized for any Controlled Substance Act violation, 21 U.S.C. 853,[88] of which conspiracy is one, 21 U.S.C. 846. The same can be said of racketeering conspiracy provisions of 18 U.S.C. 1962(d).[89]

Relation of Conspiracy to Other Crimes

Conspiracy is a completed crime upon agreement, or upon agreement and the commission of an overt act under statutes with an overt act requirement. Conviction does not require commission of the crime that is the object of the conspiracy.[90] On the other hand, conspirators may be prosecuted for conspiracy, for any completed offense which is the object of the conspiracy, as well as for any foreseeable offense committed in furtherance of the conspiracy.[91]

Aid and Abet

Anyone who "aids, abets, counsels, commands, induces, or procures" the commission of a federal crime by another is punishable as a principal, that is, as though he had committed the offense himself, 18 U.S.C. 2. If the other agrees and an overt act is committed, they are conspirators, each liable for conspiracy and any criminal act committed to accomplish it. If the other commits the offense, they are equally punishable for the basic offense. "Typically, the same evidence will support both a conspiracy and an aiding and abetting conviction."[92] The two are clearly distinct, however, as the Ninth Circuit has noted:

> The difference between the classic common law elements of aiding and abetting and a criminal conspiracy underscores this material distinction, although at first blush the two appear similar. Aiding and abetting the commission of a specific crime, we have held, includes four elements: (1) that the accused had the specific intent to facilitate the commission of a crime by another, (2) that the accused had the requisite intent to commit the underlying substantive offense, (3) that the accused assisted or participated in the commission of the underlying substantive offense, and (4) that the principal committed the underlying offense. As *Lopez* emphasized, the accused generally must associate] himself with the venture ... participate[ ] in it as something he wish[es] to bring about, and [sought by] his action to make it succeed.
>
> By contrast, a classic criminal conspiracy as charged in 18 U.S.C. § 371 is broader. The government need only prove (1) an agreement to engage in criminal activity, (2) one or more overt acts taken to implement the agreement, and (3) the requisite intent to commit the substantive crime. Indeed, a drug conspiracy does not even require commission of an overt act in furtherance of the conspiracy.
>
> Two distinctions become readily apparent after a more careful comparison. First, the substantive offense which may be the object in a § 371 conspiracy need not be completed. Second, the emphasis in a § 371 conspiracy is on whether one or more overt acts was undertaken. This language necessarily is couched in passive voice for it matters only that a co-conspirator commit the overt act, not necessarily that the accused herself does so. In an aiding and abetting case, not only must the underlying *substantive offense* actually be completed by someone, but the accused must take some action, a *substantial step,* toward associating herself with the criminal venture. *United States v. Hernandez-Orellana*, 539 F.3d 994, 1006-1007 (9th Cir. 2008)(emphasis in the original).

Attempt

Conspiracy and attempt are both inchoate offenses, unfinished crimes in a sense. They are forms of introductory misconduct that the law condemns lest they result in some completed form of misconduct.[93] Federal law has no general attempt statute.[94] Congress, however, has outlawed attempt to commit a number of specific federal offenses.[95] Like conspiracy, a conviction for attempt does not require the commission of the underlying offense.[96] Both require an intent to commit the contemplated substantive offense.[97] Like conspiracy, the fact that it may be impossible to commit the target offense is no defense to a charge of attempt to commit it.[98] Unlike conspiracy, attempt can be committed by a single individual.[99] Attempt only becomes a crime when it closely approaches a substantive offense. Conspiracy becomes a crime far sooner. Mere acts of preparation will satisfy the most demanding conspiracy statute, not so with attempt.[100] Conspiracy requires no more than an overt act in furtherance; attempt, a substantial step to completion.[101] Moreover, unlike a conspirator, an accused may not be convicted of both attempt and the underlying substantive offense.[102]

An individual may be guilty of both conspiring with others to commit an offense and of attempting to commit the same offense, either himself or through his confederates.[103] In some circumstances, he may be guilty of attempted conspiracy. Congress has outlawed at least one example of an attempt to conspire in the statute which prohibits certain invitations to conspire, that is, solicitation to commit a federal crime of violence, 18 U.S.C. 373.

Solicitation

Section 373 prohibits efforts to induce another to commit a crime of violence "under circumstances strongly corroborative" of intent to see the crime committed, 18 U.S.C. 373(a). Section 373's crimes of violence are federal "felon[ies] that [have] as an element the use, attempted use, or threatened use of physical force against property or against the person of another," id.[104] Examples of "strongly corroborative" circumstances include "the defendant offering or promising payment or another benefit in exchange for committing the offense; threatening harm or other detriment for refusing to commit the offense; repeatedly soliciting or discussing at length in soliciting the commission of the offense, or making explicit that the solicitation is serious; believing or knowing that the persons solicited had previously committed similar offenses; and acquiring weapons, tools, or information or use in committing the offense, or making other apparent preparations for its commission."[105] As is the case of attempt, "[a]n individual cannot be guilty of both the solicitation of a crime and the substantive crime."[106] Although the crime of solicitation is complete upon communication with the requisite intent, renunciation prior to commission of the substantive offense is a defense.[107] The offender's legal incapacity to commit the solicited offense himself, however, is not a defense.[108]

Procedural Attributes

Statute of Limitations

The statute of limitations for most federal crimes is five years, 18 U.S.C. 3282.[109] The five-year limitation applies to the general conspiracy statute, 18 U.S.C. 371, and to the false claims conspiracy statute, 18 U.S.C. 286. Section 371 requires proof of an overt act;[110] section 286 does not.[111] For conspiracy offenses with an overt act requirement like those under Section 371, the statute of limitations begins with completion of the last overt act in furtherance of the conspiracy.[112] For conspiracy offenses with no such requirement like those under section 286, the statute of limitations begins with the abandonment of the conspiracy or the accomplishment of its objectives.[113]

Venue

The presence or absence of an overt act requirement makes a difference for statute of limitations purposes. For venue purposes, it apparently does not. The Supreme Court has observed in passing that "this Court has long held that venue is proper in any district in which an overt act in furtherance of the conspiracy was committed, even where an overt act is not a required element of the conspiracy offense."[114] The lower federal appellate courts are seemingly of the same view, for they have found venue proper for a conspiracy prosecution wherever an overt act occurs—under overt act statutes and non-overt act statutes alike.[115]

Joinder and Severance (One Conspiracy, One Trial)

Three rules of the Federal Rules of Criminal Procedure govern joinder and severance for federal criminal trials. Rule 8 permits the joinder of common criminal charges and defendants.[116] Rule 12 insists that a motion for severance be filed prior to trial.[117] Rule 14 authorizes the court to grant severance for separate trials as a remedy for prejudicial joinder.[118]

The Supreme Court has pointed out that "[t]here is a preference in the federal system for joint trials of defendants who are indicted together. Joint trials play a vital role in the criminal justice system. They promote efficiency and serve the interests of justice by avoiding the scandal and inequity of inconsistent verdicts."[119] In conspiracy cases, a "conspiracy charge combined with substantive counts arising out of that conspiracy is a proper basis for joinder under Rule 8(b)."[120] Moreover, "the preference in a conspiracy trial is that persons charged together should be tried together."[121] In fact, "it will be the rare case, if ever, where a district court should sever the trial of alleged co-conspirators."[122] The Supreme Court has reminded the lower courts that "a district court should grant a severance under Rule 14 only if there is a serious risk that a joint trial would compromise a specific trial right of one of the defendants, or prevent the jury from making a reliable judgment about guilt or innocence."[123] The Court noted that the risk may be more substantial in complex cases with multiple defendants, but that "less drastic measures, such as limiting instructions, often will suffice to cure any risk of prejudice."[124] Subsequently lower federal appellate court opinions have emphasized the curative effect of appropriate jury instructions.[125]

Double Jeopardy and Ex Post Facto

Because conspiracy is a continuing offense, it stands as an exception to the usual ex post facto principles. Because it is a separate crime, it also stands as an exception to the usual double jeopardy principles.

The ex post facto clauses of the Constitution forbid the application of criminal laws which punish conduct that was innocent when it was committed or punishes more severely criminal conduct than when it was committed.[126] Increasing the penalty for an ongoing conspiracy, however, does not offend ex post facto constraints as long as the conspiracy straddles the date of the legislative penalty enhancement.[127]

The double jeopardy clause of the Fifth Amendment declares that no person shall "be subject for the same offence to be twice put in jeopardy of life or limb."[128] This prohibition condemns successive prosecutions, successive punishments, and successive use of charges rejected in acquittal.[129]

For successive prosecution or punishment, the critical factor is the presence or absence of the same offense. Offenses may overlap, but they are not the same crime as long as each requires proof of an element that the other does not.[130] Since conspiracy and its attendant substantive offense are ordinarily separate crimes—one alone requiring agreement and the other alone requiring completion of the substantive offense—the double jeopardy clause poses no impediment to successive prosecution or to successive punishment of the two.[131]

Double jeopardy issues arise most often in a conspiracy context when a case presents the question of whether the activities of the accused conspirators constitute a single conspiracy or several overlapping conspiracies. Multiple conspiracies may be prosecuted sequentially and punished with multiple sanctions; single conspiracies must be tried and punished once. Asked to determine whether they are faced with one or more than one conspiracy, the courts have said they inquire whether:

1. the *locus criminis* [place] of the two alleged conspiracies is the same;
2. there is a significant degree of *temporal overlap* between the two conspiracies charged;
3. there is an overlap of personnel between the two conspiracies (including unindicted as well as indicted co-conspirators);
4. the over acts charged [are related];
5. the *role played* by the defendant [relates to both];
6. there was a common goal among the conspirators;
7. whether the agreement contemplated bringing to pass a continuous result that will not continue without the continuous cooperation of the conspirators; and
8. the extent to which the participants overlap[ped] in [their] various dealings.[132]

Co-conspirator Declarations

At trial, the law favors the testimony of live witnesses—under oath, subject to cross examination, and in the presence of the accused and the jury—over the presentation of their evidence in writing or through the mouths of others. The hearsay rule is a product of this preference. Exceptions and definitions narrow the rule's reach. For example, hearsay is usually defined to include only those out-of-court statements which are offered in evidence "to prove the truth of the matter asserted."[133]

Although often referred to as the exception for co-conspirator declarations, the Federal Rules of Evidence treats the matter within its definition of hearsay. Thus, Rule 801(d)(2)(E) of the Federal Rules provides that an out-of-court "statement is not hearsay if ... (2) The statement is offered against a party and is ... (E) a statement by a coconspirator of a party during the course and in furtherance of the conspiracy."

To admit a co-conspirator declaration into evidence under the Rule, a "court must find: (1) the conspiracy existed; (2) the defendant was a member of the conspiracy; and (3) the co-conspirator made the proffered statements in furtherance of the conspiracy."[134] The court, however, may receive the statement preliminarily subject to the prosecution's subsequent demonstration of its admissibility by a preponderance of the evidence.[135] As to the first two elements, a coconspirator's statement without more is insufficient; there must be "some extrinsic evidence sufficient to delineate the conspiracy and corroborate the declarant's and the defendant's roles in it."[136] As to the third element, "[a] statement is in furtherance of a conspiracy if it is intended to promote the objectives of the conspiracy."[137] A statement is in furtherance, for instance, if it describes for the benefit of a co-conspirator the status of the scheme, its participants, or its methods.[138] Bragging, or "mere idle chatter or casual conversation about past events," however, are not considered statements in furtherance of a conspiracy.[139]

Under some circumstances, evidence admissible under the hearsay rule may nevertheless be inadmissible because of Sixth Amendment restrictions. The Sixth Amendment provides, among other things, that "[i]n all criminal prosecutions, the accused shall enjoy the right ... to be confronted with the witnesses against him." The provision was inspired in part by reactions to the trial of Sir Walter Raleigh, who argued in vain that he should be allowed to confront the alleged co-conspirator who had accused him of treason.[140] Given its broadest possible construction, the confrontation clause would eliminate any hearsay exceptions or limitations.[141] The Supreme Court in *Crawford v. Washington* explained, however, that the clause has a more precise reach. The clause uses the word "witnesses" to bring within its scope only those who testify or whose accusations are made in a testimonial context. In a testimonial context, the confrontation clause permits use at trial of prior testimonial accusations only if the witness is unavailable and only if the accused had the opportunity to cross examine him when the testimony was taken.[142] The Court elected to "leave for another day any effort to spell out a comprehensive definition of 'testimonial,'"[143] but has suggested that the term includes "affidavits, depositions, prior testimony, or confessions [,and other] statements that were made under circumstances which would lead an objective witness reasonably to believe that the statement would be available for use at a later trial."[144]

Since *Crawford*, the lower federal courts have generally held that the confrontation clause poses no obstacle to the admissibility of the co-conspirator statements at issue in the cases before them, either because the statements were not testimonial;[145] were not offered to establish the truth of the asserted statement;[146] or because the clause does not bar co-conspirator declarations generally.[147]

End Notes

[1] Zacarias Moussaoui was convicted of conspiring to commit the terrorist attacks that occurred on September 11, 2001, *United States v. Moussaoui*, 591 F.3d 263, 266 (4th Cir. 2010); Wadih El-Hage was convicted of conspiring to bomb the U.S. embassies in Kenya and Tanzania, *In re Terrorist Bombings*, 552 F.3d 93, 107 (2d Cir. 2008).

Members of an Atlanta street gang were convicted of conspiring to engage in drug trafficking, among other offenses, *United States v. Flores*, 572 F.3d 1254, 1258 (11th Cir. 2009); motorcycle gang members were convicted of conspiracy to traffic in drugs, *United States v. Deitz*, 577 F.3d 672, 675-76 (6th Cir. 2009).

Dominick Pizzponia was convicted on racketeering conspiracy charges in connection with the activities of the "Gambino organized crime family of La Cosa Nostra," *United States v. Pizzonia*, 577 F.3d 455, 459 (2d Cir. 2009); Michael Yannotti was also convicted on racketeering conspiracy in connection with activities of the "Gambino Crime Family," *United States v. Yannotti*, 541 F.3d 112, 115-16 (2d Cir. 2008).

Jeffrey Skilling, a former Enron Corporation executive, was convicted of conspiracy to commit securities fraud and mail fraud, *United States v. Skilling*, 554 F.3d 529, 534 (5th Cir. 2009); Bernanrd Ebbers, a former WorldCom, Inc. executive, was likewise convicted of conspiracy to commit securities fraud, *United States v. Ebbers*, 458 F.3d 110, 112 (2d Cir. 2006).

[2] *Iannelli v. United States*, 420 U.S. 770, 778 (1975), quoting *Callanan v. United States*, 364 U.S. 587, 593-94 (1961).

[3] *Id.*

[4] *Id.*

[5] *Id.*

There have long been contrary views, e.g., Sayre, *Criminal Conspiracy*, 35 HARVARD LAW REVIEW 393, 393 (1922)("A doctrine so vague in its outlines and uncertain in its fundamental nature as criminal conspiracy lends no strength or glory to the law; it is a veritable quicksand of shifting opinion and ill-considered thought"); *Hyde v. United States*, 222 U.S. 347, 387 (1912)(Holmes, J, with Lurton, Hughes 7 Lamarr, JJ.)(dissenting)("And as wherever two or more have united for the commission of a crime there is a conspiracy, the opening to oppression thus made is very wide indeed. It is even wider if success should be held not to merge the conspiracy in the crime intended and achieved"), both quoted in substantial part in Katyal, *Conspiracy Theory*, 112 YALE LAW JOURNAL 1307, 1310 n. 6 (2003).

[6] Federal prosecutors have used, and been encouraged to use, the law available to them, *Harrison v. United States*, 7 F.2d 259, 263 (2d Cir. 1925)("[C]onspiracy, that darling of the modern prosecutor's nursery"); *United States v. Reynolds*, 919 F.2d 435, 439 ("[P]rosecutors seem to have conspiracy on their word processors as Count I"); Chesney, *Terrorism, Criminal Prosecution, and the Preventive Detention Debate*, 50 SOUTH TEXAS LAW REVIEW 669, 684 (2009)("What options do prosecutors have in the terrorism-prevention scenario when [other charges] are unavailable for lack of evidence linking the suspect to a designated foreign terrorist organization? One possibility is conspiracy liability").

[7] 18 U.S.C. 241 (civil rights conspiracies); 21 U.S.C. 846 (drug trafficking conspiracies).

[8] *Iannelli v. United States*, 420 U.S. 770, 777 (1975).

[9] *United States v. Rehak*, 589 F.3d 965, 971 (8th Cir. 2009); *United States v. Scaffer*, 586 F.3d 414, 423 (6th Cir. 2009); *United States v. Wittig*, 575 F.3d 1085, 1104 (10th Cir. 2009).

[10] *Whitfield v. United States*, 543 U.S. 209, 219 (2005)(18 U.S.C. 1956(h)—conspiracy to commit money laundering—has no overt act requirement); *United States v. Shabani*, 513 U.S. 10, 13-4 (1994)(21 U.S.C. 846—conspiracy to violate the Controlled Substances Act—has no overt act requirement).

[11] E.g., 18 U.S.C. 956 (conspiracy in the U.S. to commit certain violent acts overseas, acts which ordinarily are crimes under the laws of the place where they occur but which need not be separate federal crimes for purposes of a prosecution under section 956). Although it is generally known for its proscription against conspiracies to violate other federal laws, Section 371 also outlaws conspiracies to defraud the United States. Conviction under the defraud portion of Section 371 does not require that the underlying misconduct be a separate federal crime.

[12] The 20-year maximum penalties of section 1956 apply to conspiracies to launder and to the underlying laundering offense alike, 18 U.S.C. 1956(h). The penalties that apply to drug trafficking under 21 U.S.C. 841 (up to life imprisonment) apply with equal force to conspiracies to traffic, 21 U.S.C. 846.

[13] *Salinas v. United States*, 522 U.S. 52, 63 (1997).

[14] *United States v. Jimenez Recio*, 537 U.S.270, 274 (2003).

[15] *Pinkerton v. United States*, 328 U.S. 640, 647 (1946).

[16] F.R.Evid. 801(d)(2)(E).

[17] *Toussie v. United States*, 397 U.S. 112, 122 (1970)(statute of limitations begins to run with the last overt act in furtherance of the conspiracy); *Whitfield v. United States,* 543 U.S. 209, 218 (2005)(venue is proper in any district in which an overt act in furtherance of the conspiracy was committed).

[18] *Salinas v. United States*, 522 U.S. 52, 65 (1997)("conspiracy is a distinct evil, dangerous to the public, and so punishable in itself"); *United States v. Felix*, 503 U.S. 378, 390 (1992)("[T]he commission of the substantive offense and a conspiracy to commit it are separate and distinct offenses ... [a]nd the plea of double jeopardy is no defense to a conviction for both offenses"); *United States v. Munoz-Franco*, 487 F.3d 25, 55 (1st Cir. 2007)("For 'continuing offenses' such as the bank fraud and conspiracy charges at issue here, however, the critical question is when the conduct ended. As we have explained, where a 'continuing offense' straddles the old and new law ... applying the new is recognized as constitutionally sound. In other words, a conviction for a continuing offense straddling enactment of a statute will not run afoul of the Ex Post Facto clause unless it was possible for the jury, following the court's instructions, to convict '*exclusively*' on pre-enactment conduct")(here and hereafter internal citations and quotation marks have been omitted unless otherwise indicated).

[19] See generally, Bryan, THE DEVELOPMENT OF THE ENGLISH LAW OF CONSPIRACY (1909); Winfield, *The History of Conspiracy and Abuse of Legal Process*, CAMBRIDGE STUDIES IN ENGLISH LEGAL HISTORY (1921); Sayre, *Criminal Conspiracy*, 35 HARVARD LAW REVIEW 393 (1922).

[20] IV BLACKSTONE, COMMENTARIES ON THE LAWS OF ENGLAND 136 (1769) (transliteration supplied)("A conspiracy also to indict an innocent man of felony falsely and maliciously, who is accordingly indicted and acquitted, is a farther abuse and perversion of public justice; for which the party injured may either have a civil action by writ of the conspirators... or the conspirators, for there must be at least two to form a conspiracy, may be indicted at the suit of the king").

[21] III CHITTY, A PRACTICAL TREATISE ON THE CRIMINAL LAW 1138 (3d Am. ed. 1839) noting that conspiracy included combinations "to commence suits against a person with a view to extorting money from him" or "to manufacture a base material in the form and color of genuine indigo, with the intent to sell it as indigo" or to cheat a man "by making him drunk and playing falsely at cards with him, but did not include combinations "to obtain money from a bank by drawing their checks on the bank when they have no funds there" or "to cheat and defraud a man by selling him an unsound horse." Of course, this is not a situation limited to the law of conspiracy.

[22] Act of April 30, 1790, ch. IX, §12, 1 Stat. 114 (1790).

[23] *United States v. Hamilton*, 26 Fed.Cas. 259, 260 (C.C.D.Mass. 1825)(No. 15,346).

[24] Act of March 3, 1825, ch.65, §23, 4 Stat. 122 (1825)(conspiracy "to cast away, burn, or otherwise destroy, ship or vessel... with intent to injure any person ... that hath underwritten ... any policy of insurance thereon.").

[25] Act of July 31, 1861, c. 33, 12 Stat. 284 (1861), as amended 18 U.S.C. 2384.

[26] Act of March 2, 1863, c.67, §§1, 3, 12 Stat. 696, 698 (1863), as amended, 18 U.S.C. 286.

[27] Act of March 2, 1867, c.169, §30, 14 Stat. 484 (1867)("that if two or more persons conspire either to commit any offence against the laws of the United States, or to defraud the United States in any manner whatever, and one or more of said parties to said conspiracy shall do any act to effect the object thereof, the parties to said conspiracy shall be deemed guilty of a misdemeanor, and on conviction thereof shall be liable to a penalty of note less than one thousand dollars and not more than ten thousand dollars, and to imprisonment not exceeding two years. And when any offence shall be begun in one judicial district of the United State and completed in another, every such offence shall be deemed to be committed in either of the said districts, and may be dealt with, inquired of, tried, determined and punished in either of the said district, in the same manner as if it had been actually and wholly committed therein"), as amended 18 U.S.C. 371.

[28] Act of April 20, 1871, c. 22, §2, 17 Stat. 13, 14 (1871), as amended, 18 U.S.C. 241.

[29] Act of July 2, 1890, c. 647, §§1, 2, 3, 26 Stat. 209 (1890), as amended, 15 U.S.C. 1, 2, 3.

[30] P.L. 91-513, Tit. II, §406, 84 Stat. 1265 (1970), as amended, 21 U.S.C. 846, and P.L. 91-452, Tit. IX, §901(a), 84 Stat. 942 (1970), as amended, 18 U.S.C. 1962(d), respectively.

[31] *Rogers v. United States*, 340 U.S. 367, 375 (1951)("at least two persons are required to constitute a conspiracy"); *United States v. Dumeisi*, 424 F.3d 566, 580 (7th Cir. 2005)("the elements of the crime of conspiracy are not satisfied unless one conspires with at least one true co-conspirator").

[32] *Dawson v. United States*, 10 F.2d 106, 107 (9th Cir. 1926).

[33] *United States v. Dege*, 364 U.S. 51, 54-5 (1960).

[34] I BLACKSTONE, COMMENTARIES ON THE LAWS OF ENGLAND 464 (1765) (transliteration supplied)("a corporation cannot commit treason, or felony, or other crime, in it's corporate capacity: though it's members, may, in their distinct individual capacities").

[35] *United States v. Singh*, 518 F.3d 236, 249-51 (4th Cir. 2008); *United States v. Hughes Aircraft Co.*, 20 F.3d 974, 978-80 (9th Cir. 1994).

[36] *United States v. Sain*, 141 F.3d 463, 474-75 (3d Cir. 1998); *United States v. Stevens*, 909 F.2d 431, 432-35 (6th Cir. 1990).

[37] *United States v. Sanchez-Garcia*, 461 F.3d 939, 946 (8th Cir. 2006); *United States v. Price*, 258 F.3d 539, 545 (6th Cir. 2001); *United States v. Contreras*, 249 F/3d 595, 598 (7th Cir. 2001).

[38] *United States v. Lo*, 447 F.3d 1212, 1226 (9th Cir. 2006); *United States v. Johnson*, 440 F.3d 1286, 1294-295 (11th Cir. 2006); *United States v. Morton*, 412 F.3d 901, 904 (8th Cir. 2005).

[39] *Salinas v. United States*, 522 U.S. 52, 64 (1997); *United States v. Moussaoui*, 591 F.3d 263, 297 (4th Cir. 2010); *United States v. Zichettello*, 208 F.3d 72, 99 (2d Cir. 2000).

[40] *United States v. Wright*, 506 F.3d 1293, 1298 n.4 (10th Cir. 2007)("Wharton's Rule is that an agreement by two persons to commit a particular crime cannot be prosecuted as conspiracy when the crime is of such a nature as to necessarily require the participation of two persons for its commission").

[41] *Iannelli v. United States*, 420 U.S. 770, 781-82 (1975); *United States v. Bornman*, 559 F.3d 150, 156 (3d Cir. 2009).

[42] *United States v. Bornman*, 559 F.3d at 156 ("In the classic Wharton's Rule offenses – adultery, bigamy, incest, and duelling – the harms attendant upon the commission of the substantive offense are restricted to the parties in the agreement. Hence, Wharton's Rule has no applicability here [to bribery]"); *United States v. Hines*, 541 F.3d 833, 838 (8th Cir. 2008)(""Wharton's Rule ... applies when there is a general congruence of the conspiracy agreement and the completed substantive offense. This general congruence exists when the parties to the agreement are the only persons who participate in commission of the substantive offense, ... the immediate consequences of the crime rest on the parties themselves rather than on society at large, and when the agreement that attends the substantive offense does not appear like to pose the distinct kinds of threats to society that the law of conspiracy seeks to avert").

[43] *United States v. Corson*, 579 F.3d 804, 811 (7th Cir. 2009); *United States v. Paret-Ruiz*, 567 F.3d 1, 6 (1st cir. 2009); *United States v. Williams*, 547 F.3d 1187, 1195 n.7 (9th Cir. 2008).

[44] *United States v. Jimenez Recio*, 537 U.S.270, 274 (2003), citing, *Iannelli v. United States*, 420 U.S. 770, 777 (1975); *United States v. Corson*, 579 F.3d 804, 810 (7th Cir. 2009); *United States v. Chavez*, 549 F.3d 119, 125 (2d Cir. 2008)("The essence of any conspiracy, of course, is agreement").

[45] *United States v. Rodriguez-Velez*, 597 F.3d 32, 39 (1st Cir. 2010); *United States v. Johnson*, 592 F.3d 749, 754-55 (7th Cir. 2010); *United States v. Boria*, 592 F.3d 476, 481 (3d Cir. 2010); *United States v. Wardell*, 591 F.3d 1279, 1287 (10th Cir. 2009).

[46] *United States v. Wardell*, 591 F.3d at 1287-288.

[47] *United States v. Donnell*, 596 F.3d 913, 924-25 (8th Cir. 2010)("Mere proof of a buyer-seller agreement without any prior or contemporaneous understanding does not support a conspiracy conviction because there is no common illegal purpose: In such circumstances, the buyer's purpose is to buy; and the seller's purpose is to sell"); *United States v. Bacon*, 598 F.3d 772, 777 (11th Cir. 2010)("... the joint objective necessary for a conspiracy conviction is missing where the conspiracy is based simply on an agreement between a buyer and a seller for the sale of drugs").

[48] *United States v. Johnson*, 592 F.3d 749, 754 (7th Cir. 2010)("When the alleged coconspirators are in a buyer-seller relationship, however, we have cautioned against conflating the underlying buy-sell agreement with the drug-distribution agreement that is alleged to form the basis of the charge conspiracy. To support a conspiracy conviction there must be sufficient evidence of an agreement to commit a crime other than the crime that consists of the sale itself"); *United States v. Deitz*, 577 F.3d 672, 680 (6th Cir. 2009)("Generally, a buyer-seller relationship alone is insufficient to tie a buyer to a [larger] conspiracy because mere sales do not prove the existence of the agreement that must exist for there to be a conspiracy").

[49] *United States v. Parker*, 554 F.3d 230, 234-35 (2d Cir. 2009)("As a literal matter, when a buyer purchases illegal drugs from a seller, two persons have agreed to a concerted effort to achieve the unlawful transfer of the drugs from the seller to the buyer. According to the customary definition, that would constitute a conspiracy with the alleged objective of a transfer of drugs. Our case law, however, has carved out a narrow exception to the general conspiracy rule for such transactions... . [If] an addicted purchaser, who acquired drugs for his own use and without intent to distribute it to others, were deemed to have joined a conspiracy with his seller for the illegal transfer of the drugs form the seller to himself, the purchaser would be guilty of substantially the same crime, and liable for the same punishment, as the seller. The policy to distinguish between transfer of an illegal drug and the acquisition of possession of the drug would be frustrated. The buyer-seller exception thus protects a buyer or transferee from the severe liabilities intended only for transferors").

[50] *United States v. Bacon*, 598 F.3d. at 777 ("Jamison was highly involved in the drug operation.... Jamison's drug transactions were larger than those that an ordinary buyer would make... . From this evidence, the jurors could reasonably infer that Jamison was a distributor"); *United States v. Johnson*, 592 F.3d at 754 ("Articulating this principle is somewhat easier than applying it; it is often difficult to determine what proof is sufficient to establish that individuals in a buyer-seller relationship also agreed to distribute drugs. Certain characteristics inherent in any ongoing buyer-seller relationships will also generally suggest the existence of a conspiracy. For example, sales of large quantities or drugs, repeated and/or standardized transactions, and a prolonged relationship between the parties constitute circumstantial evidence of a conspiracy"); *United States v. Parker*, 554 F.3d at 235 ("While providing that the unlawful transfer from seller to buyer cannot serve as the basis for a charge that the seller and buyer conspired with one another to make the illegal transfer from seller to buyer,

the rule does not protect either the seller or buyer from a charge they conspired together to transfer drugs if the evidence supports a finding that they shared a conspiratorial purpose to advance other transfers, whether by the seller or by the buyer").

[51] *Id.* at 1288; see also *United States v. Tran*, 568 F.3d 1156, 1165 9th Cir. 2009).

[52] *Kotteakos v. United States*, 328 U.S. 750, 755 (1946).

[53] *Id.* at 754-55("As the Circuit Court of Appeals said, there were at least eight, and perhaps more, separate and independent groups, none of which had any connection with any other, though all dealt independently with Brown as their agent. As the Government puts it, the pattern was that of separate spokes meeting at a common center, though, we may add, without the rim of the wheel to enclose the spokes").

[54] *United States v. Brown*, 587 F.3d 1082, 1089 (11th Cir. 2009)("Separate transactions are not necessarily separate conspiracies, so long as the conspirators act in concert to further a common goal. If a defendant's actions facilitated the endeavors of others co-conspirators, or facilitated the venture as a whole, a single conspiracy is established"); *United States v. Baldridge*, 559 F.3d 1126, 1136 (10th Cir. 2009)(emphasis in the original) ("A single conspiracy does not exist solely because many individuals deal with a common central player. What is required is a *shared* single criminal objective, not just similar or parallel objectives between similarly situated people").

[55] *United States v. Calderon*, 578 F.3d 78, 89 (1st Cir. 2009); see also *United States v. Franklin*, 561 F.3d 632, 402 (5th Cir. 2009); *United States v. Brown*, 587 F.3d 1082, 1089 (11th Cir. 2009).

[56] *United States v. Wardell*, 591 F.3d 1279, 1291 (10th Cir. 2009).

[57] *United States v. Johnson*, 592 F.3d 749, 754 (7th Cir. 2010)("To convict a defendant of conspiracy, the government must prove that (1) two or more people agreed to commit an unlawful act, and (2) the defendant knowingly and intentionally joined in the agreement"); *United States v. Boria*, 592 F.3d 476, 481 (3d Cir. 2010); *United States v. Franklin*, 561 F.3d at 402.

[58] *United States v. Reed*, 575 F.3d 900, 924 (9th Cir. 2009)("Once a conspiracy is established, only a slight connection to the conspiracy is necessary to support conviction. The term slight connection means that a defendant need not have known all the conspirators, participated in the conspiracy from its beginning, participated in all its enterprises, or known all its details"); *United States v. Brown*, 587 F.3d at 1089; *United States v. Robinson*, 547 F.3d 632, 642 (6th Cir. 2009); *United States v. Eppolito*, 543 F.3d 25, 47-8 (2d Cir. 2008).

[59] 18 U.S.C. 371 ("and one or more of such persons do any act to effect the object of the conspiracy"); *United States v. Wardell*, 591 F.3d 1279, 1287 (10th Cir. 2009); *United States v. Schaffer*, 586 F.3d 414, 422 (6th Cir. 2009); *United States v. Kingrea*, 573 F.3d 186, 195 (4th Cir. 2009).

[60] *Braverman v. United States*, 317 U.S. 49, 53 (1942); *United States v. Rehak*, 589 F.3d 965, 971 (8th Cir. 2009); *United States v. Soy*, 454 F.3d 766, 768 (7th Cir. 2006); *United States v. Lukens*, 114 F.3d 1220, 1222 (D.C.Cir. 1997).

[61] *United States v. LaSpina*, 299 F.3d 165, 176 (2d Cir. 2002); *United States v. Schlei*, 122 F.3d 944, 975 (11th Cir. 1997); *United States v. Nelson*, 66 F.3d 1036, 1044 (9th Cir. 1995).

[62] See note 55 and accompanying text.

[63] *United States v. Saybolt*, 577 F.3d 195, 202 (3d Cir. 2009); *United States v. Dedman*, 527 F.3d 577, 594 n.7 (6th Cir. 2008); *United States v. Lanier*, 920 F.2d 887, 892 (11th Cir. 1991).

[64] See generally Goldstein, *Conspiracy to Defraud the United States*, 68 YALE LAW JOURNAL 405 (1958).

[65] *United States v. Root*, 585 F.3d 145, 157 (3d Cir. 2009); *United States v. World Wide Moving, N.V.*, 411 F.3d 502, 516 (4th Cir. 2005).

[66] *Tanner v. United States*, 483 U.S. 107, 128 (1987), citing, *Dennis v. United States*, 384 U.S. 855, 861 (1966); *Glasser v. United States*, 315 U.S. 60, 66 (1942); *Hammerschmidt v. United States*, 265 U.S. 182, 188 (1924); and *Haas v. Henkel*, 216 U.S. 462, 479 (1910).

[67] *Glasser v. United States*, 315 U.S. at 66; *Hammerschmidt v. United States*, 265 U.S. at 188; *United States v. Stewart*, 590 F.3d 93, 109 (2d Cir. 2009)("In order to establish a conspiracy-to-defraud offense under 18 U.S.C. §371 ... a reasonable jury must have been able to conclude beyond a reasonable doubt (1) that the defendants entered into an agreement (2) to obstruct a lawful function of the government in this case, the administration and enforcement of the SAMs (3) by deceitful or dishonest means and (4) at least one overt act in furtherance of the conspiracy").

[68] *Tanner v. United States*, 483 U.S. 107, 128-32 (1987); *United States v. Mendez*, 528 F.3d. 811, 814-15 (11th Cir. 2008).

[69] *Hammerschmidt v. United States*, 265 U.S. at 188 ("It is not necessary that the government shall be subjected to property or pecuniary loss by the fraud, but only that its legitimate official action and purpose shall be defeated by misrepresentation"); *United States v. Ballistrea*, 101 F.3d 827, 832 (2d Cir. 1996)(This provision not only reaches schemes which deprive the government of money or property, but also is designed to protect the integrity of the United States and its agencies"); *United States v. Dean*, 55 F.3d 640, 647 (D.C. Cir. 1995)("If the government's evidence showed that Dean conspired to impair the functioning of the Department of Housing and Urban Development, no other form of injury to the Federal Government need be established for the conspiracy to fall under §371").

[70] "Whoever enters into any agreement, combination, or conspiracy to defraud the United States, or any department or agency thereof, by obtaining or aiding to obtain the payment or allowance of any false, fictitious, or fraudulent claim, shall be fined under this title or imprisoned not more than ten years, or both," 18 U.S.C. 286.

[71] *United States v. Dedman*, 527 F.3d 577, 593-94 (6th Cir. 2008). At least one other circuit also includes a materiality requirement, *i.e.*, the false, fictitious, or fraudulent assertion must be one which naturally have a material effect on the government's decision to pay or deny the claim, *United States v. Saybolt*, 577 F.3d 195, 201-204 (3d Cir. 2009).

[72] *United States v. Saybolt*, 577 F.3d 195, 202 (3d Cir. 2009); *United States v. Dedman*, 527 F.3d 577, 594 n.7 (6th Cir. 2008); *United States v. Lanier*, 920 F.2d 887, 892 (11th Cir. 1991).

[73] *United States v. Payne*, 591 F.3d 46, 69 (2d Cir. 2010)("Conspiracy is a continuing offense ... one that involves a prolonged course of conduct; its commission is not complete until the conduct has run its course"); *United States v. Caldwell*, 589 F.3d 1323, 1330 (10th Cir. 2009).

[74] *United States v. Hodge*, 594 F.3d 614, 619 (8th Cir. 2010); *United States v. Caldwell*, 589 F.3d at 1330; *United States v. Egbert*, 562 F.3d 1092, 1098 (10th Cir. 2009).

[75] *United States v. Hodge*, 594 F.3d at 619; *United States v. Mangual-Santiago*, 562 F.3d 411, 423 (1st Cir. 2009); *United States v. Eppolito*, 543 F.3d 25, 49 (2d Cir. 2008).

[76] *United States v. Gonzalez*, 596 F.3d 1228, 1234 (10th Cir. 2010)("The defense of termination by withdrawal requires that the defendant show that he or she has done some act to disavow or defeat the purpose of the conspiracy. Affirmative acts inconsistent with the object of the conspiracy and communicated in a manner reasonably calculated to reach co-conspirators have generally been regarded as sufficient to establish withdrawal"); *United States v. Spotted Elk*, 548 F.3d 641, 673 (8th Cir. 2008)("To withdraw from a conspiracy at common law, a conspirator must show not only that he ceased activities in furtherance of the conspiracy, but also that he either made a 'clean breast' to the government or else communicated the fact of withdrawal to his co-conspirators in a manner reasonably calculated to reach them"); *United States v. Eppolito*, 543 F.3d at 49.

[77] *United States v. Bornman*, 559 F.3d 150, 153 (3d Cir. 2009), citing *Grunewald v. United States*, 353 U.S. 391, 413 (1957); *United States v. Turner*, 548 F.3d 1094, 1097 (D.C. Cir. 2008).

[78] *United States v. Upton*, 559 F.3d 3, 10 (1st Cir. 2009); *United States v. Weaver*, 507 F.3d 178, 185-86 (3d cir. 2007).

[79] 18 U.S.C. 371, 3571. An offender may fined twice of the amount of the gain or loss associated with the offense, even when such a fined would exceed the otherwise applicable $250,000/$500,000 maximums, 18 U.S.C. 3571(b)(2), (d).

[80] *Gall v. United States*, 552 U.S. 38, 49 (2007).

[81] *Gall v. United States*, 552 U.S. at 46, citing *United States v. Booker*, 543 U.S. 220, 260-62 (2005).

[82] *Rita v. United States*, 551 U.S. 338, 347 (2007).

[83] U.S.S.G. Sentencing Table.

[84] E.g., *United States v. Stewart*, 590 F.3d 93, 136 (2d Cir. 2009)("The district court initially calculated Yousry's Guidelines range based on a total offense level of 28 criminal history category of I, for a range of 78 to 97 months. According to the government, Yousry's applicable Guidelines range should have been enhanced in accordance with the terrorism enhancement provided by the Guidelines, U.S.S.G. §3A1.4. The district court concluded to the contrary that the terrorism enhancement did not apply to Yousry because he did not act with the requisite state of mind.).

[85] *United States v. Farish*, 535 F.3d 815, 826 (8th Cir. 2008)("If the jury had clearly convicted Farish of conspiracy to commit arson at the Diamond Lake Road West home, then the district court's entire restitution order would have been appropriate"); *United States v. Brock-Davis*, 504 F.3d 991, 999 (9th Cir. 2007)("Even were the law of restitution not more expansive for convictions for conspiracy than for other crimes, the district would not have committed error [in ordering restitution pursuant to a conspiracy conviction].... Finally, [omission] in the indictment is immaterial ... *United States v. Boyd*, 222 F.3d 47, 50 (2d Cir. 2000)(finding restitution payable under the MVRA [18 U.S.C. 3663A] 'by all convicted co-conspirators in respect of damage suffered by all victims of a conspiracy, regardless of the facts underlying courts of conviction in individual prosecutions')").

[86] *United States v. Gutierrez-Avascal*, 542 F.3d 495, 498 (5th Cir. 2008)("The language of [21 U.S.C. 846] is clear: those convicted of a conspiracy are subject to the same punishment as the target of that conspiracy. It is undisputed that a district court, in its discretion, has authority under [18 U.S.C. 3663] to order a defendant convicted under § 841 to pay restitution. The same authority exists, under the express terms of § 846, against those who conspire to commit that crime"); *United States v. Lanzotti*, 205 F.3d 951, 958 (7th Cir. 2000)("In other words, the burden is on the defendant to show why restitution [under 18 U.S.C. 3663] is not warranted.... Lanzotti, as a member of the conspiracy, is liable for the actions of his co-conspirators, which includes restitution where appropriate. *United States v. Brewer*, 983 F.2d 181, 185 (10th Cir. 1993); *United States v. Chaney*, 964 F.2d 437, 452-53 (5th Cir. 1992)").

[87] *United States v. Elson*, 577 F.3d 713, 724-25 (6th Cir. 2009)("Elson's plea agreement explicitly provides that Elson will 'pay restitution to victims of the conspiracy to defraud orchestrated by Richard D. Schultz (J.A. 209), which is an offense different from his offense conviction – conspiracy to obstruct a grand jury

investigation.... Accordingly, the district court properly ordered Elson to pay restitution to the victims of the conspiracy to defraud Schultz's creditors").

[88] 21 U.S.C. 853(a)("Any person convicted of a violation of this subchapter [the Controlled Substances Act]... shall forfeit ... (1) any property constituting... any proceeds... . the result of such violation; (2) any ... property used ... to commit, or to facilitate the commission of, such violation...").

[89] 18 U.S.C. 1963(a)("Whoever violates any provision of section 1962 ... shall forfeit to the United States... (3) any property constituting... any proceeds ... obtained ... from racketeering activity ... in violation of section 1962").

[90] *United States v. Jimenez Recio*, 537 U.S. 270, 274 (2003)(the conspiratorial "agreement is a distinct evil, which may exist and be punished whether or not the substantive offense ensues"); *United States v. Mincoff*, 574 F.3d 1186, 1198 (9th Cir. 2009); *United States v. Eppolito*, 543 F.3d 25, 47 (2d Cir. 2008).

[91] *Pinkerton v. United States*, 328 U.S. 640, 646-47 (1946); *Callanan v. United States*, 364 U.S. 587, 593 (1961); *United States v. Wardell*, 591 F.3d 1279, 1291 (10th Cir. 2009); *United States v. Simmons*, 581 F.3d 582, 587 (7th Cir. 2009).

[92] *United States v. Rodriguez*, 553 F.3d 380, 391 (5th Cir. 2008).

[93] *United States v. Rehak*, 589 F.3d 965, 971 (8th Cir. 2009); *United States v. Iribe*, 564 F.3d 1155, 1160 (9th Cir. 2009).

[94] *United States v. Douglas*, 525 F.3d 225, 251 (2d Cir. 2008).

[95] E.g., 18 U.S.C.32(b)(4)(attempts to sabotage commercial aircraft), 33 (attempts to sabotage commercial motor vehicles); 37(a) (attempted violation at international airports), 43(a)(2)(C)(attempted violence directed at animal enterprises), 81 (attempted arson within the special maritime or territorial jurisdiction of the United States), 175 (attempt use of biological weapons), 351(c)(attempted murder or kidnapping of a Member of Congress), 1512 (attempted obstruction of justice), 1956 (attempted money laundering). There are dozens of other attempt statutes in title 18 of the United States Code and many others scattered throughout the other titles.

[96] *United States v. Macias-Valencia*, 510 F.3d 1012, (9th Cir. 2007)("conspiracy and attempt are inchoate crimes that do not require completion of the criminal objective"); *United States v. Vigil*, 523 F.3d 1258, 1267 (10th Cir. 2008)(attempt)("We do not require that a defendant be on the verge of committing the specific act, rather the law allows criminal liability to attach at some point prior to the last proximate act"); *United States v. Rehak*, 589 F.3d at 971 (conspiracy)("The crime of conspiracy is complete on the agreement to violate the law implemented by one or more overt acts... and it is not dependent on the success or failure of the planned scheme").

[97] *United States v. Wahlstrom*, 588 F.3d 538, 543 (8th Cir. 2009)(attempt); *United States v. Bristol-Martir*, 570 F.3d 29, 39 (1st Cir. 2009)(attempt); *United States v. Boria*, 592 F.3d 476, 481 (3d Cir. 2010)("To establish a charge of conspiracy, the Government must show ... (2) an intent to achieve a common illegal goal").

[98] *United States v. Rehak*, 589 F.3d at 971 (""Factual impossibility is not a defense to an inchoate offense such as conspiracy or attempt"'); *United States v. Coté*, 504 F.3d 682, 687 (7th Cir. 2007)(attempt); *United States v. Williams*, 547 F.3d 1187, 1197 (9th Cir. 2008)(conspiracy).

[99] *United States v. Iribe*, 564 F.3d at 1160 ("Each of those crimes contains an element that the other does not: Conspiracy does not require a 'substantial step,' while attempt does not require an 'agreement'").

[100] *United States v. DeMarce*, 564 F.3d 989, (8th Cir. 2009)("The requisite elements of attempt are: 1) an intent... and 2) conduct constituting a substantial step toward the commission of the substantive offense which strongly corroborates the actor's criminal intent. A substantial step goes beyond 'mere preparation'..."); *United States v. Barrow*, 568 F.3d 215, 219 ("We have defined a 'substantial step' as 'conduct which strongly corroborates the firmness of [the] defendant's criminal attempt.' 'Mere preparation' is not enough"); *United States v. Morris*, 549 F.3d 548, 550 (7th Cir. 2008)("The 'substantial step' [required for conviction of attempt] toward completion is the demonstration of dangerousness, and has been usefully described as 'some over act adapted to, approximating, and which in the ordinary and likely course of things will result in, the commission of the particular crime").

[101] *United States v. Iribe*, 564 F.3d at 1160.

[102] *United States v. Rivera-Relle*, 333 F.3d 914, 921 n.11 (9th Cir. 2003)("Unlike conspiracy, the prosecution may not obtain convictions for both the completed offense and the attempt if the attempt has in fact been completed. the attempt is an offense included in the completed crime, and, therefore, cannot support a separate conviction and sentence").

[103] *United States v. Iribe*, 564 F.3d at 1161 ("Here, Defendant conspired to commit an actual kidnapping. He also committed a substantial step toward kidnapping. Thus, he was properly convicted of both conspiring to kidnap and attempting to kidnap").

[104] *United States v. Korab*, 893 F.2d 212, 215 (9th Cir. 1989)("Section 373(a) encompasses only solicitations of federal felonies").

[105] *United States v. Hale*, 448 F.3d 971, 983 (7th Cir. 2006), citing *United States v. McNeil*, 887 F.2d 448, 450 (3d Cir. 1989).

[106] *United States v. Korab*, 893 F.3d 212, 213 (9th Cir. 1989).

[107] 18 U.S.C. 373(b)("It is an affirmative defense to a prosecution under this section that, under circumstances manifesting a voluntary and complete renunciation of his criminal intent, the defendant prevented the commission of the crime solicited. A renunciation is not "voluntary and complete" if it is motivated in whole or in part by a decision to postpone the commission of the crime until another time or to substitute another victim or another but similar objective. If the defendant raises the affirmative defense at trial, the defendant has the burden of proving the defense by a preponderance of the evidence").

[108] 18 U.S.C. 373(c)(" It is not a defense to a prosecution under this section that the person solicited could not be convicted of the crime because he lacked the state of mind required for its commission, because he was incompetent or irresponsible, or because he is immune from prosecution or is not subject to prosecution").

[109] A few crimes, such as certain terrorism and child abuse offenses have special loner statute of limitations, e.g., 18 U.S.C. 3283, 3286. Capital offenses may be tried at any time, 18 U.S.C. 3281.

[110] 18 U.S.C. 371 ("... and one or more of such persons do any act to effect the object of the conspiracy..."); *United States v. Wardell*, 591 F.3d 1279, 1287 (10th Cir. 2009); *United States v. Schaffer*, 586 F.3d 414, 422 (6th Cir. 2009); *United States v. Kingrea*, 573 F.3d 186, 195 (4th Cir. 2009).

[111] *United States v. Saybolt*, 577 F.3d 195, 202 (3d Cir. 2009); *United States v. Dedman*, 527 F.3d 577, 594 n.7 (6th Cir. 2008); *United States v. Lanier*, 920 F.2d 887, 892 (11th Cir. 1991).

[112] *United States v. Bornman*, 559 F.3d 150, 153 (3d Cir. 2009)(prosecution under Section 371)("For a conspiracy indictment to fall within the statute of limitations, it is incumbent on the Government to prove that at least one overt act in furtherance of the conspiracy was performed within five years of the date the Indictment was returned"); *United States v. Thompson*, 518 F.3d 832, 857 (10th Cir. 2008)(prosecution under Section 371); *United States v. Useni*, 516 F.3d 634, 656 (7th Cir. 2008)(same).

[113] *United States v. Seher*, 562 F.3d 1344, 1364 (11th Cir. 2009)(prosecution under 18 U.S.C. 1956(h) which has no over act requirement)("The government satisfies the requirements of the statute of limitations for a non-overt act conspiracy if it alleges and proves that the conspiracy continued into the limitations period. A conspiracy is deemed to continue as long as its purposes have neither been abandoned nor accomplished, and no affirmative showing has been made that it has terminated"); *United States v. Yannotti*, 541 F.3d 112, 123 (2d Cir. 2008) (prosecution under 18 U.S.C. 1962(d) a non-overt act statute); *United States v. Saadey*, 393 F.3d 669, 677 (6th Cir. 2005)(same).

[114] *Whitfield v. United States*, 543 U.S. 209, 218 (2005).

[115] *United States v. Brodie*, 534 F.3d 259, 273 (D.C. Cir. 2008); *United States v. Nichols*, 416 F.3d 811, 824 (8th Cir. 2005); *United States v. Geibel*, 369 F.3d 682, 696 (2d Cir. 2004)(each of these cases involves conspiracy under 18 U.S.C. 371 which carries an overt act requirement); *United States v. Morales*, 445 F.3d 1081, 1084 (8th Cir. 2006); *United States v. Haire*, 371 F.3d 833, 838 (D.C. Cir. 2004); *United States v. Carbajal*, 290 F.3d 277, 289 (5th Cir. 2002) (each of these cases involves conspiracy under 21 U.S.C. 846 which does not include an overt act requirement).

[116] "(a) **Joinder of Offenses.** The indictment or information may charge a defendant in separate counts with 2 or more offenses if the offenses charged – whether felonies or misdemeanors or both – are of the same or similar character, or are based on the same act or transaction, or are connected with or constitute parts of a common scheme or plan.

"(b) **Joinder of Defendants.** The indictment or information may charge 2 or more defendants if they are alleged to have participated in the same act or transaction, or in the same series of acts or transactions, constituting an offense or offenses. The defendants may be charged in one or more counts together or separately. All defendants need not be charged in each count," F.R.Crim.P 8.

[117] "The following must be raised before trial: ... (D) a Rule 14 motion to sever charges or defendants," F.R.Crim.P. 12(b)(3)(D). If the motion is denied, the courts will require that the motion be renewed at the close of the presentation of evidence or it will be considered waived, *United States v. Williams*, 553 F.3d 1073, 1079 (7th Cir. 2009); *United States v. Sullivan*, 522 F.3d 967, 981 (9th Cir. 2008).

[118] "(a) Relief. If the joinder of offenses or defendants in an indictment, an information, or a consolidation for trial appears to prejudice a defendant or the government, the court may order separate trials of counts, sever the defendants' trials, or provide any other relief that justice requires.

"(b) Defendant's Statements. Before ruling on a defendant's motion to sever, the court may order an attorney for the government to deliver to the court for in camera inspection any defendant's statement that the government intends to use as evidence," F.R.Crim.P. 14.

[119] *Zafiro v. United States*, 5056 U.S. 534, 537 (1993).

[120] *United States v. Williams*, 553 F.3d 1073, 78-79 (7th Cir. 2009).

[121] *United States v. Zapata*, 546 F.3d 1179, 1191 (10th Cir. 2008); *United States v. Lewis*, 557 F.3d 601, 609 (8th Cir. 2009); *United States v. Saunders*, 553 F.3d 81, 85 (1st Cir. 2009); *United States v. Wilson*, 481 F.3d 475,482 (7th Cir. 2007).

[122] *United States v. Spotted Elk*, 548 F.3d 641, 658 (8th Cir. 2008).

[123] *Zafiro v. United States*, 506 U.S. at 539; see also *United States v. Lewis*, 557 F.3d at 609 ("To demonstrate the severe and compelling prejudice necessary to show that the court abused its discretion in denying severance, a

defendant must show that his defense was irreconcilable with that of the codefendant or that the jury was unable to compartmentalize the evidence")

124 *Zafiro v. United States*, 506 U.S. at 539.

125 *United States v. Williams*, 553 F.3d 1073, 1079 (7th Cir. 2009)("[T]he district court gave a limiting instruction both before the presentation of the evidence and again at closing arguments that the jury should consider the evidence regarding each defendant separately. Such instructions are normally sufficient to cure any possibility of prejudice"); *United States v. Spotted Elk*, 548 F.3d at 658 ("As a practical matter, disparity among the defendant s in extent of involvement and culpability is commonplace in conspiracy cases and does not alone show the kind of prejudice that would require a district court to sever, rather than to respond with some less drastic measure such as a curative instruction"); *United States v. Reyeros*, 537 F.3d 270, 286 (3d Cir. 2008)("Even if there were some risk of prejudice, here it is of the type that can be cured with proper instructions, and juries are presumed to follow their instructions").

126 U.S. Const. Art.I, §§9, 10; *Stogner v. California*, 539 U.S. 607, 612 (2003).

127 *United States v. Julian*, 427 F.3d. 471, 482 (7th Cir. 2005)("It is well established that a statute increasing a penalty with respect to a criminal conspiracy which commenced prior to, but was continued beyond the effective date of the statute, is not *ex post facto* as to that crime"); *United States v. Valladares*, 544 F.3d 1257, 1270-271 (11th Cir. 2008);

128 U.S. Const. Amend. V.

129 *United States v. Dixon*, 509 U.S. 688, 696 (1993)("The prohibition applies both to successive punishments and to successive prosecutions for the same offense"); *Yeager v. United States*, 129 U.S. 2360, 2366 (2009)("[T]he Double Jeopardy Clause precludes [as collateral estoppel] the Government from relitigating any issue that was necessarily decided by a jury's acquittal in a prior trial"); *United States v. Wittig*, 575 F.3d 1085, 1100-101 (10th Cir. 2009)("[W]hen the only way the government can prove one of the elements of a conspiracy offense is to prove the same facts decided against it in a prior trial on a substantive offense, collateral estoppel bars the attempt").

130 *Rutledge v. United States*, 517 U.S. 292, 297 (1996).

131 *United States v. Felix*, 503 U.S. 378, 391 (1992); *United States v. Yearwood*, 518 F.3d 220, 223 (4th Cir. 2008).

132 *United States v. Rigas*, 584 F.3d 594, (3d Cir. 2009)(emphasis in the original); see also, *United States v. Wheeler*, 535 F.3d 446, 449 (6th Cir. 2008)(citing factors [1] through [4] in addition to :the statutory offenses charged in the indictments)

133 F.R.Evid. 801(c).

134 *United States v. Warman*, 578 F.3d 320, 335 (6th Cir. 2009); *United States v. Flores*, 572 F.3d 1254, 1264 (11th Cir. 2009); *United States v. Harris*, 585 F.3d 394, 398 (7th Cir. 2009); *United States v. Mitchell*, 596 F.3d 18, 23 (1st Cir. 2010).

135 *United States v. Warman*, 578 F.3d at 335; *United States v. Dowdell*, 595 F.3d 50, 74 (1st Cir. 2010).

136 *United States v. Mitchell*, 596 F.3d at 23; *United States v. Llera*, 585 F.3d 1237, 1245-246 (9th Cir. 2009); *United States v. Benson*, 591 F.3d 491, 502 (6th Cir. 2010).

137 *United States v. Warman*, 578 F.3d at 338; *United States v. Flores*, 572 F.3d at 1264.

138 *United States v. Warman*, 578 F.3d at 338; *United States v. Alviar*, 573 F.3d 526, 545(7th Cir. 2009)("In conspiracy cases statements that are part of the information flow between conspirators intended to help each perform his role satisfy the 'in furtherance' requirement of Rule 801(d)(2)(E)"); *United States v. Flores*, 572 F.3d at 1264.

139 *United States v. Warman*, 578 F.3d at 338.

140 *Crawford v. Washington*, 541 U.S. 36, 44, 52 (2004)("One of Raleigh's trial judges later lamented that the justice of England has never been so degraded and injured as by the condemnation of Sir Walter Raleigh. Through a series of statutory and judicial reforms, English law developed a right of confrontation that limited these abuses.... Raleigh's trial has long been thought as a paradigmatic confrontation violation").

141 "If taken literally, the Clause would bar all hearsay, or at least all hearsay uttered by a declarant unavailable for examination at trial," Trachtenberg, *Coconspirator, "Coventurers," and the Exception Swallowing the Hearsay Rule*, 61 HASTINGS LAW JOURNAL 581, 637 (2010).

142 *Crawford v. Washington*, 541 U.S. at 68 ("Where nontestimonial hearsay is at issue, it is wholly consistent with the Framers' design to afford the States [and Congress] flexibility in their development of hearsay law ... as would an approach that exempted such statements from Confrontation Clause scrutiny altogether. Where testimonial evidence is at issue, however, the Sixth Amendment demands what the common law required: unavailability and a prior opportunity for cross-examination").

143 *Id.*

144 *Melendez-Diaz v. Massachusetts*, 129 S.Ct. 2527, 2531 (2009), quoting *Crawford v. Washington*, 541 U.S. at 51-2 (2004).

145 *United States v. Hyles*, 521 F.3d 946, 960 (8th Cir. 2008)("Neither ... were ... formal statements, nor were [the] statements elicited in response to government interrogation. In other words, they did not bear testimony. Therefore, *Crawford* is inapplicable"); *United States v. Spotted Elk*, 548 F.3d 641, 662 (8th Cir. 2008)("Blue Bird's reported utterance was not a statement of fact, but a proposal of a future course of action (i.e., what to

say in the future), uttered not to any official, but to a co-defendant. Blue Bird's reported words were not testimonial, and therefore Frogg's account of them could not have violated Spotted Elk's Sixth Amendment rights"); *United States v. US Infrastructure, Inc.*, 576 F.3d 1195, 1209 (11th Cir. 2009)("Given that McNair's statement to Dawson was part of a private conversation, it is 'nontestimonial' within the meaning of *Crawford*, and *Crawford*'s strict Confrontation Clause requirements do not apply").

146 *United States v. Cesareo-Ayala*, 576 F.3d 1120, 1127-128 (10th Cir. 2009)("The government contends that Mendez' statements in the two conversations are not hearsay and do not implicate the Confrontation Clause because they were not offered in evidence to prove the truth of the matter asserted. We agree"); *United States v. Brown*, 560 F.3d 754, 765 (8th Cir. 2009)("Because Williams's statement was not admitted for the truth of the matter asserted, it does not implicate the confrontation clause").

147 *United States v. Hargrove*, 508 F.3d 445, 449 (7th Cir. 2007)("Under Rule 801(d)(2)(E) the statements of coconspirators made during the course and in furtherance of the conspiracy are considered admissions by a party opponent and are not hearsay. The use of this sort of evidence does not implicate the Confrontation Clause"); *United States v. Singh*, 494 F.3d 653, 659 (8th Cir. 2007)("[C]o-conspirators' statements made in furtherance of a conspiracy and admitted under Rule 801(d)(2)(E) are generally non-testimonial and, therefore, do not violate the Confrontation Clause as interpreted by the Supreme Court"); but see *United States v. Warman*, 578 F.3d 320, 346 (6th Cir. 2009) ("[S]tatements of a confidential informant are testimonial in nature and therefore, may not be offered by the government to establish the guilt of an accused absent an opportunity for the accused to cross-examine the informant").

In: Forfeiture, Conspiracy, Venue: Federal Crime Law
Editors: Ryan E. McGowan and Colin H. Grovsten
ISBN: 978-1-61209-315-4

Chapter 3

VENUE: A LEGAL ANALYSIS OF WHERE A FEDERAL CRIME MAY BE TRIED

Charles Doyle

SUMMARY

Federal law promises criminal defendants a proper venue, that is, trial in the district in which the federal crime was committed. A crime is committed in any district in which any of its "conduct" elements are committed. Some offenses are committed entirely within a single district; there they must be tried. Others begin in one district and are completed in another. They may be tried where they occur unless Congress has limited the choice of venue for the particular offense. Still others, while fully committed in one district, continue on through one or more other districts. They too may be tried where they occur unless Congress elected to limit where they may be tried. Conspiracy is one of the continuing offenses, and so it may be tried in any district in which an overt act in its furtherance is committed.

Crimes for which there is otherwise no proper venue within the United States because they have been committed entirely overseas are usually tried in the district into which the accused is first brought.

The court may grant a change of venue at the behest of the defendant to avoid undue prejudice, for the convenience of the parties, or for sentencing purposes.

This report is available in an abridged form as CRS Report RS22361, *Venue: A Brief Look at Federal Law Governing Where a Federal Crime May Be Tried*, by Charles Doyle, stripped of the footnotes and most of the citations to authority found inthis chapter

INTRODUCTION

The Constitution states that those accused of a federal crime shall be tried in the state in which the crime occurred (venue) by a jury selected from the district in which the crime was committed (vicinage).

> The Trial of all Crimes ... shall be by Jury ... held in the State where the said Crimes shall have been committed; but when not committed within any State, the Trial shall be at such Place or Places as the Congress may by Law have directed, U.S. Const. Art. III, §2, cl.3.
>
> In all criminal prosecutions, the accused shall enjoy the right to ... trial, by an impartial jury of the State and district wherein the crime shall have been committed, which district shall have been previously ascertained by law. . .. U.S. Const. Amend. VI.

The Constitution's demands are deceptively simple: juries must be drawn and federal crimes must be tried where the crimes occur; jury selection and the place of trial for crimes that occur beyond the bounds of any state shall be as Congress by law provides. Rule 18 of the Federal Rules of Criminal Procedure is if anything more cryptic, "Unless a statute or these rules permit otherwise, the government must prosecute an offense in a district where the offense was committed." But what exceptions exist by statute or rule? What marks the district where the offense was committed? Suppose the crime appears to have been committed in more than one district? How does Congress provide for the trial of overseas crimes? When should the request of an accused for a change of venue be granted?

The Constitution describes venue as the *state* where trial is proper and vicinage as the *district* from which the jury is to be drawn, but with a single recently added exception the two are generally thought of as one and their dual requirements are generally referred to simply as "venue."[1]

Background: The Melding of Venue and Vicinage

The melding of venue and vicinage is something of an American phenomenon. Of the two concepts we now think of as venue where a trial must be held and where the jury must come from—the common law spoke more often of vicinage. The theory that the jury in a criminal trial ought to come from the neighborhood in which the crime was committed predates and is acknowledged in the Magna Carta, which declared that "no freeman shall be aken or imprisoned ... unless by the lawful judgment of his peers" and that punishment would not be "assessed but by the oath of honest men *in the neighborhood*," Magna Carta, XXXIX, XX. Of course, the jury of Runnymede was a far cry from the jury of today. Then and for sometime thereafter, it was the body whose verdict rested upon the knowledge of its members—their prior knowledge of the circumstances of the offense, of the character of the defendant, and of the credibility of the witnesses.[2] By the beginning of the colonial period, however, the English jury had been transformed into an institution more familiar to us, an impartial panel rather than one necessarily convened with prior knowledge and thus perhaps with bias. By then, a jury panel could no longer be challenged simply because none of its members came from the neighborhood where the offense had occurred; it was enough that the panel was drawn from the county where the offense had occurred.[3]

In turbulence that lead to the American Revolution, grievances over venue seemed to roil as much as those over vicinage. Unrest in Massachusetts spurred the British Parliament to enact measures under which misconduct in the colonies might be tried in England or Canada. This denied the colonial suspect the advantages of both venue and vicinage, since jurors for a trial in London or Halifax were not likely to be drawn from a county in any of the 13 colonies. The famous protest of the Virginia House of Burgesses spoke candidly of disadvantages of the change in venue—the hardships faced while awaiting trial and the difficulty of securing the attendance of witnesses. It spoke somewhat more cryptically of the disadvantages of the loss of vicinage, "not to await his Trial before a ... Jury ... from a Knowledge of whom [he] is encouraged to hope for speedy Justice."[4] Yet when the First Continental Congress later echoed the same objections it did so in terms more clearly grounded in both vicinage and venue:

> Whereas ... it has lately been resolved in Parliament, that by force of a statute made in the thirty-fifth year of the reign of king Henry the Eighth, colonists may be transported to England, and tried there upon accusations for treasons and misprisions, or concealments of treasons committed in the colonies ... Resolved, That the following acts of Parliament are infringements and violations of the rights of the colonists; and that the repeal of them is essentially necessary, in order to restore harmony between Great Britain and the American colonies ... 12 Geo.3, ch. 24 ... which declares a new offense in America, and deprives the American subject of a constitutional trial by jury of the vicinage, by authorizing the trial of any person charged with the committing [of] any offense described in the said act, out of the realm, to be indicted and tried for the same in shire or county within the realm ... 1 JOURNAL OF THE CONTINENTAL CONGRESS 69 (Oct. 14, 1774).

On the other hand, when it came time to list colonial complaints against the British Crown in the Declaration of Independence, that document mentioned only venue:

> "He [the King of Great Britain] has combined with others to subject us to a jurisdiction foreign to our constitution, and unacknowledged by our laws; giving his Assent to their acts of pretended Legislation: . . .
>
> For transporting us beyond Seas to be tried for pretended offenses.

The men who drafted the Constitution apparently never seriously questioned the proposition that became Article III, §2, cl.3 ("The trial of all Crimes ... shall be by Jury; and such Trial shall be held in the State where the said Crimes shall have been committed"), for it was feature of each of the preliminary proposals—as language in the Pinckney Plan,[5] as well as in the Hamilton Plan,[6] and in all probability figured in the formulation of the New Jersey or Patterson Plan.[7] But vicinage was nowhere mentioned.

Some of the delegates to the various states conventions called to ratify the Constitution objected to the omission,[8] and when the First Congress convened James Madison attempted to meet the objection. He proposed an amendment to appear not as a Sixth Amendment in a Bill of Rights but in Article III of the Constitution under which criminal trials would "be by an impartial jury of freeholders of the vicinage."[9] Although the provision passed the House, the Senate would not agree, perhaps because the laws of some of the states permitted jurors to be drawn from anywhere within the state.[10] The language upon which the two Houses ultimately agreed is found in the Sixth Amendment today: "In all criminal prosecutions, the accused shall enjoy the right to a speedy and public trial, by an impartial jury of the state and district wherein the crime shall have been committed."[11] Story explained the compromise as an effort to ensure that the accused would not be unfairly inconvenienced nor the beneficiary of too parochial a jury.[12]

By the time the amendments were sent to the states for ratification, the geographical distinction between venue (state in which the crime occurs) and vicinage (district in which the crime occurs) made little difference, for Congress had established the federal courts with a single district for each state, except in Virginia and Massachusetts, where separate districts were created for portions of those states that would soon become the states of Kentucky and Maine.[13] Congress preserved a semblance of common law vicinage distinct from venue, however, when it decreed that in federal capital cases trial had to be held in the county in which the offense occurred, if possible, and jurors had to be drawn from there in any event.[14]

The county venue requirement in capital cases survives to this day,[15] but the distinct vicinage component that insisted that jurors be drawn from the county of the crime was repealed in 1862.[16] Thereafter, other explicit vicinage components, distinct from constitutional venue and vicinage requirements, surfaced occasionally when Congress divided districts into divisions.[17] The Judicial Code revision of 1911 eliminated the explicit statutory basis for all of these,[18] but up until 1966 divisional vicinage practices continued in some districts under the umbrella of the venue provisions of Rule 18 of the Federal Rules of Criminal Procedure.[19] When the division clause was eliminated from Rule 18 in 1966 at least one commentator concluded that for purposes of federal law the venue has consumed vicinage;[20] the questions of where have become one: In what district[s] is venue (venue/vicinage) proper?

Threshold Issues

Before a court decides whether venue in a particular district is proper, it would confront the questions of who bears the burden of persuasion on the issue, to what level of persuasion, and whether waiver by the accused obviates the need for further inquiry. It is generally agreed that the government bears the burden of establishing that venue is proper, that is, that the offense is being prosecuted in the district in which it was committed.[21] This obligation extends to every count within the indictment or information.[22] Venue, however, is not a substantive element of the offense and consequently the government need only establish venue by a preponderance of the evidence.[23] Moreover, venue is not jurisdictional.[24] Therefore, a court in an improper venue enjoys the judicial authority to proceed to conviction or acquittal, if the accused waives objection.[25] If the absence of proper venue is apparent on the face of indictment or information, failure to object prior to trial constitutes waiver.[26] If the failure of proper venue is not apparent on the face of the charging document and is not established during the presentation of the government's case in the main, objection may be raised at the close of the government's case.[27]

In What District Did the Crime Occur?

The district in which venue is proper, the district in which the offense was committed, "the '*locus delicti* [of the charged offense,] must be determined from the nature of the crime alleged and the location of the act or acts constituting it.' In performing this inquiry, a court must initially identify the conduct constituting the offense (the nature of the crime) and then discern the location of the commission of the criminal acts."[28] Which is to say, the inquiry begins by identifying (1) the statutory prohibition charged, (2) what acts or omissions of the accused are alleged to have been committed in violation of the prohibition, and (3) where those acts or omissions occurred.

The words Congress uses when it drafts a criminal proscription will establish where the offense occurs and therefore the district or districts in which venue is proper. For some time, the courts and academics used a so-called "verb test" as one means of identifying where an offense was committed.[29] The test may still be useful to determine where venue is proper, but particularly in the case of purported multi-district offenses it is not necessarily dispositive of where venue is not proper. In the words of the Supreme Court, "the 'verb test' certainly has value as an interpretative tool, it cannot be applied rigidly, to the exclusion of other relevant statutory language. The test unduly limits the inquiry into the nature of the offense and thereby creates a danger that certain conduct prohibited by statute will be missed," *United States v. Rodriguez-Moreno*, 526 U.S. 275, 280 (1999).[30] The test endorsed in *Rodriguez-Moreno*, is: where did the activity or omission that offends the statute's "conduct element" occur? Id.

Crimes Continuing Through More than One District

Some statutes limit venue to a particular district even though the offense could be said to have been committed in more than one district and thus otherwise might have been tried in any of the two or more districts in which it was committed. Others simply clarify the several districts in which venue for the trial of certain offenses is proper. The general statute that seeks to clarify venue in the case of multi-district crimes is 18 U.S.C. 3237. It consists of three parts: one for continuing offenses generally, another for offenses involving elements of the mails or interstate commerce, and a third for tax offenses.

The first paragraph of section 3237 is the oldest portion of the statute. Originally enacted during Reconstruction as part of the general conspiracy statute now found in 18 U.S.C. 371,[31] the Revised Statutes made it applicable to all multi-district federal crimes.[32] Slightly modified in the 1948 revision, it now provides:

> Except as otherwise expressly provided by enactment of Congress, any offense against the United States begun in one district and completed in another, or committed in more than one district, may be inquired of and prosecuted in any district in which such offense was begun, continued, or completed.

Over the years, there has been a certain ebb and flow of the Supreme Court's reading of venue requirements of the section. The Court first considered the provision in *Palliser v. United States*, 136 U.S. 257, 267-68 (1890), when it held that prosecution of an offense under the postal bribery statute might be held in the district in Connecticut in which the letter offering the bribe was received even though the accused had acted entirely outside of the district. The Court expressed no opinion as to whether the offense might also have been tried in the district in New York from which the letter had been sent, 136 U.S. at 268. Two years later the Court held that the trial of an indictment for causing the mail delivery of lottery material might be held in the district in which the mail was delivered, but observed that "perhaps" trial might also be held in the district in which the material was deposited in the mail, *Horner v. United States*, 143 U.S. 207, 211-12 (1892).

In later years, it concluded that the failure to file required documentation with immigration officials was not a continuous offense and must be prosecuted in the district where the document had to be filed; *United States v. Lombardo*, 241 U.S. 73, 76-9 (1916), but that an alien crewman's unlawfully remaining in the United States was a continuous offense and consequently that venue "lies in any district where the crewman willfully remains, " *United States v. Cores*, 356 U.S. 405, 409 (1958).

More recently, it held that money laundering and the crimes that generated the tainted funds did not *automatically* form one continuous criminal episode so as to permit trial of the laundering offense in the foreign district in which money-generating offense occurred, *United States v. Cabrales*, 524 U.S. 1, 5-6 (1998). The Court was quick to point out, however, that under different circumstances, venue over a money laundering charge might be proper in the district in which its predicate offenses occurred. "Notably, the counts at issue do not charge Cabrales with conspiracy; they do not link her to, or assert her responsibility for, acts done by others. Nor do they charge her as an aider or abettor in the Missouri drug trafficking ... Cabrales is charged in the money-laundering counts with criminal activity 'after the fact' of an offense begun and completed by others," 524 U.S. at 7. Further, "[m]oney laundering ... arguably might rank as a continuing offense triable in more than one place, if the launderer acquired the funds in one district and transported them into another. But that is tellingly not this case," 524 U.S. at 8.

Conspiracy

Conspiracy may be the most commonly recognized "continuing offense," although whether conspiracy is really a continuing offense or merely shares the attributes of a continuing offense is not clear. When the present, general federal conspiracy statute was first drafted it contained an overt act requirement,[33] as it does today.[34] The crime under the general statute was not, and is not, complete until one of the conspirators takes some affirmative action in furtherance of the criminal scheme. An overt act is an element of the crime.[35] In such cases, it would come as no surprise if venue were said to be proper wherever an overt act was committed—was proper wherever a conduct element of the crime occurred. Under several individual federal conspiracy statutes, however, an overt act is not required and therefore is not an element of the offense.[36] In such cases, is venue nevertheless proper wherever an overt act in furtherance of the conspiracy is committed? It appears so.

Some time ago, the Supreme Court pointed out that conspiracy could be considered something akin to a continuous offense. Conspiracy, it declared, may be tried in any district in which an overt act in its furtherance is committed, at least when the conspiracy statute has an overt act requirement, *Hyde v. United States*, 225 U.S. 347, 360-61 (1912)("[I]f the unlawful combination and the overt act constitute the offense ... marking its beginning and its execution or a step in its execution, §731 of the Revised Statutes [18 U.S.C. 3237's predecessor] must be applied"). Even for those conspiracy offenses for which an overt act is not an element, the Court in *Hyde* implied that a prosecution might be had in any district in which an overt act in their furtherance was committed.[37] Without apparent exception, the lower federal appellate courts have followed *Hyde's* lead and found venue proper for trial of conspiracy charges in any district in which an overt act is committed, regardless of whether the conspiracy statute in question requires proof of an overt act[38] or not.[39] It is interesting to note that in *Cabrales* when the Court noted that the money launderer might have been tried as a conspirator in the district where the predicate offense (drug trafficking) occurred, it referred to the general conspiracy statute that requires an overt act, 18 U.S.C. 371, rather than the equally applicable drug trafficking conspiracy statute that does not, 21 U.S.C. 846.[40] Nevertheless, the Court later in *Whitfield* observed in passing that "this Court has long held that venue is proper in any district in which an overt act in furtherance of the conspiracy was committed, even where an overt act is not a required element of the conspiracy offense."[41]

Venue in the Place of Impact

Continuing offenses and the first paragraph of subsection 3237(a) present one other puzzle: when is venue proper in any district in which the crime's effects are felt? The Court expressly declined to address the issue in *Rodriguez-Moreno*: "The Government argues that venue also may permissibly be based upon the effects of a defendant's conduct in a district other than the one in which the defendant performs the acts constituting the offense. Brief for the United States 16-17. Because this case only concerns the *locus delicti*, we express no opinion as to whether the Government's assertion is correct," 526 U.S. at 279 n.2. The Brief declares that "[v]enue may also be based on the effects of a defendant's conduct in another district," and cites *Armour Packing Co.* (rail transportation at unlawful rate), *supra*, and the mail cases discussed below, Brief for the United States at 16-17. It also cites the lower court obstruction of justice and Hobbs Act cases, *id.*

The Hobbs Act outlaws the obstruction of interstate or foreign commerce through the use of violence or extortion.[42] Venue for a Hobbs Act violation is generally considered proper in any district in which there is an obstruction of commerce.[43] Yet obstruction is an element of the offense.[44] The act is drafted in such a way that obstruction is arguably a "conduct" element ("Whoever in any way or degree obstructs"); if so, it would seem to provide little support for "impact" venue in the case of those crimes for whom the effect is not a conduct element.

An earlier line of cases suggested that an obstruction of justice—intimidation or bribery of witness, bail jumping, or the like—might be tried in the district in which the proceedings were conducted even when the act of obstruction was committed elsewhere.[45] The line gave birth to a suggestion that venue might be predicated upon the impact of the crime within a particular district especially when the offense involved other "substantial contacts" with the district of victimization.[46]

After *Rodriguez-Moreno*, the courts continue to recognize an "effects" or "substantial contacts" test for venue,[47] but generally hold that the effect must also constitute a "conduct element" under the statute defining the offense,[48] and that venue may not be based on elements of the offense which are not conduct elements.[49]

Mail and Commerce Cases

The second paragraph of subsection 3237(a) expands the number of districts where prosecutions for offenses involving smuggling, the mails or commerce may be brought to any district from, through, or into which "commerce, mail matter, or [an] imported object or person moves."[50] The paragraph was added when title 18 of the United States Code was revised in 1948. Interstate transportation and mail cases had previously been resolved under the continuing offense language of the first paragraph discussed above. Professor Wright has suggested that the paragraph stems from a misreading of the Supreme Court's opinion in *United States v. Johnson* and that at its outer limits the paragraph may lie beyond constitutional expectations.[51] Perhaps for this reason although the paragraph has been used under a wide range of circumstances, its invocation has not always been successful.[52]

Tax Cases

The tax provision, subsection 3237(b), is in fact a limited transfer provision under which the accused may opt for trial in the district in which he resided at the time when the alleged offense occurred.[53] The subsection was added in 1958 upon the view that prosecution in the district where a return was received or due rather than the district in which the taxpayer resided visited inappropriate inconvenience and expense upon taxpayers, their attorneys and witnesses.[54] The subsection is only available in the case of prosecutions under 26 U.S.C. 7203 (willful failure to file a return, supply information or pay a tax),[55] or, if the government seeks to prosecute in a district where venue exists solely because of a mailing to the Internal Revenue Service, under 26 U.S.C. 7201 (attempted tax evasion) or 7206(1), (2), or (5)(various frauds and false statements).[56]

Other Continuous Offenses

In *Armour Packing Co. v. United States*, 209 U.S. 56, 77 (1908), the Supreme Court upheld a conviction following a trial in the Western District of Missouri for the offense of continuous carriage by rail of the defendant's products from Kansas to New York at an illegally reduced rate. The Court concluded that "[t]his is a single continuing offense ... continuously committed in each district through which the transportation is received at the prohibited rate," *id.* The Court's most recent venue decision confirmed the continued vitality of this view when it held that if Congress so crafts a criminal offense as to embed within it a continuing offense as one of the conduct elements of the new crime, venue over the new crime is proper wherever trial over the continuing offense may be had. In *United States v. Rodriguez-Moreno*, 526 U.S. 275, 281 (1999), it held that the constitutional right to a jury trial in the state and district in which the crime occurs did not preclude trial for use of a firearm during the commission of a predicate offense in a state and district, New Jersey, other than that in which the firearm was used, Maryland. The crime in question, 18 U.S.C. 924(c)(1), "contains two distinct conduct elements—as is relevant in this case, the 'using and carrying' of a gun and the commission of a kidnaping," 526 U.S. at 280. A defendant commits a crime and may be tried where *he* commits any of its *conduct* elements.[57] Kidnaping is a crime that continues from capture until release and therefore can be tried in any place from, through or into which the victim is taken, and the appended gun charge travels with it:

> The kidnaping, to which the §924(c)(1) offense is attached, was committed in all of the places that any part of it took place, and venue for the kidnaping charge against respondent was appropriate in any of them. (Congress has provided that continuing offenses can be tried 'in any district in which such offense was begun, continued, or completed,' 18 U.S.C. §3237(a).) Where venue is appropriate for the underlying crime of violence [, in this case kidnaping,] so too it is for the §924(c)(1) offense. 526 U.S. at 282.

In addition to kidnaping, the lower federal appellate courts have found venue proper based on the continuing nature of violations involving, *inter alia*:

- false statements (18 U.S.C. 1001);[58]
- wire fraud (18 U.S.C.1343);[59]

- mail fraud (18 U.S.C. 1341);[60]
- bank fraud (18 U.S.C. 1344);[61]
- possession of controlled substances with the intent to distribute (21 U.S.C. 841);[62]
- Hobbs Act (violent interference with interstate commerce) (18 U.S.C. 1951);[63]
- unlawful possession of a firearm (18 U.S.C. 922(g));[64]
- Travel Act (interstate travel in aid of racketeering)(18 U.S.C. 1952);[65]
- violent crimes in aid of racketeering (18 U.S.C. 1959);[66] and
- failure to pay child support (18 U.S.C. 228).[67]

Aiding and Abetting

Those who aid and abet the commission of a federal crime are punishable as principals, 18 U.S.C. 2. *Cabrales* suggests they may be prosecuted wherever the underlying offense was committed, 524 U.S. at 7 ("Nor do they charge her as an aider or abettor in the Missouri drug trafficking"). Subsequent lower federal appellate courts have so held.[68]

Venue in Murder Cases

Sections 3235 and 3236 provide special venue requirements in murder cases. Section 3235 dates from the First Congress, 1 Stat. 88 (1789), and states that "the trial of offenses punishable with death shall be had in the county where the offense was committed, where that can be done without great inconvenience." The cases under the section are few and rarely seem to favor the accused. For instance, more than one court has held that the section does not apply to offenses punishable with death unless the charges are for "unitary" murder offenses.[69] As in other instances, the benefits of section 3235 can be waived if the accused fails to move to dismiss for improper venue.[70] Moreover, the determination of the benefit can be afforded "without great inconvenience" is a matter within the trial court's discretion.[71] Great inconvenience has been found when there was no federal courthouse within the county in which the crime was committed;[72] when a majority of the government's witnesses were located outside of the county in which the crime was committed;[73] and when observance would overburden court resources.[74]

Section 3236 provides that for venue purposes in murder and manslaughter cases, the offense will be deemed to have occurred where the death-causing act is committed.[75] Congress enacted section 3236 in apparent reaction to a Supreme Court observation that a federal murder case could not be brought if an injury were inflicted within a district in the United States but death occurred elsewhere.[76] Here too the case law is sparse. Two trial courts have held that the section only applies to "unitary" murder cases and thus does not apply to murders committed in aid of racketeering in violation of 18 U.S.C. 1959.[77] A third held that section must yield where section 3237 (venue in multiple districts) is applicable.[78] And an appellate court has held that under the section a father who battered his three-year-old daughter in one district may be tried in a second district where she died of pneumonia as a consequence of his negligence there.[79]

Crimes with Individual Venue Statutes

In a few instances, Congress had enacted special venue provisions for particular crimes. The provisions dictate venue decisions unless they contravene constitutional requirements. The list includes

- 8 U.S.C. 1328 (importation of aliens for immoral purposes);[80]
- 8 U.S.C. 1329 (immigration offenses generally);[81]
- 15 U.S.C. 78aa (securities offenses);[82]
- 15 U.S.C. 80a-43 (investment company offenses);[83]
- 15 U.S.C. 298 (falsely stamped gold or silver);[84]
- 18 U.S.C. 228(e) (failure to pay legal child support obligations);[85]
- 18 U.S.C. 1073 (flight to avoid prosecution);[86]
- 18 U.S.C. 1074 (flight to avoid prosecution for property damage);[87]
- 18 U.S.C. 1512(*i*) (obstruction of justice);[88]
- 18 U.S.C. 1752(c) (secret service offenses);[89]
- 18 U.S.C. 1956(*i*) (money laundering);[90]
- 18 U.S.C. 2339(b) (harboring terrorists);[91]
- 18 U.S.C. 2339A(a)(material support of terrorists).[92]

A few others have special venue provisions that simply replicate the features of rule 18—that is, a violation is to be prosecuted in the district in which it occurs:

- 15 U.S.C. 78aa (securities offenses);
- 15 U.S.C. 79y (public utility holding company violations);
- 15 U.S.C. 80a-43 (investment company offenses generally);
- 15 U.S.C. 80b-14 (investment adviser offenses);
- 15 U.S.C. 715i (interstate transportation of petroleum products);
- 15 U.S.C. 717u (natural gas offenses);
- 21 U.S.C. 17 (falsely labeled dairy or food products).

Venue for Crimes Committed Outside Any District

The Constitution recognizes that certain crimes, like piracy, may be committed beyond the geographical confines of any federal judicial district. Article III after declaring that the trial of crimes shall be in the state in which they are committed provides that, "but when not committed within any State, the Trial shall be at such Place or Places as the Congress may by Law have directed."[93] The First Congress decided that "the trial of crimes committed on the high seas, or in any place out of the jurisdiction of any particular state, shall be in the district where the offender is apprehended, or into which he may first be brought."[94] The approach changed little over the years until the early 1960s.[95] Then, it was amended to address two problems: (1) to permit a single trial for crimes committed overseas by a group of offenders who scattered when they returned to this country, and (2) to toll the statute of limitations by permitting indictment when the suspect was overseas but not clearly a fugitive.[96] It now reads:

> The trial of all offenses begun or committed upon the high seas, or elsewhere out of the jurisdiction of any particular State or district, shall be in the district in which the offender, or any one of two or more joint offenders, is arrested or is first brought; but if such offender or offenders are not so arrested or brought into any district, an indictment or information may be filed in the district of the last known residence of the offender or of any one of two or more joint offenders, or if no such residence is known the indictment or information may be filed in the District of Columbia. 18 U.S.C. 3238.

Venue cannot be claimed under section 3238 for an offense committed in part within the United States, even if it were also partially committed overseas.[97]

The district to which section 3238 refers includes the districts of U.S. territorial district courts, but does not include the geographical confines of the courts of the U.S. territories that have not been designed "district courts."[98] The district in which a defendant is arrested or into which he is brought for purposes of section 3238 is the district "where the defendant is first restrained of his liberty *in connection with the offense charged*."[99] Thus, venue in a particular district by operation of section 3238 is no less proper because the defendant was initially arrested in another district under another charge,[100] or because he entered the United States in another district prior to his indictment in the District of Columbia and subsequent arrest.[101] Conversely, venue is not proper in a second district after an accused has been arrested for the extraterritorial offense in another.[102] The "last known address" or District of Columbia basis for venue under section 3238 is an alternative basis for venue over an extraterritorial offense available to the exclusion of venue elsewhere when the offender has not first been arrested in or brought to another district.[103] Of course, in the case of multiple, joint offenders, venue over an extraterritorial offense is proper for all offenders in any district in which it is proper for one of them.[104] Finally, the fact that venue may be proper elsewhere under other statutory provisions, does not preclude venue under section 3238.[105]

There is a second, alternative venue statute for certain espionage related cases:

> The trial for any offense involving a violation, begun or committed upon the high seas or elsewhere out of the jurisdiction of any particular State or district, of–
>
> (1) section 793, 794, 798, [espionage] or section 1030(a)(1)[obtaining classified information by unauthorized computer access] of this title;
>
> (2) section 601 of the National Security Act of 1947 (50 U.S.C. 421)[disclosure of the identities of covert agents]; or
>
> (3) section 4(b) or 4(c) of the Subversive Activities Control Act of 1950 (50 U.S.C. 783(b) or (c))[receipt of classified information by foreign agents];
>
> may be in the District of Columbia or in any other district authorized by law.18 U.S.C. 3239.

Section 3238 permits the government to bring an extraterritorial espionage case in the District of Columbia *if* the offender's residence is unknown. If the offender's last address in this country is known, section 3238 requires that the case be brought there or in the district in which the offender is first arrested or brought or any other district in which venue is otherwise proper. But without more the option to bring an extraterritorial espionage case in the District of Columbia is not necessarily available in all cases. Section 3239 changes that. It affords the government the option to bring an exterritorial espionage case in the District Columbia when it would otherwise be precluded from doing so.

Section 3239's limited history suggests proponents may have initially had something else in mind. It was enacted as section 320909 of the Violent Crime Control and Law Enforcement Act of 1994, 108 Stat. 2127 (1994). The committee reports accompanying that legislation barely mention it;[106] the conference report acknowledges that it comes from the Senate bill but says no more;[107] there are no Senate reports. The Senate Select Committee on Intelligence, however, had reported out a bill with identical language, the Counterintelligence and Security Enhancements Act of 1994 (S. 2056). The Committee's report indicates that the section was thought to provide a more explicit statement of extraterritorial jurisdiction rather than an expansion of venue options.[108] This may explain why there are no reported cases under section 3239.

Venue Transfers

For Prejudice

While the Constitution promises the accused a trial in the district in which the offense was committed, it also promises him a trial by an impartial jury. U.S. Const. Amend. VI. To fulfill this second promise, Rule 21(a) of the Federal Rules of Criminal Procedure entitles the accused to a change of venue for trial in another district when "so great a prejudice against the defendant exists in the transferring district that the defendant cannot obtain a fair and impartial trial there."[109]

Pre-trial publicity usually supplies the basis for a change of venue request under Rule 21(a).[110] The applicable standard is a demanding one. A transfer will ordinarily only be granted when no less disruptive curative measures will suffice. To create so great a prejudice that an impartial trial is not possible, media coverage must have been pervasive, inflammatory, contemporaneous to trial, and produced a serious contamination of the jury pool.[111] Requests for transfer under Rule 21(a) have been rejected when the coverage was less than pervasive,[112] when the coverage had subsided between the commission or discovery of the crime or arrest of the accused and the time of trial,[113] when the coverage was not overwhelmingly inflammatory or sensational,[114] or when evidence suggested that an untainted jury might nevertheless be selected.[115] In a compelling case, the court may order trial to be elsewhere within the district under Rule 18, which allows the trial court to set the place of trial,[116] and in a rare case may grant a change of venue.[117]

For Convenience

Under Rule 21(b) of the Federal Rules of Criminal Procedure, "Upon the defendant's motion, the court may transfer the proceeding, or one or more counts, against that defendant to another district for the convenience of the parties and witnesses and in the interest of justice." When weighing a motion for a transfer under Rule 21(b), the lower federal courts frequently point to the ten factors mentioned in *Platt v. Minnesota Mining & Manufacturing Co.*, 376 U.S. 240, 243-44 (1964):

1. location of [the] defendant;
2. location of possible witnesses;
3. location of events likely to be in issue;
4. location of documents and records likely to be involved;
5. disruption of defendant's business unless the case is transferred;
6. expense to the parties;
7. location of counsel;
8. relative accessibility of place of trial;
9. docket condition of each district or division involved; and
10. any other special elements which might affect the transfer.[118]

The motion runs to the discretion of the trial court, and the trial court's decision will only be overturned for an abuse of discretion[119] such as a failure to apply the proper standard.[120] The defendant bears the burden of establishing that convenience and the interests of justice compel a transfer.[121] Professor Wright has described the rule as one designed for the convenience of the accused:

> Rule 21(b) gives the court ample power in every case to provide for trial in the most convenient forum if the defendant makes such a request ... One court has said that the rule is only intended to insure defendant a fair trial, and that it must be a rare case in which mere inconvenience to him will prevent a fair and just trial. This approach seems erroneous. Rule 21(a) is intended to protect defendant's right to a fair trial, while Rule 21(b) looks to a convenient trial. The beneficent purposes of Rule 21(b) will be thwarted, also, if it is supposed that there is a "general rule that a criminal prosecution should be retained in the original district."[122]

Be that as it may, a number of courts continue to observe a general rule that prosecution should be kept in the district where the government filed it.[123] Others appear to exercise their discretion to the same effect.[124] Still others speak in terms that seem at odds with the sentiments that led to drafting of the venue provisions in Article III and the Sixth Amendment.[125] The cases suggest that few defendants are able to carry their burden,[126] but that a transfer may be granted where the interests are clearly one-sided or where the case presents extraordinary facts.[127]

For Plea and Sentencing

Defendants who wish to waive their right to trial may petition the court in the district in which they have been charged for a change of venue, for sentencing purposes, to the district in which they are being held or are present.[128] By definition, the rule requires the pendency of an indictment, information, or complaint in the district from which the accused seeks a transfer of venue.[129] Prosecutors in both districts must concur.[130] Should the defendant subsequently fail to plead as agreed or should the receiving court refuse to accept the plea, the transfer is revoked.[131] Juveniles who wish to waive federal delinquency proceedings enjoy similar benefits.[132]

End Notes

[1] 2 WRIGHT, FEDERAL PRACTICE AND PROCEDURE §301 (Crim. 3d ed. 2000)("Strictly speaking the former constitutional provision [Art.III, §2, cl.3] is a venue provision, since it fixes the place of trial, while the latter [Amend. VI] is a vicinage provision, since it deals with the place from which the jurors are to be selected. This technical distinction has been of no importance whatever"), *citing inter alia*, Orfield, *Venue of Federal Criminal Cases*, 17 UNIVERSITY OF PITTSBURGH LAW REVIEW 375, 380 (1955).
Professor Wright's observation may be subject to one small caveat. Following hurricane devastation in the Gulf states, Congress enacted legislation that authorizes the federal district courts to relocate outside their districts in emergency situations, 28 U.S.C. 141(b). The provision revives the state (venue)-district (vicinage) distinction. A district court, relocated in the different state, may try criminal cases arising in its former district with the consent of the defendant, but regardless of whether it has relocated in another state or within another district within the same state unless the defendant consents, it must draw jurors from the district in which the crime occurred, 28 U.S.C. 141(b)(2),(3).

As a general rule, each district court must establish a plan for the random selection of jurors representing "a fair cross section of the community in the district or division wherein the court convenes," 28 U.S.C. 1861, 1863.

Other than section 141 noted above there does not appear to be any authority for a district court to convene other than in the judicial district to which it is assigned.

[2] PLUCKNETT,ACONCISE HISTORY OF THE COMMON LAW, 112-24 (5th ed. 1956); II POLLOCK &MAITLAND,HISTORY OF ENGLISH LAW, 645-56 (2d ed. 1898); 1 STEPHEN,HISTORY OF THE CRIMINAL LAW OF ENGLAND, 254-65 (1883); HELLER, THE SIXTH AMENDMENT TO THE CONSTITUTION OF THE UNITED STATES, 8 (1951).

[3] III BLACKSTONE,COMMENTARIES ON THE LAWS OF ENGLAND, 359-60 (1768) ("Also, by the policy of the ancient law, the jury was to come *de vicineto*, from the neighbourhood of the vill or place where the cause of action was laid in the declaration; and therefore some of the jury were obliged to be returned from the hundred in which such vill lay; and, if none were returned, the array might be challenged for defect of hundredors ... for, living in the neighbourhood, they were properly the very country, or *pais*, to which both parties had appealed; and were supposed to know before-hand the characters of the parties and witnesses, and therefore the better knew what credit to give to the facts alleged in evidence. But this convenience was overballanced by another very natural and almost unavoidable inconvenience; that jurors, coming out of the immediate neighbourhood, would be apt to intermix their prejudices and partialities in the trial of the right. And this our law was so sensible of, that for a long time has been gradually relinquishing this practice ... At length, by statute 4 &5 Ann. c.16, it was entirely abolished upon all civil actions, except upon penal statutes; and upon those also by the 24 Geo.II. c.18. the jury being now only to come *de corpore comitatus*, from the body of the county at large, and not *de vicineto*, or from the particular neighbourhood ")); Blume, *The Place of Trial of Criminal Cases: Constitutional Vicinage and Venue*, 43 MICHIGAN LAW REVIEW 59, 60 (1944); *see generally*, Kershen, *Vicinage*, 29 OKLAHOMA LAW REVIEW 801 (1976)(Pt.I); 30 OKLAHOMA LAW REVIEW 73 (1977)(Pt.II).

[4] Letter dated May 17, 1769, to His Royal Majesty, George III, from the Virginia House of Burgesses, JOURNALS OF THE HOUSE OF BURGESSES 1766-1769, 216 ("When we consider, that by the established Laws and Constitution of this Colony, the most ample Provision is made for apprehending and punishing all those who shall dare to engage in any treasonable Practices against your Majesty, or disturb the Tranquility of Government, we cannot, without Horror, thinks of the new, unusual, and permit us, with all Humility, to add, unconstitutional and illegal Mode, recommended to your Majesty, of seizing and carrying beyond Sea, the Inhabitants of America, suspected of any Crime; and of trying such Persons in any other Manner than by the ancient and long established Course of Proceeding: For, how truly deplorable must be the Case of a wretched American, who, have incurred the Displeasure of any one in Power, is dragged from his native Home, and his dearest domestick Connections, thrown into Prison, not to await his Trial before a Court, Jury, or Judges, from a Knowledge of whom is encouraged to hope for speedy Justice; but to exchange his Imprisonment in his own Country, for Fetters amongst Strangers? Conveyed to a distant Land, where no Friend, no Relation, will alleviate his Distresses, or minister to his Necessities; and where no Witness can be found to testify [to] his Innocence; shunned by the reputable and honest, and consigned to the Society and Converse of the wretched and abandoned; he can only pray that he may soon end his Misery with his life").

[5] III FARRAND,RECORDS OF THE FEDERAL CONVENTION OF 1787, 600 (1966) ("All Criminal offenses, (except in cases of impeachment), shall be tried in the State where they shall be committed—the trial shall be open & public & be by Jury ... ").

[6] III FARRAND,RECORDS OF THE FEDERAL CONVENTION OF 1787, 626 (1966) ("All crimes, except upon impeachment, shall be tried by a Jury of twelve men; and if they shall have been committed within any State, shall be tried within such State ... ").

[7] Farrand quotes the proposals of Convention delegate Roger Sherman of Connecticut which Farrand believed "more probably present[ed] the ideas of the Connecticut delegation in forming the New Jersey Plan," III FARRAND,RECORDS OF THE FEDERAL CONVENTION OF 1787, 615 (1966). Sherman proposed, *inter alia*, "That no person shall be liable to be tried for any criminal offence, committed within any of the United States, in any other state than that wherein the offence shall be committed, nor be deprived of the privilege of trial by a jury, by virtue of any law of the United States," ID. at 616.

[8] II ELLIOT,DEBATES ON THE ADOPTION OF THE FEDERAL CONSTITUTION 109-10 (Holmes-Mass.)("It is a maxim universally admitted, that the safety of the subject consists in having a right to a trial as free and impartial as the lot of humanity will admit of. Does the Constitution make provision for such a trial? I think not; for in a criminal process, a person shall not have a right to insist on a trial in the vicinity where the fact was committed where a jury of the peers would, from their local situation, have an opportunity to form a judgment of the *character* of the person charged with the crime, and also to judge of the *credibility* of the witnesses. There a person must be tried by a jury of strangers; a jury who *may* be interested in his conviction; and where he *may* by reason of the distance of his residence from the place of trial, be incapable of making such a defence as he is, in justice, entitled to, and which he could avail himself of, if his trial was in the same county where the crime is said to have been committed"); see also, ID. AT 400 (TREADWAY-N.Y.); III ELLIOT,DEBATES ON THE

ADOPTION OF THE FEDERAL CONSTITUTION 545 (HENRY-VA.); ID. at 569 (Grayson-Va.); IV ELLIOT,DEBATES ON THE ADOPTION OF THE FEDERAL CONSTITUTION 150 (McDowall-N.C.).

[9] 1 ANNALS 436 (1789).

[10] Letter from James Madison to Edmund Pendleton, dated September 14, 1789, "The Senate have sent back the plan of amendments with some alternations which strike in my opinion at the most salutary articles. In many of the States juries even in criminal cases, are taken from the State at large—in others from districts of considerable extent—in very few from the County alone. Hence a dislike to the restraint with respect to *vicinage*, which has produced a negative on that clause, "12 THE PAPERS OF JAMES MADISON 402.

[11] 1 Stat. 98 (1789).

[12] II STORY,COMMENTARIES ON THE CONSTITUTION §1781 (1833)("It is observable, that the trial of all crimes is not only to be by jury, but to be held in the State where they are committed. The object of this clause is to secure the party accused from being dragged to a trial in some distant State, away from his friends, and witnesses, and neighborhood, and thus to be subjected to the verdict of mere strangers, who may feel on common sympathy, or who may even cherish animosities or prejudices against him. Besides this, a trial in a distant State or territory might subject the party to the most oppressive expenses, or perhaps even to the inability of procuring the proper witnesses to establish his innocence. There is little danger, indeed, that Congress would ever exert their power in such an oppressive and unjustifiable a manner. But upon a subject so vital to the security of the citizen, it was fit to leave as little as possible to mere discretion. By the common law, trial of all crimes is required to be in the county where they are committed. Nay, it originally carried its jealousy still further, and required that the jury itself should come from the vicinage of the place where the crime was alleged to be committed. This was certain a precaution which, however, justifiable in an early and barbarous state of society, is little commendable in its more advance stages. It has been justly remarked, that in such cases to summon a jury laboring under local prejudices is laying a snare for their consciences; and though they should have virtue and vigor of mind sufficient to keep them upright, the parties will grow suspicious, and indulge other doubts of the impartiality of the trial").

[13] 1 Stat. 73 (1789).

[14] 1 Stat. 88 (1789)("[I]n cases punishable with death, the trial shall be held in the county where the offence was committed, or where that cannot be done without great inconvenience, twelve petit jurors at least shall be summoned from thence"). Early federal capital offenses included piracy, treason, murder, and counterfeiting, 1 Stat. 112-14 (1789).

[15] 18 U.S.C. 3235.

[16] 12 Stat. 588 (1862).

[17] E.g., 20 Stat. 102 (1878)("All offenses committed in either of the subdivisions shall be cognizable and indictable within said division ... All grand and petit jurors summoned for service in each division shall be residents of such division"); *see also*, 21 Stat. 64 (1880), 21 Stat. 176 (1880), 25 Stat. 388 (1988), 28 Stat. 68 (1894), 31 Stat. 6 (1900).

[18] 36 Stat. 1169 (1911).

[19] F.R.Crim.P. 18 (1964 ed.)(" ... if the district consists of two or more divisions the trial shall be had in a division in which the offense was committed").

[20] Kershen, *Vicinage*, 30 OKLAHOMA LAW REVIEW 3, 65, 72, 74-5 (1977)("After 1911, so far as Congress was concerned, the concept of vicinage had disappeared as an independent, significant concept ... Hence, after 1911, the federal courts, just like Congress, totally identified the geographical source from which petit jurors were summoned with the place at which the trial was being held. For the courts, too, the concept of vicinage had been subsumed within the concept of venue ... In light of the legislative and decisional history of the concepts of venue and vicinage ... it is understandable that Professor Wright could say ... that the distinction between venue and vicinage is a 'technical distinction having no importance.' It is also understandable that Professor Blue could write as early as 1944: 'The tendency of modern law is to think of the place of trial rather than the place from which the jury must be summoned. From vicinage to venue has been the pattern of development, and the transition is about complete.' With the deletion of the divisional venue in 1966 ... the transition was complete"), quoting, I WRIGHT,FEDERAL PRACTICE AND PROCEDURE §301, at 579 (Crim. 1969) and Blume, *The Place of Trial of Criminal Cases: Constitutional Vicinage and Venue*, 43 MICHIGAN LAW REVIEW 59, 91 (1944); *see also*, *United States v. Wipf*, 397 F.3d 677, 685-86 (8th Cir. 2005)(the Sixth Amendment does not require summoning jurors from the division of the district in which the crime occurred); *United States v. Miller*, 116 F.3d 641, 659 (2d Cir. 1997)("The [Sixth] Amendment's guarantees of an impartial jury 'of the State and district' in which the crime was committed does not require a narrower geographical focus than the district itself").

For arguments in favor of recognizing a community right to vicinage see, Engel, *The Public's Vicinage Right: A Constitutional Argument*, 75 NEW YORK UNIVERSITY LAW REVIEW 1658 (2000); Levenson, *Change of Venue and the Role of the Criminal Jury*, 66 SOUTHERN CALIFORNIA LAW REVIEW 1533 (1992).

[21] *United States v. Root*, 585 F.3d 145, 155 (3d Cir. 2009); *United States v. Brodie*, 524 F.3d 259, 273 (D.C.Cir. 2008); *United States v. Johnson*, 510 F.3d 521, 524 (4th Cir. 2007); *United States v. Johnson*, 462 F.3d 815, 820 (8th Cir. 2006); *United States v. Ramirez*, 420 F.3d 134, 139 (2d Cir. 2005).

[22] *United States v. Royer*, 549 F.3d 886, 893 (2d Cir. 2008)(venue must be laid in a district where all the counts may be tried"); *United States v. Haire*, 371 F.3d 833, 837 (D.C.Cir. 2004); *United States v. Wood*, 364 F.3d 704, 710 (6th Cir. 2004); *United States v. Villarini*, 238 F.3d 530, 533 (4th Cir. 2001).

[23] *United States v. Root*, 585 F.3d 145, 155 (2d Cir. 2009); *United States v. Delgado*, 545 F.3d 1195, 1206 (9th Cir. 2008); *United States v. Kelly*, 535 F.3d 1229, 1233 (10th Cir. 2008);*United States v. Brodie*, 534 F.3d 259, 273 (D.C. Cir. 2008); *United States v. Muhammad*, 502 F.3d 646, 652 (7th Cir. 2007); *United States v. Strain*, 396 F.3d 689, 692 (5th Cir. 2005).

[24] *United States v. Calderon*, 243 F.3d 587, 590-91 (2d Cir. 2001); *United States v. Cordova*, 157 F.3d 587, 597 (8th Cir. 1998).

[25] *United States v. Ebersole*, 411 F.3d 517, 524 (4th Cir. 2005); see also, *United States v. Matera*, 489 F.3d 115, 124 (2d cir. 2007)(defendant waived when he failed to object to venue during district court proceedings).

[26] *United States v. Kelly*, 535 F.3d 1229, 1234 (10th Cir. 2008); *United States v. Novak*, 443 F.3d 150, 161 (2d Cir. 2006); *United States v. Grenoble*, 413 F.3d 569, 573 (6th Cir. 2005); *United States v. Strain*, 396 F.3d 689, 693 (5th Cir. 2005).

[27] *United States v. Strain*, 396 F.3d 689, 693 (5th Cir. 2005); *United States v. Collins*, 372 F.3d 629, 633 (4th Cir. 2004); *United States v. Roberts*, 308 F.3d 1147, 1152 (11th Cir. 2002); *United States v. Ringer*, 300 F.3d 788, 790 (7th Cir. 2002).

[28] *United States v. Rodriguez-Moreno*, 526 U.S. 275, 279 (1999), quoting, *United States v. Cabrales*, 524 U.S. 1, 6-7 (1998), and *United States v. Anderson*, 326 U.S. 699, 703 (1946).

[29] Dobie, *Venue in Criminal Cases in the United States District Court*, 12 VIRGINIA LAW REVIEW 287, 289-90 (1926)(emphasis in the original)("All federal crimes are statutory, and these crimes are often defined, hidden away amid pompous verbosity, in terms of a single verb. That essential verb usually contains the key to the solution of the question: In what district was the crime committed ... So in the celebrated Burton case, twice before the Supreme Court, the statute said: 'No Senator * * * shall *receive or agree to receive* any compensation' for a certain kind of service. In the first opinion, the question was where was the compensation *received*, at St. Louis, where the check was mailed and where the ban was on which it was drawn, or in Washington, where defendant deposited it in another bank which placed the amount of the check unconditionally to his credit. The *receipt* was held to be in Washington and the St. Louis conviction reversed[, *United States v. Burton*, 196 U.S. 283 (1906)]. But the second opinion dealt with where the defendant *agreed to receive* the compensation. This the court said, was in St. Louis, the place where the *agreement* was finally accepted and ratified[, *United States v. Burton*, 202 U.S. 344(1906)]"); *United States v. Palma-Ruedas*, 121 F.3d 841, 847-51 (3d Cir. 1997), *rev'd sub nom., United States v. Rodriguez-Moreno*, 526 U.S. 275 (1999).

[30] For a critical review of *Rodriguez-Moreno see*, *Stretching Venue Beyond Constitutional Recognition*, 90JOURNAL OF CRIMINAL LAW &CRIMINOLOGY 951 (1999).

[31] 14 Stat. 484 (1867).

[32] Rev. Stat. §731 (1878).

[33] 14 Stat. 484 (1867).

[34] 18 U.S.C. 371.

[35] *United States v. Dowlin*, 408 F.3d 647, 659 (10th Cir. 2005); *United States v. Beverly*, 369 F.3d 516, 532 (6th Cir. 2004); *United States v. Svoboda*, 347 F.3d 471, 476 (2d Cir. 2003); *United States v. Guerra*, 293 F.3d 1279, 1285 (11th Cir. 2002).

[36] *United States v. Shabani*, 513 U.S. 10, 13-4 (1994)(21 U.S.C. 846, conspiracy to violate the Controlled Substances Act, has no overt act requirement); *Whitfield v. United States*, 543 U.S. 209, 214 (2005)(18 U.S.C. 1956, conspiracy to commit money laundering, has no overt act requirement).

[37] "The court, passing on the ruling of the trial court, said by District Judge Carland, and we quote its language to avail ourselves not only of the citation of cases, but of the comments upon them: ' ... [At common law] no overt act need be shown or ever performed to authorize a conviction. If conspirators enter into the illegal agreement in one county, the crime is perpetrated there, and they may be immediately prosecuted; but the proceedings against them must be in that county. If they go into another county to execute their plans of mischief, and there commit an overt act, they may be punished in the latter county without any evidence of an express renewal of their agreement ... If this was the law of venue in conspiracies at common law, where proof of an overt act was not necessary to show a completed offense, the same rule can be urged with much greater force [here], as the offense described [here] for all practical purposes is not complete until an overt act is committed ... It seems clear, then, that whether we place reliance on the common law or on §731, Rev. Stat., the venue of the offense was correctly laid ... '" 225 U.S. at 365-66. For a more extensive discussion of *Hyde, see*, Abrams, *Conspiracy and Multi-Venue in Federal Criminal Prosecutions: The Crime Committed Formula*, 9 UCLA LAW REVIEW 751 (1962).

[38] *United States v. Brodie*, 534 F.3d 259, 273 (D.C. Cir. 2008); *United States v. Nichols*, 416 F.3d 811, 824 (8th Cir. 2005); *United States v. Geibel*, 369 F.3d 682, 696 (2d Cir. 2004); *United States v. Pearson*, 340 F.3d 459, 467 (7th Cir. 2003); *United States v. Robinson*, 275 F.3d 371, 379 (4th Cir. 2002); *United States v. Smith*, 198 F.3d 377, 382 (2d Cir. 1999); *United States v. Schlei*, 122 F.3d 944, 975 (11th Cir. 1997). Each of these cases involves conspiracy under 18 U.S.C. 371 which carries an overt act requirement.

[39] *United States v. Morales*, 445 F.3d 1081, 1084 (8th Cir. 2006); *United States v. Haire*, 371 F.3d 833, 838 (D.C. Cir. 2004); *United States v. Carbajal*, 290 F.3d 277, 289 (5th Cir. 2002); *United States v. Crozier*, 259 F.3d 503, 519 (6th Cir. 2001); *United States v. Antonakeas*, 255 F.3d 714, 726 (9th Cir. 2001); *United States v. Matthews*, 168 F.3d 1234, 1246 (11th Cir. 1999); *United States v. Cordova*, 157 F.3d 587, 597 (8th Cir. 1998). Each of these cases involves conspiracy under 21 U.S.C. 846 which does not include an overt act requirement (*United States v. Shabani*, 513 U.S. 10 (1994)); see also, *United States v. Rommy,* 506 F.3d 108, 111 (2d Cir. 2007)(conspiracy under 21 U.S.C. 963, no overt act requirement); *United States v. Royer*, 549 F.3d 886, 896 (2d Cir. 2008)(RICO conspiracy under 18 U.S.C. 1962(d), no overt act requirement); *United States v. Moussaoui*, 591 F.3d 263, 300 (4th Cir. 2010)(venue was proper in the Eastern District of Virginia when co-conspirators committed overt acts in furtherance of conspiracies outlawed under different statutes, some of which had an overt act requirement (e.g., 18 U.S.C. 1117) and some of which did not (e.g., 18 U.S.C. 2332a).

[40] "If the Government can prove the [conspiratorial] agreement it has alleged, Cabrales can be prosecuted in Missouri for that confederacy, and her money laundering in Florida could be shown as overt acts in furtherance of the conspiracy. See 18 U.S.C. §371 (requiring proof of an act to effect the object of the conspiracy)," 524 U.S. at 9.

[41] *Whitfield v. United States*, 543 U.S. 209, 218 (2005); *United States v. Valdez-Santos*, 457 F.3d 1044, 1046 (9th Cir. 2006)("[A]n aider and abetter to a continuing crime may be tried anywhere a part of the crime occurred").

[42] "Whoever in any way or degree obstructs, delays, or affects commerce or the movement of any article or commodity in commerce, by robbery or extortion or attempts or conspires so to do, or commits or threatens physical violence to any person or property in furtherance of a plan or purpose to do anything in violation of this section shall be fined under this title or imprisoned not more than twenty years, or both," 18 U.S.C. 1951(a).

[43] *United States v. Lewis*, 797 F.2d 358, 367 (7th Cir. 1986)("[V]enue for a Hobbs Act prosecution lies in any district where the requisite effect on commerce is present, even if the acts of extortion occur outside the jurisdiction"); *United States v. Stephenson*, 895 F.2d 867, 875 (2d Cir. 1990)("Venue under the Hobbs Act is proper in any district where the interstate commerce is affected or where the alleged acts took place").

[44] *Stirone v. United States*, 361 U.S. 212, 218 (1960); *United States v. Vega Molina*, 407 F.3d 511, 526-27 (1st Cir. 2005); *United States v. McCarter*, 406 F.3d 460, 462 (7th Cir. 2005); *United States v. Verbitskaya*, 406 F.3d 1324, 1330-331 (11th Cir. 2005).

[45] *United States v. O'Donnell*, 510 F.2d 1190, 1192-195 (6th Cir. 1975); *United States v. Tedesco*, 635 F.2d 902, 904-906 (1st Cir. 1980); *United States v. Barham*, 666 F.2d 521, 523-24 (11th Cir. 1982); *United States v. Kibler*, 667 F.2d 452, 454-55 (4th Cir. 1975); *United States v. Reed*, 773 F.2d 477, 484-86 (2d Cir. 1985); *United States v. Frederick*, 835 F.2d 1211, 1213-214 (7th Cir. 1988); *contra, United States v. Swann*, 441 F.2d 1053, 1055 (D.C. Cir. 1971); *see generally, Criminal Venue in the Federal Courts: The Obstruction of Justice Puzzle*, 82 MICHIGAN LAW REVIEW 90 (1983).

[46] *United States v. Reed*, 773 F.2d 477, 481, 482 (2d Cir. 1985)(emphasis added)("[A] review of relevant authorities demonstrates that there is no single defined policy or mechanical test to determine constitutional venue. Rather, the test is best described as a substantial contacts rule that takes into account a number of factors—the site of the defendant's acts, the elements and nature of the crime, *the locus of the effect of the criminal conduct*, and the suitability of each district for accurate factfinding ... places that suffer the effects of a crime are entitled to consideration for venue purposes"); *see also*, *United States v. Williams*, 788 F.2d 1213, 1215 (6th Cir. 1986)(applying "the substantial contacts test as well as the rationale and framework of analysis articulated by the *Reed* court" to venue in a bail jumping case); *United States v. Beddow*, 957 F.2d 1330, 1336 (6th Cir. 1992)("[T]he funds involved in both money laundering counts were acquired by selling drugs in the Western District of Michigan ... Under the substantial contacts test used in the Sixth Circuit, venue was proper in the Western District of Michigan"); *United States v. Newsom*, 9 F.3d 337, 339 (4th Cir. 1993); *United States v. Bagnell*, 679 F.2d 826, 832 (11th Cir. 1982)("[P]rosecution [of the use of interstate carrier to transport obscene material] in the district of receipt is eminently reasonable in view of the fact that it is the recipient community that suffers the deleterious effects of pornography distribution").

[47] *United States v. Ramirez*, 420 F.3d 134, (2d Cir. 2005)("[W]hen venue may properly lie in more than one district under a continuing offense theory, we should also ask whether the criminal acts in question bear substantial contacts with any given venue"); *United States v. Brika*, 416 F.3d 514, 527 (6th Cir. 2005)("The crime is also one in which the locus of the effect of the criminal conduct is to be found more in the district in which the call is received that in the district in which it is placed, meeting the third factor of the substantial contacts test").

[48] *United States v. Bowens*, 224 F.3d 302, 311 (4th Cir. 2000)("[T]he government argues, venue for a §1071 prosecution should lie in the district where the effects of the criminal conduct are felt ... Instead, we conclude that the Supreme Court's recent decisions in *Cabrales* and *Rodriguez-Moreno* require us to determine venue solely by reference to the essential conduct elements of the crime, without regard to Congress's purpose in forbidding the conduct"); *United States v. Peterson*, 357 F.Supp.2d 748, 752 (S.D.N.Y. 2005)("[A]ll three crimes alleged are continuing offenses that involved conduct in New York and elsewhere. Wire fraud clearly is a continuing offense. The crime of engaging in the insurance business following a felony conviction likewise is a crime that spans space and time, and here Peterson is alleged to have conducted the business of insurance

over a period of time, with actions occurring in and having an effect on a number of jurisdictions. The money laundering charge also involves, in the context alleged here, a continuing offense, as the Government alleges that Peterson caused illegal proceeds of his insurance fraud scheme to be cleared through New York for transmission to a bank account in the Cayman Islands ... All three of these offenses alleged involved some conduct in New York, the effects of the conduct are felt here ... and this Court certainly is a suitable forum for accurate fact-finding"); *United States v. D-1 Mikell*, 163 F.Supp.2d 720, 733 (E.D.Mich. 2001) ("[A]lthough venue may lie where the effects of the defendant's conduct are felt, this is true only when Congress had defined the essential conduct elements in terms of those effects").

[49] *United States v. Ramirez*, 420 F.3d 134, 144-45 (2d Cir. 2005)("While a scheme to defraud is certainly one of three essential elements of mail fraud, it is not an essential conduct element ... [Thus,] having devised or intending to devise a scheme or artifice to defraud, while an essential element, is not an essential conduct element for purposes of establishing venue"); *United States v. Strain*, 396 F.3d 689, 694 (5th Cir. 2005)("The issuance of the warrant and Strain's knowledge of it, however, are 'circumstance elements' of the offense of harboring, insofar as they do not involve any proscribed conduct by the accused. As such neither may serve as a basis for establishing venue"); *United States v. Clenney*, 434 F.3d 780, 781-82 (5th Cir. 2005)("The government argues that venue exists under the terms of the statute [(18 U.SA.C. 1204)] because intent to obstruct the lawful exercise of parental rights is an element of the offense, and Carmichael's parental rights were violated in the Northern District. We disagree, because this element merely speaks to the offender's *mens rea* as he commits the conduct essential to the crime; it is plainly not an 'essential conduct element' as required by *Rodriguez-Moreno").*

[50] " ... Any offense involving the use of the mails, transportation in interstate or foreign commerce, or the importation of an object or person into the United States is a continuing offense and, except as otherwise expressly provided by enactment of Congress, may be inquired of and prosecuted in any district from, through, or into which such commerce, mail matter, or imported object or person moves," 18 U.S.C. 3237(a).

[51] "Four years earlier the Supreme Court had held that an offense under the Federal Denture Act was complete when the goods are deposited in the mails, and that prosecution could be had at the place of delivery. This construction was required the Court thought, by 'the large policy back of the constitutional safeguards.' The Reviser of the Criminal Code read that decision, however, as having 'turned on the absence of a special venue provision in the Denture Act' and added the second paragraph to §3237(a) that 'removes all doubt as to the venue of continuing offenses and makes unnecessary special venue provisions* * *.' This of course presupposes that wide choice of venue is necessarily a good thing, a view prosecutors are likely to share but that many persons, include not infrequently a majority of the Supreme Court, have rejected," 2 WRIGHT,FEDERAL PRACTICE AND PROCEDURE, §303 (Crim. 3d ed. 2000), referring to *United States v. Johnson*, 323 U.S. 273 (1944).

[52] ID. and cases cited therein; *see also, United States v.Kapordelis*, 569 F.3d 1291, 1307-308 (11th Cir. 2009)(venue for prosecution of use of a minor in the production of child pornography, knowingly transported in interstate commerce, was proper in the district through which it was transported); *United States v. Rowe*, 414 F.3d 271, (2d Cir. 2005)(venue for prosecution of an Internet offer, transmitted in interstate commerce, to exchange or distribute child pornography was proper in the district were it was received); *United States v. Haire*, 371 F.3d 833, 838 (D.C. Cir. 2004)(venue for unlawful importation of cocaine prosecution was proper under the second paragraph of §3237(a) in the district into which the cocaine was imported); *United States v. Cole*, 262 F.3d 704, 710 (8th Cir. 2001)(venue for prosecution of a charge of interstate transportation for immoral purposes was proper under the second paragraph of §3237(a) in the district in which the victim was transported); *United States v. Sutton*, 13 F.3d 595, 598-99 (2d Cir. 1994)(venue for prosecution of a charge of producing and transferring false documents was proper under the second paragraph of §3237(a) either in the district in which they were produced or the district into which they were mailed); *contra,United States v. Morgan*, 393 F.3d 192, 197-200 (D.C.Cir. 2004)(venue in the district for the District of Columbia was not proper under the second paragraph of §3237(a) for prosecution of a charge of receiving, in Maryland, federal property stolen in the District of Columbia); *United States v. Villarini*, 238 F.3d 530, 535-36 (4th Cir. 2001)(venue for prosecution of a money laundering charge was not proper under the second paragraph of §3237(a) in the district where the offenses which generated the tainted cash were committed when the laundering occurred elsewhere); *United States v. Brennan*, 183 F.3d 139, 144-49 (2d Cir. 1999)(venue for prosecution of a mail fraud charge was not proper under the second paragraph of §3237(a) in a district through which mail passed from another district in which it was mailed to destinations outside the district of transit).

[53] "Notwithstanding subsection (a), where an offense is described in section 7203 of the Internal Revenue Code of 1986, or where venue for prosecution of an offense described in section 7201 or 7206(1), (2), or (5) of such Code (whether or not the offense is also described in another provision of law) is based solely on a mailing to the Internal Revenue Service, and prosecution is begun in a judicial district other than the judicial district in which the defendant resides, he may upon motion filed in the district in which the prosecution is begun, elect to be tried in the district in which he was residing at the time the alleged offense was committed: *Provided,* That the motion is filed within twenty days after arraignment of the defendant upon indictment or information," 18 U.S.C. 3237(b).

[54] "The cost and inconvenience to the defendant may be substantial especially in the case of an extended trial. The additional expense to the defendant of living away from home, the problem of getting his local attorneys to leave their offices and practices for several days or weeks and the increased cost incurred thereby, the inconvenience to witnesses, these are all factors which the committee believes place a heavy burden upon the defendant which can be better borne by the Government. The committee believes, further, that, in the type of case covered by this bill, the acts for which the defendant is really being tried are generally committed in the district in which he resides and certainly bear little or no relationship to the place where his tax return is received," H.Rept. 85-1952, at 2 (1958); *see also*, S.Rept. 85-1890 (1958).

[55] As originally enacted, subsection 3237(b) included only 26 U.S.C. 7201 and 7206(1),(2) and (5) cases. Section 7203 cases were added in 1966 for the same reasons as the originals: relative cost and inconvenience to the taxpayers, their attorneys, and witnesses, H.Rept. 89-1915, at 5 (1966).

[56] The transfer option for cases under 26 U.S.C. 7201 (attempted tax evasion) or 7206(1),(2), or (5)(various frauds and false statements) does not apply when venue is proper in a nonresidential district for reasons other than a mailing, *United States v. Humphreys*, 982 F.2d 254, 260 (8th Cir. 1993).

[57] This is the difference between *Cabrales* and *Rodriguez-Moreno*: "The existence of criminally generated proceeds [in *Cabrales*] was a circumstance element of the offense but the proscribed conduct, defendant's money laundering activity, occurred after the fact of an offense begun and completed by others. [In *Rodriguez-Moreno*], by contrast, given the 'during and in relation to' language, the underlying crime of violence is a critical part of the §924(c)(1) offense," 526 U.S. at 280-81 n.4.

[58] *United States v. Ramirez*, 420 F.3d 134, 142-43 (2d Cir. 2005).

[59] *United States v. Ebersole*, 411 F.3d 517, 525-27 (4th Cir. 2005); *United States v. Pace*, 314 F.3d 344, 350 (9th Cir. 2002); *United States v. Kim*, 246 F.3d 186, 192 (2d Cir. 2001).

[60] *United States v. Woods*, 364 F.3d 704,710 (6th Cir. 2004).

[61] *United States v. Scott*, 270 F.3d 30, 36 (1st Cir. 2001).

[62] *United States v. Zidell*, 323 F.3d 412 (6th Cir. 2003); *United States v. Solis*, 299 F.3d 420, 445 n.76 (5th Cir. 2002); *United States v. Uribe*, 890 F.2d 554, 559 (1st Cir. 1989); *United States v. Baskin*, 886 F.2d 383, 388 (D.C.Cir. 1989).

[63] *United States v. Fabian*, 312 F.3d 550, 557 (2d Cir. 2002).

[64] *United States v. Fleischli*, 305 F.3d 643, 658 (7th Cir. 2002).

[65] *United States v. Williams*, 291 F.3d 1180, 1189 (9th Cir. 2002).

[66] *United States v. Saavedra*, 223 F.3d 85, 91 (2d Cir. 2000).

[67] *United States v. Muench*, 153 F.3d 1298, 1303-305(11th Cir. 1998); *United States v. Crawford*, 115 F.3d 1397, 1406 (8th Cir. 1997).

[68] *United States v. Stewart*, 256 F.3d 231, 244 (4th Cir. 2001); *United States v. Smith*, 198 F.3d 377, 382 (2d Cir. 1999). Where conduct which constitutes the aiding and abetting is itself a crime, at least one court has held that a defendant may not be tried in one district for selling a precursor chemical and then tried in another district for aiding and abetting the manufacture of a controlled substance by selling the chemical to the manufacturer, *United States v. Valdez-Santos*, 370 F.Supp.2d 1051, 1055 (E.D.Cal. 2005).

[69] *United States v. Barnette*, 211 F.3d 803, 814 (4th Cir. 2000)(18 U.S.C. 924(c), (j)(use or carriage of a firearm to commit murder during the commission of crime of violence or drug trafficking crime)); *United States v. Aiken*, 76 F.Supp.2d 1346, 1349-351 (S.D.Fla. 1999)(18 U.S.C. 1959 (murder in aid of racketeering)).

[70] *Hayes v. United States*, 296 F.2d 657, 667 (8th Cir. 1961); *Bickford v. Looney*, 219 F.2d 555, 556 (10th Cir. 1955); *United States v. Taylor*, 316 F.Supp.2d 722, 728 (N.D.Ind. 2004).

[71] *United States v. Parker*, 103 F.2d 857, 861 (3d Cir. 1939); *Barrett v. United States*, 82 F.2d 528, 534 (7th Cir. 1936); *Davis v. United States*, 32 F.2d 860, 860 (9th Cir. 1929).

[72] *Hayes v. United States*, 296 F.2d 657, 667 (8th Cir. 1961); *Davis v. United States*, 32 F.2d 860, 860 (9th Cir. 1929).

[73] *United States v. Parker*, 103 F.2d 857, 861 (3d Cir. 1939).

[74] *United States v. Taylor*, 316 F.Supp.2d 722, 728 (N.D.Ind. 2004).

[75] "In all cases of murder or manslaughter, the offense shall be deemed to have been committed at the place where the injury was inflicted, or the poison administered or other means employed which caused the death, without regard to the place where the death occurs," 18 U.S.C. 3236.

[76] *Ball v. United States*, 140 U.S. 118, 136 (1891)("If this section [relating venue over offenses occurring in more than one district] is applicable to the crime of murder, it certainly could not apply if the stroke were given in one district and the death ensued in some other country than the United States"). In *Ball,* the Court also noted that at common law, jurisdiction over the offense of murder required that the assault and resulting death occur within the same jurisdiction, 140 U.S. at 133.

[77] *United States v. Perez*, 940 F.Supp. 540, 548-49 (S.D.N.Y. 1996); *United States v. Aiken*, 76 F.Supp.2d 1346, 1349-351 (S.D.Fla. 1999).

[78] *United States v. Gotti*, 660 F.Supp.2d 512, 517 (S.D.N.Y. 2009).

[79] *United States v. Eder*, 836 F.2d 1145, 1148 (8th Cir. 1988). *Eder* is reminiscent of the cases that cite section 3236 for the proposition that a violation of 18 U.S.C. 1111, murder within the special maritime and territorial

jurisdiction of the United States, occurs when a victim is assaulted outside the territorial jurisdiction of the United States and then brought by the defendant within U.S. territorial jurisdiction and abandoned to the elements there under conditions that lead to the victim's death, *United States v. Todd*, 657 F.2d 212, 215 (8th Cir. 1981); *United States v. Parker*, 622 F.2d 298, 301 (8th Cir. 1980).

80 " ... The trial and punishment of offenses under this section may be in any district to or into which such alien is brought in pursuance of importation by the persons or persons accused, or in any district in which a violation of any of the provisions of this section occurs ... " 8 U.S.C. 1328.

81 " ... [S]uch prosecutions ... may be instituted at any place in the United States at which the violation may occur or at which the person charged with a violation under section 1325 or 1326 of this title may be apprehended ... " 8 U.S.C. 1329. *Unites States v. Uribe-Rios*, 558 F.3d 347, 357 (4th Cir. 2009), citing *United States v. Herrera-Ordones*, 190 F.3d 504, 511 (7th Cir. 1999), ("Courts have interpreted this provisions [(8 U.S.C. 1329)] as placing venue for a section 1326 offense in any district where an alien is 'found,'" whether his presence is voluntary or the authorities have brought him there).

82 "Any criminal proceeding may be brought in the district wherein any act or transaction constituting the violation occurred." *United States v. Royer*, 549 F.3d 886, 894 (2d Cir. 2008)("We have stated that venue is proper in a district where (1) the defendant intentionally or knowingly causes an act in furtherance of the charged offense to occur in the district of venue or (2) it is foreseeable that such an act would occur in the district of venue and it does").

83 " ... Any criminal proceeding may be brought in the district wherein any act or transaction constituting the violation occurred. A criminal proceeding based upon a violation of section 80a-33 of this title [destruction and falsification of records], or upon a failure to file a report other document required to be filed under this subchapter, may be brought in the district wherein the defendant is an inhabitant or maintains his principal office or place of business," 15 U.S.C. 80a-43.

84 " ... the district in which such violation was committed or through which has been conducted the transportation of the article in respect to which such violations has been committed ... " 15 U.S.C. 298.

85 "With respect to an offense under this section, an action may be inquired of and prosecuted in a district court of the United States for– (1) the district in which the child who is the subject of the support obligation involved resided during a period during which a person described in subsection (a) (referred to in this subsection as an 'obliger') failed to meet that support obligation; (2) the district in which the obliger resided during a period described in paragraph (1); or (3) any other district with jurisdiction otherwise provided for by law," 18 U.S.C. 228(e).

86 " ... Violations of this section may be prosecuted only in the Federal judicial district in which the original crime was alleged to have been committed, or in which the person was held in custody or confinement, or in which an avoidance of service of process or a contempt referred to in clause (3) of the first paragraph of this section is alleged to have been committed, and only upon formal approval in writing by the Attorney General, the Deputy Attorney General, the Associate Attorney General, or an Assistant Attorney General of the United States, which function of approving prosecutions may not be delegated," 18 U.S.C. 1073.

87 "Violations of this section may be prosecuted in the Federal judicial district in which the original crime was alleged to have been committed or in which the person was held in custody or confinement: Provided, however, That this section shall not be construed as indicating an intent on the part of Congress to prevent any State, Territory, Commonwealth, or possession of the United States of any jurisdiction over any offense over which they would have jurisdiction in the absence of such section," 18 U.S.C. 1074(b).

88 "A prosecution under this section [witness tampering] or section 1503 [obstruction of judicial proceedings] may be brought in the district in which the official proceeding (whether or not pending or about to be instituted) was intended to be affected or in the district in which the conduct constituting the alleged offense occurred," 18 U.S.C. 1512(*i*).

89 "Violation of this section, and attempts or conspiracies to commit such violations, shall be prosecuted by the United States attorney in the Federal district court having jurisdiction of the place where the offense occurred," 18 U.S.C. 1752(c).

90 "(1) Except as provided in paragraph (2), a prosecution for an offense under this section or section 1957 may be brought in – (A) any district in which the financial or monetary transaction is conducted; or (B) any district where a prosecution for the underlying specified unlawful activity could be brought, if the defendant participated in the transfer of the proceeds of the specified unlawful activity from that district to the district where the financial or monetary transaction is conducted. (2) A prosecution for an attempt or conspiracy offense under this section or section 1957 may be brought in the district where venue would lie for the completed offense under paragraph (1), or in any other district where an act in furtherance of the attempt or conspiracy took place. (3) For purposes of this section, a transfer of funds from one place to another, by wire or any other means, shall constitute a single, continuing transaction. Any person who conducts (as that term is defined in subsection (c)(2)) any portion of the transaction may be charged in any district in which the transaction takes place," 18 U.S.C. 1956(*i*).

91 "A violation of this section may be prosecuted in any Federal judicial district in which the underlying offense was committed, or in any other Federal judicial district as provided by law," 18 U.S.C. 2339(b).

[92] "... A violation of this section may be prosecuted in any Federal judicial district in which the underlying offense was committed or in any other Federal judicial district as provided by law," 18 U.S.C. 2339A(a).

[93] U.S.Const. Art.III, §2, cl.3.

[94] 1 Stat. 114 (1790).

[95] *See* Rev.Stat. §729 (1878)("The trial of all offenses committed upon the high seas, or elsewhere out of the jurisdiction of any particular state or district, shall be in the district where the offender is found, or into which he may first be brought"); 18 U.S.C. 3238 (1956 ed.)("The trial of all offenses begun or committed upon the high seas, or elsewhere out of the jurisdiction of any particular state or district, shall be in the district where the offender is found, or into which he may first be brought").

[96] S.Rept. 88-146 (1963); *see generally*, 2 WRIGHT, FEDERAL PRACTICE AND PROCEDURE §304 (Crim. 3d ed. 2000).

[97] *United States v. Pace*, 314 F.3d 344, 351 (9th Cir. 2002).

[98] *United States v. Lee*, 472 F.3d 638, 644-45 (9th Cir. 2006).

[99] *United States v. Wharton*, 320 F.3d 526, 536-37 (5th Cir. 2003)(emphasis in the original), quoting, *United States v. Erdos*, 474 F.2d 157, 160 (4th Cir. 1973); *see also*, *United States v. Feng*, 277 F.3d 1151, 1155 (9th Cir. 2002); *United States v. Catino*, 735 F.2d 718, 724 (2d Cir. 1984).

[100] *United States v. Wharton*, 320 F.3d 526, 536-37 (5th Cir. 2003).

[101] *United States v. Gurr*, 471 F.3d 144, 155 (D.C.Cir. 2006)

[102] *United States v. Liang*, 224 F.3d 1057, 1060-62 (9th Cir. 2000).

[103] *United States v. Feng*, 277 F.3d 1151, 1155 (9th Cir. 2002); *United States v. Fraser*, 709 F.2d 1556, 1558 (6th Cir. 1983); *United States v. Hsin-Yung*, 97 F.Supp.2d 24, 28 (D.D.C. 2000).

[104] *United States v. Pearson*, 791 F.2d 867, 869-70 (11th Cir. 1986)(venue over offenders first brought into the Southern District of Florida was proper in the Southern District of Alabama into which a joint offender had been first brought).

[105] *United States v. Levy Auto Parts*, 787 F.2d 946, 950-52 (4th Cir. 1986); *United States v. Erwin*, 602 F.2d 1183, 1185 (5th Cir. 1979); *United States v. Stickle*, 355 F.Supp.2d 1317, 1331-333 (S.D.Fla. 2004), aff'd, 454 F.3d 1265 (11th Cir. 2006).

[106] H.Rept. 103-324; H.Rept. 103-489 (1994).

[107] H.Rept. 103-711, at 408, *reprinted in*, 1994 U.S.C.C.A.N. 1876 ("Section 320909 – House recedes to Senate section 2961, optional venue for espionage").

[108] S.Rept. 103-296, at 27 (1994)("Section 6 would give the U.S. District Court for the District of Columbia and other federal district court authorized by law jurisdiction over trials of offenses involving violations of U.S. espionage statutes and related statutes where the alleged misconduct took place outside the United States. According to Justice Department representatives, the lack of such jurisdiction in U.S. courts has posed, from time to time, a substantial problem in terms of trying U.S. citizens in U.S. courts even [though] their conduct allegedly violated U.S. law, e.g., passing classified U.S. information to a foreign agent. This has led to prosecutions in foreign courts even though the United States had the predominant interest in prosecution. Section 6 is intended to provide an alternative in such circumstances"). This suggests the alternative sought was trial in U.S. courts rather than trial in foreign courts; not trial in the District of Columbia rather than in some other U.S. judicial district. Venue is not mentioned; jurisdiction is.

[109] F.R.Crim.P. 21(a); *United States v. Rodriguez*, 581 F.3d 775, 785 (8th Cir. 2009)("A motion to change venue must be granted if pretrial publicity was so extensive that reviewing court is required to presume unfairness of constitutional magnitude"); *see generally*, *The Right to Venue and the Right to an Impartial Jury: Resolving the Conflict in the Federal Constitution*, 52 UNIVERSITY OF CHICAGO LAW REVIEW 729 (1985).

[110] Requests have also been made on the basis of the demographic composition of the district, but the standard here seems even more demanding than that used in the press cases, e.g., *United States v. Granillo*, 288 F.3d 1071 (8th Cir. 2002)("Notwithstanding defendant's evidence suggesting that Hispanics comprise a small portion of the population in the State of Iowa, defendant did not present evidence indicating that his ethnic background would prevent jurors from being fair and impartial or that Hispanics were otherwise the target of purposeful discrimination in the jury selection process within the Southern District of Iowa").

[111] *United States v. Higgs*, 353 F.3d 281, 307-308 (4th Cir. 2003)("[T]he determination of whether a change of venue is required as a result of pretrial publicity involves a two-step process. First, the district court must determine whether the publicity is so inherently prejudicial that trial proceedings must be presumed to be stained, and , if so, grant a change of venue prior to jury selection. However, only in extreme circumstances may prejudice to a defendant's right to a fair trial be presumed from the existence of pretrial publicity itself. Ordinarily the trial court must conduct a *voir dire* of prospective jurors to determine if actual prejudice exists"); *United States v. Campa*, 459 F.3d 1121, 1143 (11th Cir. 2006); *United States v. Nelson*, 347 F.3d 701, 707-708 (8th Cir. 2003).

[112] *United States v. Campa*, 459 F.3d 1121, 1144-145 (11th Cir. 2006); *United States v. Jamieson*, 427 F.3d 394, 413 (6th Cir. 2005); *United States v. Sherwood*, 98 F.3d 402, 410 (9th Cir. 1996); *United States v. Brandon*, 17 F.3d 409, 441 (1st Cir. 1994).

[113] *United States v. Nelson*, 347 F.3d 701, 709 (8th Cir. 2003); *United States v. Allee*, 299 F.3d 996, 1000 (8th Cir. 2002); *United States v. Yousef*, 327 F.3d 56, 155 (2d Cir. 2003); *United States v. Johnson*, 354 F.Supp.2d 939, 982 (N. D. Iowa 2005).

[114] *United States v. Nettles*, 476 F.3d 508, 513 (7th Cir. 2007); *United States v. Jamieson*, 427 F.3d 394, 413 (6th Cir. 2005); *United States v. Higgs*, 353 F.3d 281, 308 (4th Cir. 2003); *United States v. Blom*, 242 F.3d 799, 804 (8th Cir. 2001); *United States v. Brandon*, 17 F.3d 409, 441 (1st Cir. 1994).

[115] *United States v. Nelson*, 347 F.3d 701, 709 (8th Cir. 2003)(jury pool survey indicated "only 29% of those jurors had formed strong or fixed opinions about the case"); *United States v. Blom*, 242 F.3d 799, 804 (8th Cir. 2001)(jury pool drawn from the entire state, questionnaires to probe impartiality sent to prospective jurors, increase in the number of peremptory strikes).

[116] *United States v. Knox*, 363 F.Supp.2d 845, 847 (W.D.Va. 2005)(scheduling retrial in another division following media attention surrounding the racketeering trial that ended in a hung jury); *United States v. Dakota*, 197 F.3d 821, 826-27 (6th Cir. 2000)(finding no abuse of discretion when the district court scheduled trial in different city within the same district in a case involving an anonymous jury empanelled "to minimize the prejudicial effects of pretrial publicity and an emotional, political atmosphere"); *but see*, *United States v. Lentz*, 352 F.Supp.2d 718, 722-23 (E.D.Va. 2005)(denying motion for retrial in another division until after voir dire established it was necessary since nature and level of media coverage was not so inherently prejudicial that taint had to be assumed).

[117] *United States v. McVeigh*, 918 F.Supp. 1467 (W.D.Okla. 1996)(Oklahoma City bombing case); *United States v. Gordon*, 380 F.Supp.2d 356, 365 (D.Del. 2005)(extensive press coverage, much of it adverse; substantial evidence that a high percentage of potential jurors had made up their minds and concluded the accused were guilty; trial could be transferred from Wilmington to Philadelphia with little difficulty or inconvenience).

[118] *In re United States*, 273 F.3d 380, 387-88 (3d Cir. 2001); *United States v. Morrison*, 946 F.2d 484, 490 (7th Cir. 1991); *United States v. Motz,* 652 F.Supp.2d 284, 290-91 (E.D.N.Y. 2009); *United States v. Balsiger*, 644 F.Supp.2d 1101, 1121 (E.D.Wis. 2009); *United States v. Burke*, 607 F.Supp.2d 1314, 1323 (M.D.Fla. 2009); *United States v. Radley*, 558 F.Supp.2d 865, 877 (N.D.Ill. 2008); *United States v. Moncrieffe*, 485 F.Supp.2d 1059, 1060 (S.D. Iowa 2007).

[119] *United States v. Jordan*, 223 F.3d 676, 685 (7th Cir. 2000); *United States v. Perry*, 152 F.3d 900, 904 (8th Cir. 1998); *United States v. Maldonado-Rivera*, 922 F.2d 934, 966 (2d Cir. 1990); *United States v. Fagan*, 821 F.2d 1002, 1008 (5th Cir. 1987).

[120] *In re United States*, 273 F.3d 380, 389 (3d Cir. 2001)(record was unclear whether the trial court had required the accused to bear the burden of proof on the Rule 21(b) motion); *In re Balsimo*, 68 F.3d 185, 187 (7th Cir. 1995)(trial court erroneously applied a presumption against transfers to a contiguous district except on a showing of truly compelling circumstances); *United States v. McManus*, 535 F.2d 460, (8th Cir. 1976)(finding an abuse of discretion in granting a change of venue to the California district of residence of the defendants because, "in view of the recent decisions of the Supreme Court that obscenity vel non must be determined on a local community standard, we have no choice but to order that this case be tried in Iowa ... A stronger showing than made here, such as intentional overreaching by the government, must be made, however, to overcome the government's choice of forum in postal obscenity cases").

[121] *In re United States*, 273 F.3d 380, 388 (3d Cir. 2001); *United States v. Crutchfield*, 379 F.Supp.2d 913, 923 (W.D. Tenn. 2005); *United States v. Stickle*, 355 F.Supp.2d 1317, 1321 (S.D.Fla. 2004)), aff'd, 454 F.3d 1265 (11th Cir. 2006); *United States v. Quattrone*, 277 F.Supp.2d 278, 279-80 (S.D.N.Y. 2003); *United States v. Carey*, 152 F.Supp.2d 415, 421-23 (S.D.N.Y. 2001).

[122] 2 WRIGHT,FEDERAL PRACTICE AND PROCEDURE 401-403 (Crim. 3d ed. 2000), citing *United States v. Hinton*, 268 F.Supp. 728, 731 (E.D.La. 1967), and quoting, *United States v. Bloom*, 78 F.R.D. 591, 608 (E.D.Pa. 1977); *see also*, Marcus, *Re-Evaluating Large Multiple-Defendant Criminal Prosecutions*, 11 WILLIAM &MARY BILL OF RIGHTS JOURNAL 67 (2002)("Federal Rule of Criminal Procedure 21(b) allows the trial judge to transfer the proceedings, at the defendant's request, 'in the interest of justice.' However, the hope of deference to negatively-impacted defendants never has been realized. These provisions ... often are not applied in favor of criminal defendants. To the contrary, they usually are construed quite narrowly in response to removal motions based on venue hardships").

[123] *United States v. Motz,* 652 F.Supp.2d 284, 291 (E.D.N.Y. 2009); *United States v. Carey*, 152 F.Supp.2d 415, 421 (S.D.N.Y. 2001); *United States v. Guastella*, 90 F.Supp.2d 335, 338 (S.D.N.Y. 2000); *United States v. Spy Factory, Inc.*, 951 F.Supp. 450 (S.D.N.Y. 1997); *United States v. Wecker*, 620 F.Supp. 1002, 1004 (D.Del. 1985).

[124] *United States v. Stickle*, 355 F.Supp.2d 1317, 1321 (S.D.Fla. 2004)), aff'd, 454 F.3d 1265 (11th Cir. 2006)("The burden falls on the defendant to demonstrate a substantial imbalance of inconvenience to himself if he is to succeed in nullifying the prosecutor's choice of venue").

[125] *United States v. McDade*, 827 F.Supp. 1153, 1191 (E.D.Pa. 1993)("[T]he government points out that it would be equally, if not more, difficult to get a fair trial in the Scranton area, where nearly everyone at least knows of Mr. McDade, and where his case has received plentiful press coverage. For this reason, the practical effect of this motion is substantial. At oral argument, counsel for Mr. McDade conceded that Mr. McDade would be

more likely to get a favorable array of prospective jurors when picking from his friends, neighbors, and constituents, than he would in a relatively strange vicinage ... It must be remembered that it is not just the defendant, but also the government, that is entitled to a fair trial").

[126] *United States v. Motz,* 652 F.Supp.2d 284, 292 (E.D.N.Y. 2009), quoting *United States v. United States Steel Corp.*, 233 F.Supp.2d 154, 157 (S.D.N.Y. 1964)("'To warrant a transfer ... it should appear that a trial there would be so unduly burdensome that fairness requires the transfer to another district of proper venue where a trial would be less burdensome' and that the Court's inquiry 'must take into account any countervailing considerations which may militate against removal'"). This is not to suggest that inconvenience to the defendant is always greater than inconvenience to the government. Several cases seem to involve some governmental administrative inconvenience and relatively little defendant inconvenience, e.g., cases where defendants sought a transfer between the Eastern District and Southern District of New York or between the Eastern District of Virginia and District for the District of Columbia, *United States v. Smallwood*, 293 F.Supp.2d 631, 639-44 (E.D.Va. 2003); *United States v. Elson*, 968 F.Supp. 900, 902-904 (S.D.N.Y. 1997); *United States v. Persico*, 621 F.Supp. 842, 858-59 (S.D.N.Y. 1985).

[127] *United States v. Burke*, 607 F.Supp.2d 1314, 1324 (M.D.Fla. 2009)("[T]he United States is not entitled to staff a prosecution awkwardly or unnaturally to manufacture for tactical advantage an inconvenience or a burden that weighs against the Rule 21(b) interest of the defendant"); *United States v. Ferguson*, 432 F.Supp.2d 559, 570 (E.D.Va. 2006)("Defendants have demonstrated that having this matter adjudicated in this district will result in a substantial balance of inconvenience to the defendants"); *United States v. McDonald*, 740 F.Supp. 757, 764 (D.Alaska 1990)("The unpredictability and probability of volcanic activity could radically disrupt the orderly course of trial. Erratic accessibility is not an asset. Under the circumstances, [the] western [district of] Washington is more accessible than [the district of] Alaska"); *United States v. Coffee*, 113 F.Supp.2d 751, 759 (E.D.Pa. 2000) (facts so one-sided that the court was driven to observe, "one wonders why the Government brought this prosecution in this district in the first place ... the Government assures us that this was not a tactic to maximize the pressure for guilty pleas").

[128] "A prosecution may be transferred from the district where the indictment or information is pending, or from which a warrant on a complaint has been issued, to the district where the defendant is arrested, held, or present if: (1) the defendant states in writing a wish to plead guilty or nolo contendere and to waive trial in the district where the indictment, information, or complaint is pending, consents in writing to the court's disposing of the case in the transferee district, and files the statement in the transferee district; and (2) the United States attorneys in both districts approve the transfer in writing," F.R.Crim.P. 20(a).

[129] *Id.*; *United States v. Sevick*, 234 F.3d 248, 250 (5th Cir. 2000).

[130] "A prosecution may be transferred from the district where the indictment or information is pending, or from which a warrant on a complaint has been issued, to the district where the defendant is arrested, held, or present if: ... (2) the United States attorneys in both districts approve the transfer in writing," F.R.Crim.P. 20(c); *United States v. Lovell*, 81 F.3d 58, 60-1 (7th Cir. 1996); *United States v. French*, 787 F.2d 1381, 1384-385 (9th Cir. 1986); *United States v. Herbst*, 565 F.2d 638, 643 (10th Cir. 1977).

[131] "If the defendant pleads not guilty after the case has been transferred under Rule 20(a), the clerk must return the papers to the court where the prosecution began, and that court must restore the proceeding to its docket. The defendant's statement that the defendant wished to plead guilty or nolo contendere is not, in any civil or criminal proceeding, admissible against the defendant," F.R.Crim.P. 20(c); *United States v. Khan*, 822 F.2d 451, 455 (4th Cir. 1987)(following transfer under the rule, a district court has no authority to *sua sponte* withdraw the defendant's guilty plea, substitute a plea of nolo contendere, and acquit the defendant); *In re Arvedon*, 523 F.2d 914, 916 (1st Cir. 1975) ("[R]ules 11 and 20 should be read in harmony with one another. The court is, of course, not obliged to accept an involuntary or improvident plea of guilty because the defendant comes before it on a rule transfer. But, since every defendant who invokes Rule 20 does so from a desire not to return to the indicting district, that desire, by itself, is an impermissible reason to reject a proffered plea of guilty under Rule 11").

[132] "A juvenile, as defined in 18 U.S.C. § 5031, may be proceeded against as a juvenile delinquent in the district where the juvenile is arrested, held, or present if: (A) the alleged offense that occurred in the other district is not punishable by death or life imprisonment; (B) an attorney has advised the juvenile; (C) the court has informed the juvenile of the juvenile's rights—including the right to be returned to the district where the offense allegedly occurred—and the consequences of waiving those rights; (D) the juvenile, after receiving the court's information about rights, consents in writing to be proceeded against in the transferee district, and files the consent in the transferee district; (E) the United States attorneys for both districts approve the transfer in writing; and (F) the transferee court approves the transfer," F.R.Crim.P.20(d)(1).

Chapter Sources

The following chapters have been previously published:

Chapter 1 – This is an edited, reformatted and augmented edition of a Congressional Research Service publication, Report 97-139A, dated May 9, 2007.

Chapter 2 – This is an edited, reformatted and augmented edition of a Congressional Research Service publication, Report 7-5700, dated April 30, 2010.

Chapter 3 – This is an edited, reformatted and augmented edition of a Congressional Research Service publication, Report RL33223 dated December 28, 2005.

INDEX

D

E

F

R

S

Y